MORE PRAISE FOR
EASY CULINARY SCIENCE FOR BETTER COOKING

"Is cooking an art or is it a science? Why can't it be both?! Jessica Gavin may not be Bill Nye, but I sense that she may be a much better cook. Sorry, Bill . . ."

—MARTIN YAN, celebrity chef and TV host of *Yan Can Cook*

"Jessica has found the perfect formula to capture the attention and imagination of the new generation of foodies who also like science and have good taste! I will use this book with my talks directed to our Culinology orientation at my institution."

—DR. RAFAEL JIMÉNEZ-FLORES, Professor and JT Parker Chair in Dairy Foods at The Ohio State University

"*Easy Culinary Science for Better Cooking* is like a mini culinary course in book form and is the perfect primer for today's new crop of home cooks! Jessica excellently demonstrates the intricate science involved in cooking, while remaining approachable and easy to read. With gorgeous photography and skillfully crafted recipes, this book will be an interesting and tasty read for cooks of any level."

—BETH MONCEL, founder of BudgetBytes.com and Saveur Blog Award winner

"*Easy Culinary Science for Better Cooking* is full of delicious, foolproof recipes, beautiful photos and helpful cooking tips. Jessica's food science background shines through on every page!"

—JACLYN BELL, founder of CookingClassy.com

"From the lovely stories and delicious recipes to the captivating science, Jessica will become your instant best friend and culinary companion in the kitchen!"

—SALLY MCKENNEY QUINN, author of *Sally's Baking Addiction*

easy
CULINARY SCIENCE
FOR BETTER COOKING

**RECIPES FOR EVERYDAY MEALS
MADE EASIER, FASTER AND MORE DELICIOUS**

JESSICA GAVIN

CERTIFIED CULINARY SCIENTIST

PAGE STREET
PUBLISHING CO.

PAGE STREET
PUBLISHING CO.

First published in 2018 by

Page Street Publishing Co.

27 Congress Street, Suite 105

Salem, MA 01970

www.pagestreetpublishing.com

Distributed by Macmillan, sales in Canada by The Canadian Manda Group.

22 21 20 19 18   1 2 3 4 5

ISBN-13: 978-1-62414-484-4

ISBN-10: 1-62414-484-5

Library of Congress Control Number: 2017954053

Cover and book design by Page Street Publishing Co.

Photography by Anne Watson

Printed and bound in China

Page Street Publishing protects our planet by donating to nonprofits like The Trustees, which focuses on local land conservation.

TO MY HUSBAND, JASON, YOU PROMISED A LIFETIME OF ADVENTURE AND NEVER DISAPPOINT. FOREVER MY ROCK, BEST FRIEND AND MOTIVATOR.

TO MY SON JAMES AND MY DAUGHTER OLIVIA, THE BEST KITCHEN HELPERS.

TO MY MOM, JANET, MY GUIDING LIGHT AND DAILY INSPIRATION.

table of contents

INTRODUCTION | 9

WHAT IS CULINARY SCIENCE? | 13

DRY-HEAT COOKING | 15
Turn Up the Heat for Quick Flavor

MOIST-HEAT COOKING | 67
Let the Water Do the Work

BRAISING & STEWING | 93
When Two Techniques are Better Than One

SLOW COOKING | 117
Save Time with a Slow Cooker

EMULSIFICATION & THICKENING | 135
Elevated Add-Ons

CHEMICAL LEAVENING | 153
Speed Up Baking with Quick Shortcuts

YEAST LEAVENING | 177
A Foolproof Way to Rise Up

TEST KITCHEN TOOLS & TIPS | 193

CONVERSIONS & EQUIVALENTS | 207

ACKNOWLEDGMENTS | 212

ABOUT THE AUTHOR | 215

INDEX | 216

introduction

I used to be scared of science. It seemed intimidating and technical, reserved only for the bright and gifted to explore. That is until I eventually figured out how to use its potential to my advantage in the kitchen. Once I could actually see, smell, touch and taste the practical application of science in everyday cooking, my passion to learn skyrocketed. The information is out there for all to use; I'm just here to share it with you in an approachable way!

Culinary science will empower you as a cook. It helps you take the guesswork and mystery out of the process so you can enjoy the tasty results. By understanding the basic principles of cooking and using tools to achieve your culinary goals, you can unlock your inner chef and scientist!

A LOVE STORY AND PEEK INTO MY FOOD JOURNEY

An undeniable passion for food and cooking runs deep in my family's roots. My grandparents Bing Chow and Kam Kwei Yee, and Cheung Fung and Fay Ching Huie emigrated from China to the San Francisco Bay Area. This is where my grandfathers became rival chefs working at the same Chinese restaurant in Walnut Creek, California. Little did they know that their children Rick and Janet would someday marry and build a clan of their own. My brothers Sydney and Blandon and I grew up in a family where food was not only nourishment, it was the essential way to connect with others and cultivate bonds.

I grew up in the East Bay Area of Northern California, a melting pot of various cultures and cuisines. This is where I embraced my curiosity and appreciation for food. My fondest memories consist of weekend visits to Oakland Chinatown with family to shop for fresh vegetables, roasted meats and special pink bakery boxes loaded with Chinese sweets. From a very young age, I noticed how food brought people together and built connections—I knew then that food would have a very important role in my life.

I remember the exact moment that my love for food turned into something much greater. I was fifteen years old and watching a cooking show called *Dessert Circus* with Jacques Torres. This incredibly talented and entertaining French pastry chef turned simple household ingredients into playful, artistic culinary masterpieces. After that episode, I recall running downstairs to the kitchen and attempting to temper chocolate for the first time. From then on, I was compelled to cook, insatiably curious to try new things and to see how far my imagination would take me.

Throughout high school, I worked at a European patisserie called Boniere Bakery, in the heart of Alameda, the quaint little town where I lived. The jaw-dropping pastries and cakes Chef Donna Meadows and her team produced were incredible. This is where I first dreamed about a career in culinary and fell madly in love with chocolate croissants, fruit tarts and opera cake.

My plan was to attend culinary school right after high school. I remember declaring to my family that I wanted to be the next Emeril Lagasse! The thought of working at a popular restaurant with talented culinarians, creating extravagant menus and dishes made my heart full. However, my plan did not take me straight to the kitchen as I had imagined. Instead of up to my elbows in flour, I found myself in the lab and lecture halls at California Polytechnic State University in San Luis Obispo, as a budding food scientist.

To be honest, this was uncomfortable at first because I never excelled at math or science, and I felt out of place. It was only after a few lectures in Food Science 101 that I had an "aha!" moment. I realized my untapped knowledge of food chemistry and how ingredients functioned together could elevate my awareness about what happens in the kitchen. I was learning the science behind culinary arts! Now I could understand why my custard sauces were turning into scrambled eggs, how to keep my salad dressings from separating and why Grandma Kam's rice was always so light and fluffy.

Culinary science has allowed me to become a better cook because with knowledge comes the confidence to apply solutions when problems arise in recipes. These little wins keep me motivated to continue my food quest, sharing what I've learned along the way with others who are just as hungry and curious.

After pursuing a bachelor's degree in food science and a master's in dairy products technology, I was ready to hit the working world. Over the last 10 years, I have been extremely fortunate to be able to apply my knowledge to a career in product development. As a senior research scientist for a global nutrition company, I get to design food and supplement formulations that help people around the world achieve optimal health.

During my career as a scientist, my heart never stopped yearning to learn more about cooking in the kitchen. While working full time, I pursued a culinary arts education. In culinary school, I learned how to combine my food science knowledge with the dishes I produced in each class. The hours were crazy, but it was pure bliss.

WHEN YOU OPEN YOUR MIND TO NEW IDEAS, TREMENDOUS THINGS CAN HAPPEN . . .

Along the way, I happened to fall in love with a remarkable man I met in college—Jason. He grew up eating traditional Italian cuisine handmade with lots of love. Good thing for him, I loved to cook, especially his favorite meals, like Grandma's Italian Meatballs (page 133) and Classic Pineapple Upside Down Cake (page 170). The thing about Jason is that he's full of ideas. A true entrepreneur at heart, he's always looking for ways to create business opportunities out of his passions.

In 2012, a year after we were married, we found ourselves in Napa Valley, California, dining at The French Laundry for our anniversary. An epicurean dream come true in itself! I had just graduated from culinary school and the conversation switched to "What's next?" I knew that I couldn't handle the grueling hours of working on the line in a restaurant, but I wanted to do something with my culinary degree. I also really enjoyed the application of food science. Was there a way I could do both?

Jason cunningly mentioned starting a food blog. A food what? I had no experience with websites, back-end coding, food photography or any of the other terrifying technical aspects of running a food blog. I just wanted to cook! We made a deal: I would be in charge of content creation and he would handle the website operations.

Though reluctant at first, I eventually immersed myself in this unknown world of blogging, and I'm so happy that I did! My culinary science website (www.jessicagavin.com) and mobile app are my portfolio and places to teach readers kitchen confidence through delicious and approachable recipes and tips. It's hard work, but I can't help but keep coming back to create and share more! I cherish the ability to instantly interact with home cooks from around the world, getting feedback on what I've shared and being part of a community of food lovers and science seekers.

Now that we are busy working parents to James and Olivia, I am challenged with getting creative in the kitchen. I want to cook healthy, fast, flavorful meals and, of course, occasional sweet indulgences. That challenge inspired me to write this book. The bonus is that I get to share these recipes with people like you, who also have the same mealtime needs.

In this cookbook I've included a few cherished childhood recipes like Chinese Steamed Custard Buns (page 183), Chinese Sticky Rice (page 78) and Grandma's Ginger Beef Stew (page 107). I've also featured new family favorites, inspired by the most influential cooks in my life, our mothers and grandparents. These special recipes are part of who I am, and I'm so ecstatic that they get to be a part of this collection. I still pinch myself that I've been given the opportunity to publish my very own cookbook! This accomplishment is something I've dreamed of since I was a young girl watching *Dessert Circus*.

HOW THIS COOKBOOK WILL TRANSFORM THE WAY YOU INTERACT WITH FOOD . . .

Easy Culinary Science for Better Cooking will teach you the essential techniques and tips that will help you expand your skill set and confidence in the kitchen! Each chapter will explore the basic concepts of cooking. This abbreviated background information will provide key insights before you jump into the recipes. My hope is that you approach a recipe using the new awareness of the science behind it. Culinary science is essential every time you cook, and having the insider knowledge will elevate your game.

As you continue your culinary science journey, I recommend you have two important tools that will ensure you have the most success with this book: a digital thermometer and a kitchen scale. The Test Kitchen Tools & Tips section (page 193) also provides information about a few more cooking essentials. These tools will give you more control and insight as you experiment in the kitchen. As you begin to trust the science and use data to help make important culinary decisions, cooking and baking will become easier and more intuitive.

Embrace your inner geek, have fun and turn your kitchen into a food lab. As long as you are willing to learn and be playful in your culinary adventures, tasty meals will flow from your mind, to your hands, and onto the plate. The best part is sharing your flavorful experiments with the ones you love, and when they ask you to make it again. I know you can do this! You already love food and are interested in the science; let's take you closer to your goals.

I am grateful every day that I get to share my perspective with others as a culinary scientist. I get to infuse my cooking skills with the scientific and technical knowledge behind each recipe and technique. I'm thrilled that I can share my passion with my family, friends and now you!

Happy cooking!

Jessica

what is culinary science?

The moment you step into a kitchen and begin to measure, chop and cook, science is happening—even if you don't realize it. Each decision you make affects your finished dish, and that is powerful. As you discover the scientific side of food, such as how ingredients function together, or how to manipulate heat transfer to enhance textures, you will naturally become a better cook.

Culinary Arts: The art of preparation, cooking and presentation of food for individuals. People working in this field especially in establishments such as restaurants are commonly called chefs or cooks. Chefs must be able to identify, purchase, utilize and prepare a wide variety of foods.

Food Science: Focuses on delivering food products to the masses. Food science and technology is the study of the physical, biological and chemical composition of food and its commercial application. It's a fascinating field that is integral to the food system we have established today. Researchers, scientists and engineers get the incredible task of developing safe, wholesome and innovative food products for people around the world.

Culinary Science: The blending of both food science and culinary arts allows for a deeper understanding of how foods interact from a cooking or baking perspective and how to leverage those characteristics for the desired gastronomic outcome. The combination of theory, practice and intuition will help you gain the confidence you need to create flavorful meals consistently.

Food brings immense joy to our brains, with each bite delivering nourishment and engaging all of our senses. Through the research fields of food and culinary science, we can dive deeper into the chemical and physical study of food to understand how to maximize and preserve the flavor potential of each ingredient.

While you explore this book, I want you to try your own experiments. Each time you enter the kitchen, imagine that you are a scientist. When you read the ingredients and instructions, think about why certain ingredients are used and combined together. Be inquisitive about why particular cooking methods or techniques are applied and how it changes the food. If you think you can make a tweak to improve the recipe, be fearless and give it a try. Knowledge, investigation and practice will help you excel in your skills as a cook.

As you learn more through hands-on practice in the kitchen, you'll begin to notice why your recipes are a success, or how you could make them better through science.

Just remember, science is a framework for discovery. Each recipe is a guideline, but your experience may be slightly different because you are unique and so is your test kitchen. If you find a technique that works, write down how you did it, and try it again and again until it's repeatable. Don't be afraid to play in the kitchen; it's your edible playground!

There are no real failures, as long as you stay curious, are brave enough to try a new way and embrace the learning. Use these simple tools to take control of your cooking for tasty results!

dry-heat cooking

TURN UP THE HEAT FOR QUICK FLAVOR

Learn how dry-heat cooking methods like grilling, roasting, baking, sautéing, pan-frying and deep-frying create the most interesting textures through the molecular act of browning. It's simple and it's all about knowing how to use heat combined with air or fat to develop visible flavor.

the simple science

When you want a burst of flavor, dry-heat cooking is your go-to method. It utilizes air or fat to cook food, and the result is layers of flavor with a nice brown color. Direct heat can be used to cook the food with an open flame (think campfire marshmallows) or with heated air (grilling, roasting, baking, broiling) or fat (deep-frying, sautéing, pan-frying). Learn about how to select the right oil for cooking in the Test Kitchen Tools & Tips section (page 193).

THE MAILLARD BROWNING REACTION: THE KEY TO FLAVOR DEVELOPMENT

You've seen it countless times: the visible color change from a piece of raw meat to a golden brown surface. This complex chemical interaction is called the Maillard reaction, and it's responsible for flavor development when cooking with high, dry heat. You may not realize it, but as this physical change happens, a chain reaction of flavor compounds is being created. When foods like beef or chicken that contain protein and amino acids are heated, a reaction with reducing sugars like fructose and glucose occurs. New flavor compounds called dicarbonyls are created, but the process does not stop there. The sugars continue to react with amino acids, quickly creating an abundance of flavors on the food and in the cooking vessel. What you see is the final transformation of melanoidin pigment molecules naturally present in the food as a deep brown color appears. Different flavor compounds are formed depending on the type of protein being cooked and the sugars present. Therefore beef and chicken will taste different after cooking at high temperatures. This Maillard reaction happens when the surface temperature of the food reaches 300°F (149°C). The key is to make sure the surface of the food being cooked is dry to prevent steaming and promote the maximum amount of browning.

dry-heat cooking basics

Broiling: Broiling is a great option for quickly cooking food. Using an upper heat source like in an oven, the extreme heat radiating from above (scorching temperatures of up to 2,000°F [1,093°C]) makes for a rapid meal. If broiling in the oven, place the food about 6 to 7 inches (15 to 18 cm) away from the heat source and keep an eye on the food to make sure it doesn't burn.

Grilling: For lovers of the outdoors, grilling uses radiant heat from beneath the food to give gorgeous surface color, especially if you like those characteristic diamond-shaped cross marks. Grilling can take flavor to the next level if you are using wood, cedar or coal to infuse different layers of smoky flavors into the food.

Roasting: The oven uses hot air radiating from the nearby heating elements and walls to cook the food by convection. Temperatures can range from 200 to 500°F (90 to 260°C) depending on the type of meat or vegetable. Higher temperature encourages quicker browning and cooking, while lower temperature cooks more evenly and has more moisture retention, but takes longer. A combination of high-to-low heat may be used for initial browning on the surface, finished with low-temperature roasting, especially for larger roasts like beef, turkey or chicken.

Baking: The heat transfer process is very similar to roasting, yet is often used for fish, vegetables, bread, cookies, cakes and pastries. The goal in baking is to use the hot oven air to promote uniform cooking, while using the heat to achieve dry, browned surfaces and flavorful crusts over a period of time.

Sautéing: A fast and flavorful method of conduction cooking, where the heat transferred from the hot pan cooks the food. A little bit of oil or butter is used to just lightly coat the bottom of the pan, which helps keep the ingredients from sticking, while adding color and some flavor. The key for sautéing is using hot oil that is near its smoke point to cook the ingredients, but not burning the surface. Cutting foods to similar sizes, cooking in a single layer (while not overcrowding the pan) and briefly tossing the ingredients to encourage color development helps to ensure sauté success. Stir-frying utilizes the same method but a different cooking vessel, a wok. The round shape of the pan efficiently transfers the heat to the vessel, and then to the food. The sloped sides makes it easy for stirring the vegetables.

Pan-Frying: This method uses a sauté pan filled about one-third of the way or up to halfway with oil to cook the food. It's a popular technique to use for breaded food, like chicken Parmesan, when you want to achieve a crisp, golden crust and tender meat. Heating starts with conduction from the pan to the fat, then continues with convection of the hot oil to the food. The oil temperature should be below the smoking point. You can see the food sizzling and gently spattering in the oil, making a crackling sound.

Deep-Frying: This method completely submerges the breaded or battered food in hot oil for conduction and convection cooking. Depending on the type of oil chosen to fry the food, high temperatures of around 400°F (204°C) are reached to create beautiful golden brown textures on the surface in a short amount of time. Canola, peanut and soybean oils are most commonly used because they have a high smoke point, the temperature when the fat breaks down and begins to visibly smoke. The goal is to have the hot oil instantly seal and fry the outside, and cook the inside, without burning the surface. The temperature of the oil can be adjusted based on the type that is selected; however, a typical range of 325 to 375°F (160 to 191°C) is used. Make sure to have an instant-read thermometer that can read above 400°F (204°C) before you start deep-frying. The differences in temperature can change quickly and will greatly impact the fried product if not closely monitored throughout the process.

dry-heat cooking methods

METHOD	HEAT TRANSFER	MEDIUM	EQUIPMENT	FOOD
Broiling	Radiant	Electromagnetic waves	Oven broiler, rotisserie, salamander	Fish, seafood, meat, bread, poultry
Grilling	Radiant	Air	Barbecue grill	Meats, poultry, fish, vegetables
Roasting	Convection/Conduction	Air	Oven	Meats, poultry, fish, vegetables
Baking	Convection/Conduction	Air	Oven	Fish, vegetables, fruit, bread, poultry
Sautéing	Conduction	Fat	Stove top, sauté pan, wok (stir-frying)	Meats, poultry, fish, vegetables
Pan-frying	Convection/Conduction	Fat	Stove top, skillet, sauté pan	Breaded foods
Deep-frying	Convection/Conduction	Fat	Fryer, basket, tongs, spider	Breaded or battered foods

blackened salmon tacos with avocado yogurt lime sauce

SAUTÉ | GLUTEN-FREE | QUICK (30 MINUTES OR LESS)

These blackened salmon tacos are reminiscent of eating fresh seafood by the ocean during college road trips down to Baja California in Mexico. To make these tacos healthier, spices are used to achieve a low-calorie explosion of flavor. To instantly boost the taste of the salmon, a blend of earthy cumin, garlic, onion and paprika, balanced with a hint of heat from chipotle chilis and sweetness from brown sugar creates savory, smoky, spicy notes in each bite! The volatile molecules are sent rushing to your nose and provide the initial characteristic flavor impact. Pan-frying the spice-coated salmon in oil additionally helps to release fat-soluble flavor compounds. The cool and creamy avocado sauce complements the spicy notes of the seasoning for an irresistible handheld meal.

SERVES: 4 | PREP TIME: 15 minutes | COOK TIME: 5 minutes

SAUCE

1 serrano chili pepper, cut in half and seeded

½ cup (123 g) plain Greek yogurt or low-fat sour cream

1 avocado, pitted

2 tbsp (30 ml) lime juice

½ tsp lime zest

¼ cup (4 g) cilantro leaves, packed

¼ tsp kosher salt

¼ cup (60 ml) water

SALMON TACOS

1 tsp paprika

1 tsp dark brown sugar

¾ tsp garlic powder

¾ tsp onion powder

¾ tsp cumin

¼ tsp chipotle chili powder, or chili powder

½ tsp kosher salt

¼ tsp black pepper

1 lb (454 g) salmon fillet, skin removed and cut into 8 even pieces

1 tbsp (15 ml) vegetable oil

8 corn tortillas

Suggested toppings: cilantro, serrano peppers, cabbage, limes, avocado, pickled onions (page 124)

To make the sauce, process the serrano peppers, yogurt, avocado, lime juice, lime zest, cilantro, salt and water in a food processor or blender until smooth. Transfer to a bowl and set aside.

To make the seasoning, combine the paprika, brown sugar, garlic powder, onion powder, cumin, chipotle chili powder, salt and black pepper in a small bowl. Season the salmon with about ½ teaspoon of the spice blend on each side.

In a large, 12-inch (30-cm) cast-iron skillet or sauté pan, heat the vegetable oil over medium-high heat until very hot. Place the salmon in the pan, and cook until the surface is browned and crisp, and the fish flakes easily with a fork, about 2 to 3 minutes on the first side. Flip the fish over and cook for 1½ to 2 minutes. Make sure to turn on a cooking vent or open the windows as the hot skillet may smoke due to the smoke point of the oil and the hot temperature required to achieve the blackened appearance and flavor.

Serve the blackened salmon in warmed tortillas and topped with the avocado yogurt lime sauce.

COOK'S NOTES:

To achieve a crispy blackened surface, a small amount of brown sugar is added to the dry rub and the fish is pan-fried in smoking hot oil.

Blooming the spices in the oil intensifies the flavors and aromas, which are quickly transferred to the surface of the fish and the oil.

RECIPE SCIENCE:

Sugar, also known as sucrose, is a disaccharide composed of two simple sugar molecules, glucose and fructose. In the presence of heat, the sugar breaks down into these molecules. At around 200°F (93°C), the fructose begins to caramelize and deep brown pigments are formed on the surface. With a preheated pan and continuous exposure to high heat, the surface temperature of the fish easily reaches the 200-degree (93-degree) mark.

wok-fired orange garlic shrimp

SAUTÉ | GLUTEN-FREE | QUICK (30 MINUTES OR LESS) | DAIRY-FREE | ONE-PAN MEAL

Skip the takeout because this orange garlic shrimp is bursting with flavor and is ready in only 15 minutes! A complete meal of protein and vegetables all in one pot, plus a sweet and sticky sauce to coat each piece of succulent shrimp. The fresh orange juice combined with savory chicken stock, soy sauce, honey, lemon and a hint of spicy chili complements the delicate flavors of the shrimp.

SERVES: 4 | PREP TIME: 15 minutes | COOK TIME: 10 minutes

SAUCE

½ cup (118 ml) orange juice

1½ tsp (3 g) orange zest

⅓ cup (79 ml) unsalted chicken stock

2 tbsp (30 ml) soy sauce or tamari (for gluten-free option)

3 tbsp (45 ml) honey

2 tsp (10 ml) lemon juice or rice wine vinegar

⅛ tsp red chili flakes, optional

2 tsp (10 g) cornstarch

SHRIMP

1 lb (454 g) large shrimp, 16/20 count size, peeled and deveined

½ tsp kosher salt

¼ tsp black pepper

½ tsp sesame oil

1 tbsp (15 ml) vegetable oil

¾ cup (128 g) chopped red bell peppers, cut into ½-inch (1.3-cm) pieces

1¼ cups (113 g) stringless sugar snap peas

4 cloves garlic, minced

2 tsp (8 g) minced ginger

2 tbsp (7g) sliced green onions

½ tsp sesame seeds

¼ cup (4 g) cilantro leaves, packed

To make the sauce, whisk together the orange juice, orange zest, chicken stock, soy sauce, honey, lemon juice, red chili flakes (if using) and cornstarch in a medium-size bowl. Set the sauce aside.

Prepare the shrimp by patting it dry between two paper towels to remove as much moisture as possible. In a medium-size bowl, combine the shrimp, salt, pepper and sesame oil.

Cooking the shrimp and vegetables in a single layer and at separate times allows for maximum browning. Heat a wok or 12-inch (30-cm) skillet over high heat. Add the oil and heat until just beginning to smoke. Add the shrimp to the pan in a single layer and cook for 1 minute. Flip the shrimp over and cook until pink, about 1 minute. Transfer the cooked shrimp to a clean plate.

Add the bell peppers and sugar snap peas to the wok in a single layer and allow to cook for 1 minute without moving. Stir the vegetables and cook until lightly browned and crisp, about 30 seconds. Add the garlic and ginger to the pan, and stir-fry until fragrant, about 30 seconds.

Whisk the orange sauce and then gradually add it to the side of the pan, stirring the sauce continuously as it gathers in the bottom of the pan. Allow the sauce to boil for 1 to 2 minutes, stirring continuously, until the sauce is thickened. Add the shrimp to the pan and allow to warm, 1 minute. Season the shrimp and vegetables with salt and pepper to taste.

Serve the shrimp garnished with green onions, sesame seeds and cilantro.

COOK'S NOTE:
Prevent sauces from becoming lumpy by mixing the cornstarch into cold water or liquid before heating. As you heat the sauce, make sure to keep stirring to allow the starch granules to swell independently for sauce-thickening success!

RECIPE SCIENCE:
The quick stir-frying method relies on selecting the right cooking vessel, heat level and not overloading the pan. Woks are unique because the round bottom shape creates a large surface area so the shrimp and vegetables can be cooked quickly. A large flat-bottomed skillet can also be used and works great for even browning of the food. It's important to preheat the wok and oil over high heat, so the oil can reach scorching-hot temperatures of 415°F (212°C). This will encourage browning of the ingredients from the Maillard reaction, imparting flavor and color to the dish.

chinese chicken lettuce wraps

SAUTÉ | ONE-PAN MEAL | QUICK (30 MINUTES OR LESS)

One of my favorite cooking vessels to use at home is my wok. I grew up to the sounds of the clanging metal spatula hitting the side of the pan when my grandparents and mom would prepare dinner, making the perfect stir-fry. Using a little bit of oil in a sizzling hot pan, a quick and flavorful meal or appetizer is ready in minutes. It's an ideal dish because one pan delivers chicken, vegetables and a savory sauce with less clean up. The seasoned chicken and vegetables in large lettuce cups, topped with green onions and crunchy peanuts, adds layers of flavors and textures to each handheld wrap.

MAKES: 12 wraps | **PREP TIME:** 20 minutes | **COOK TIME:** 10 minutes

2 tbsp (30 ml) vegetable oil, divided

1 tsp sesame oil

⅓ cup (80 g) minced shallots

⅓ cup (90 g) bamboo shoots, chopped

⅓ cup (51 g) water chestnuts, chopped

1 cup (59 g) shiitake mushrooms, chopped, stems removed

½ cup (65 g) finely diced carrots

3 cloves garlic, minced

1 tsp minced ginger

1 lb (454 g) ground chicken

4 tsp (20 ml) hoisin sauce, plus more for topping

2 tsp (10 ml) soy sauce

½ tsp kosher salt

¼ tsp black pepper

1 head butter leaf lettuce, 12 leaves washed and dried

¼ cup (12 g) sliced green onions, on the bias

¼ cup (38 g) roasted peanuts, roughly chopped

To keep the pan nice and hot, the vegetables are cooked first. Natural moisture from the vegetables can initially bring down the temperature of the wok, which is why they are stir-fried and removed from the pan. This gives the wok and additional oil time to come back to a high temperature and makes ample room for the chicken to properly brown. In a wok, heat 2 teaspoons (10 ml) of vegetable oil and sesame oil over high heat until very hot. Add the shallots to the pan and stir-fry for 1 minute. Add the bamboo shoots, water chestnuts, mushrooms and carrots, and stir-fry for 4 minutes.

Push the vegetables to the side of the pan and add 1 teaspoon of vegetable oil to the center of the pan. Once the oil heats up, add the garlic and ginger, and cook until fragrant but not overly browned, about 15 seconds. Mix the vegetables back in with the garlic and ginger. Transfer the vegetables to a medium-size bowl and set aside.

Return the wok to the stove and heat the remaining tablespoon (15 ml) of vegetable oil over high heat. Draining any residual liquid from the ground chicken will help the chicken brown instead of steam when it hits the pan. Add the ground chicken to the hot pan and stir-fry, breaking up the chicken into smaller chunks, about 4 minutes or until the meat is no longer pink. Add the hoisin sauce, soy sauce, stir-fried vegetables, salt and pepper to the meat, and stir to combine.

To serve, add about ¼ cup (58 g) of chicken filling to each lettuce leaf, and garnish with the green onion and peanuts. Drizzle the lettuce wraps with the hoisin sauce if desired.

COOK'S NOTE:
Many traditional Chinese stir-fry recipes call for the garlic and ginger to be cooked first thing in the hot oil. This is okay if using large slices of ginger or garlic. However, when minced, there is a higher chance of burning the aromatics. That's why the garlic and ginger are added at the end of cooking the vegetables and only heated for a few seconds. This will still impart pungent flavor without scorched notes.

RECIPE SCIENCE:
Cooking over high heat in the round bottom vessel encourages quick browning of the ingredients through the Maillard reaction. However, the oil must reach 415°F (212°C) for browning to occur. This imparts flavors to the chicken, even before the sauce is added.

pan-seared scallops with garlic sauce

SAUTÉ | GLUTEN-FREE | ONE-PAN MEAL

My husband, Jason, and I are big fans of the television show *Hell's Kitchen*. It reminds me of the pure adrenaline rush while working the grill station during culinary school! Every season, a cook brings up raw or rubbery scallops to the pass for Chef Gordon Ramsay, resulting in lots of profanity and plate-slamming. I wanted to see for myself just how difficult it was to make beautifully caramelized scallops. Ever since I learned the correct method, I never feared making it at home again. Nailing this pan-searing technique will certainly impress your dinner guests and elevate your cooking status to gourmet. The lemon caper wine sauce is a delicate and luscious complement to the crusted scallops.

SERVES: 4 | PREP TIME: 25 minutes | COOK TIME: 20 minutes

⅓ cup (95 g) kosher salt, plus more for seasoning

1 cup (240 ml) hot water

4 cups (960 ml) ice water

1 lb (454 g) large scallops, 10 to 20 per pound, about 2 inches (5 cm) wide each

3 tbsp (45 ml) grapeseed or olive oil

Black pepper, for seasoning

Salt, for seasoning

3 tbsp (42 g) unsalted butter, divided

3 cloves garlic, minced

½ cup (120 ml) white wine (Chardonnay recommended)

1 cup (240 ml) unsalted chicken stock or broth

Zest of one lemon

2 tbsp (30 ml) lemon juice

2 tbsp (17 g) capers, rinsed

1 tbsp (4 g) chopped parsley

In a medium-size bowl, combine ⅓ cup (95 g) of salt and the hot water, stirring to dissolve the salt. Add the ice water to cool the brine. Line a sheet pan with paper towels, and set aside.

Add the scallops to the brine and let stand for 10 minutes. To drain the scallops, rinse under cold water and arrange in a single layer on the paper towel–lined sheet pan. Place the paper towels on top of the scallops and gently press to remove additional moisture. Remove as much surface moisture as possible for the best browning results when cooked. Allow the scallops to sit for 10 minutes at room temperature before cooking.

Heat a 12-inch (30-cm) sauté pan or cast-iron pan over medium-high heat. Add the grapeseed oil and heat until the oil ripples and just begins to smoke. Lightly season the scallops with salt and black pepper. Add the scallops to the hot pan, spacing to avoid crowding. Gently press the scallops to make direct contact with pan. Sear the scallops without moving them, until the bottoms are a rich golden brown, 3 to 3½ minutes.

Add 1 tablespoon (14 g) of butter to the pan. Once the scallops are in the pan, do not even think of moving them—they need uninterrupted contact for even and effective browning. Turn the scallops over and cook the second side. Use a spoon to baste the scallops with the butter, tilting the pan so the butter moves to one side and can easily be collected for basting. Basting the scallops with butter helps to promote additional browning. The milk proteins and natural sugar lactose in butter enhances the browning reaction so the crust is beautifully formed.

Cook until the scallops are opaque in color and firm to the touch, about 1 to 2 minutes. Turn off the heat and transfer to a plate; do not discard the pan drippings.

(continued)

COOK'S NOTE:

The scallops are briefly brined in a saltwater solution because it delicately seasons the seafood and helps it retain moisture. This prevents the scallops from becoming tough in the high-heat cooking environment. The scallops are an extremely lean protein so the salt dissolves and reshapes some of the protein molecules in the seafood. The dissolved protein forms a gel so it can hold on to the added water after cooking and stay tender.

pan-seared scallops with garlic sauce (cont.)

In the same pan used for cooking the scallops, turn the heat to medium. Add 1 tablespoon (14 g) of butter and the garlic. Stir and cook the garlic until fragrant but not browned, about 1 minute. Increase the heat to medium-high and add the wine. Simmer, stirring as needed, until the wine is reduced by half to about ¼ cup (60 ml), about 3 minutes.

Turn the heat to high and add the chicken stock, lemon zest, lemon juice and capers to the pan. Cook until the sauce is reduced to about ½ cup (120 ml), 8 to 10 minutes. Turn off the heat and add 1 tablespoon (14 g) of butter, and whisk to combine.

Turn the heat to medium and add the scallops back to the pan, and cook until warm, 2 minutes. Season the sauce with salt and pepper to taste. Top the scallops with chopped parsley.

RECIPE SCIENCE:

Pan-searing scallops in extremely hot oil is a dry-heat method that uses conduction heat from the pan to the fat, and convection of the hot oil to cook the scallops. There are a few key tips to achieve the highly sought after golden crust color and tender scallops. The scallops must be very dry on the surface so that they will sear instead of steam. I use a stainless steel or cast-iron pan because it gives a more attractive caramel-colored surface compared to a nonstick pan. The scallops are seared over very high heat so the Maillard reaction, which is initiated when the surface temperature of the seafood reaches 300°F (149°C), begins very soon after the scallops hit the pan.

chicken egg rolls

DEEP-FRY | DAIRY-FREE | FREEZER-FRIENDLY

Ever since I was a little girl sitting at the big round table with my family at our favorite local Chinese restaurant, when the lazy Susan spun around with a plate of crispy egg rolls I had to grab one or two! This recipe makes large golden-brown egg rolls stuffed with a seasoned chicken and vegetable filling. These egg rolls have a nice brown, crisp exterior and a slight chew. A quick sweet and sour orange sauce is the perfect condiment for these golden rolls. Each sticky, sweet and crunchy bite from the freshly fried egg rolls is a great way to start any meal!

MAKES: 12 to 15 rolls | **PREP TIME:** 30 minutes | **COOK TIME:** 30 minutes

ORANGE DIPPING SAUCE

½ cup (120 ml) orange juice

1 tbsp (15 ml) soy sauce

2 tbsp (30 ml) honey

2 tsp (10 ml) rice vinegar

¼ tsp chili paste, plus more as desired

1 tsp cornstarch

EGG ROLLS

2 tbsp (30 ml) vegetable oil, divided

1 cup (73 g) shredded carrots

2 cups (80 g) thinly shredded napa cabbage

1 cup (67 g) bean sprouts

3 tbsp (45 ml) soy sauce, divided

1 tsp honey

2 cloves garlic, minced

1 tsp minced ginger

1 lb (454 g) ground chicken

1 tbsp (16 ml) hoisin sauce

¼ tsp black pepper

⅓ cup (14 g) thinly sliced green onions

15 egg roll wrappers, 6½ x 6½ inches (17 x 17 cm)

64 oz (2 L) canola oil or peanut oil

For the orange dipping sauce, whisk together the orange juice, soy sauce, honey, rice vinegar, chili paste and cornstarch in a small saucepan, until no lumps remain. Add more chili paste depending on desired spiciness level.

Heat a pan over medium-high heat until the sauce comes to a boil. Turn the heat down to medium and whisk, until the sauce thickens, about 1 to 2 minutes. Turn off the heat and transfer the sauce to a bowl and reserve.

To make the egg roll filling, heat a wok or large skillet over high heat. Add 1 tablespoon (15 ml) of vegetable oil and heat until just smoking. Add the carrot and cabbage, and stir-fry for 2 minutes. Add the bean sprouts and stir-fry 1 minute. Add 1 tablespoon (15 ml) of soy sauce and the honey; stir-fry 1 minute until the moisture has evaporated. Transfer the vegetables to a plate and allow to cool.

Heat 1 tablespoon (15 ml) of vegetable oil in wok over high heat, add the garlic and ginger, and cook 30 seconds, stirring until fragrant. Add the chicken and cook until no longer pink, breaking down the chicken into small pieces, about 4 minutes. Add 2 tablespoons (30 ml) of soy sauce, hoisin sauce and black pepper. Stir to combine, and cook until the moisture evaporates, about 2 to 3 minutes. Transfer the chicken to a medium-size bowl and allow to slightly cool. Add the vegetables and green onions to the chicken, and stir to combine.

To make the egg rolls, add some water to a small bowl, have a brush ready and set aside. On a cutting board, place one wrapper down with a corner pointed toward you. Add 3 tablespoons (32 g) of filling to the lower third of the wrapper, making a 4-inch (10-cm) wide, tight and even mound. Tightly roll from the bottom corner toward the top, until about halfway up.

Press on the edges of the filling to make sure the filling is packed and even. Brush a small amount of water on the left and right corners of the wrapper. Tightly fold the corners of the wrapper towards the center, so it looks like an opened envelope.

(continued)

COOK'S NOTE:

If you like a crunchier egg roll, fry the egg rolls at 375°F (191°C). However, cooking time will be slightly shorter, about 4 to 5 minutes. Do not exceed this temperature as going above 400°F (204°C) will cause the egg rolls to become too crisp and brown too quickly, giving an unpleasant burnt taste.

Place the wrapper with the corner pointed toward you for a better seal once rolled.

Tightly roll the wrapper halfway, making sure the filling is evenly packed.

Firmly fold the corners and remove any extra air space.

Brush the top corner of the wrapper with water. Tightly roll the egg roll until it is completely sealed. Each roll should be about 4 inches (10 cm) long. Repeat process with the remaining rolls. Egg rolls can be frozen for up to 3 months in a sealed container. If frozen, fry directly from the freezer for an additional 1 minute of fry time.

Heat the oil in a large pot or Dutch oven to 350°F (177°C) over medium heat. Add 4 to 5 egg rolls at a time, working in batches. Occasionally move the egg rolls with a large metal spoon or wire spider so that they can be evenly golden brown in color and crisp in texture, 5 to 6 minutes. Drain the egg rolls on a paper towel–lined sheet pan. Repeat with the additional egg rolls.

Serve the egg rolls hot with orange dipping sauce.

RECIPE SCIENCE:

The chicken filling is tightly folded into a wrapper, which is typically made from a combination of wheat flour, corn starch, wheat gluten, eggs and water to give an ultra-thin and pliable sheet. This egg roll recipe requires deep-frying in 350°F (177°C) canola or peanut oil, both of which have high smoke points for prolonged and successful frying. As the egg roll enters the hot oil, any surface moisture from the wrapper instantly turns to steam. These are the bubbles you see immediately surrounding the food. You will notice some porous-looking bubbles and craters on the fried egg roll skin. That is from the moisture leaving small pockets that are replaced by a small amount of oil. As the egg rolls cook, the starch that is naturally in the wrapper starts to dry, brown and become crispy, just what you want. Any excess moisture will stay on the surface of the wrapper, losing its crunch factor and feeling greasy if not fried properly.

pan-seared ribeye with miso butter

SAUTÉ | GLUTEN-FREE

Every once in a while, I crave a juicy steak with a perfectly browned crust. Until recently, this craving was only satisfied during celebrations at fancy restaurants. But I was determined to recreate the gourmet-quality steak at home so my family wouldn't have to wait so long in between. After researching and testing multiple methods, I finally found one that gives the seared-to-perfection surface and medium-rare pink center. The beef is topped with savory miso butter for the ultimate steak experience.

SERVES: 2 | **PREP TIME:** 15 minutes | **COOK TIME:** 25 minutes

MISO BUTTER

¼ cup (56 g) unsalted butter, softened

2 tbsp (39 g) yellow miso paste

1 tbsp (3 g) thinly sliced green onions

¼ tsp black pepper

RIBEYE STEAK

2 large ribeye steaks, at least 1½ inches (3.8 cm) thick

Kosher salt, as desired for seasoning

Black pepper, as desired for seasoning

1 tbsp (15 ml) vegetable oil

1 tbsp (14 g) unsalted butter

3 cloves garlic, roughly chopped

¼ cup (10 g) thinly sliced white and light green parts of green onion

¼ cup (10 g) thinly sliced on the bias green onions, for garnish

¼ cup (4 g) cilantro leaves, for garnish

For the miso butter, combine the softened butter and miso together in a small bowl. Add the green onions and pepper and combine. Keep at room temperature or roll into a 1½-inch (3.8-cm) wide log in plastic wrap and refrigerate. Cut into slices before serving.

There is one key difference to this method for thick steaks. The first step is to slightly warm the steaks in the oven before cooking on the stove. Adjust the oven rack to the center position and preheat the oven to 275°F (135°C). Add your cast-iron skillet to the oven to warm up. I like to use a preheated cast-iron pan because it retains heat very well for searing. Place a wire rack on a rimmed baking sheet, and set aside.

Pat dry the steaks with paper towels, pressing out as much surface moisture as possible. Season both sides of the steak with salt and pepper. Transfer the steaks to the wire rack and place in the oven. The heat helps to dry the free moisture on the surface of the steaks for quicker browning and cook time in the pan.

Cook the steak until the internal temperature reaches 90 to 95°F (32 to 35°C) for medium-rare, or 100 to 105°F (38°C to 41°C) for medium, about 15 to 20 minutes. The time will vary depending on the thickness of the steaks. Remove the steaks from the oven.

In the warmed 12-inch (30-cm) cast-iron skillet, heat the vegetable oil over high heat until just beginning to smoke. Carefully add the steaks and sear until browned with a nice crust, about 2 minutes. Flip the steaks with tongs and sear until browned, 1½ to 2 minutes, or until an instant-read thermometer inserted into the thickest part of steak registers 120 to 125°F (49 to 52°C) for medium-rare or 130°F (54°C) for medium.

Reduce the heat to medium and add the butter, garlic and white and light green parts of green onion. Turn the steaks onto their sides to cook and render any remaining fat, about 1 to 2 minutes. Briefly baste the steaks with the butter, garlic and green onion mixture. Basting the steaks as they cook with oil helps distribute any aromatics like herbs in the pan and evenly browns the surface. The butter is added toward the end to add flavor, mouthfeel and encourage more browning due to the milk protein solids in the butter.

Immediately transfer the steaks to a clean wire rack set on a sheet pan to rest for 10 minutes. Serve the steaks topped with the miso butter, green onions and cilantro.

COOK'S NOTE:

Rest the ribeye steak right after searing to allow for carryover cooking to finish (page 203). About 10 minutes should suffice, or until the internal temperature drops 5 degrees or below its maximum temperature right when it was taken out of the pan. The juices redistribute more evenly throughout the inside of the steak and thicken as it cools.

RECIPE SCIENCE:

Preheating the steak at low temperature activates enzymes called cathepsins in the meat that help to tenderize the beef, which occurs below 122°F (50°C). The goal with searing is to achieve a quick sear to create a thick brown crust on the steak without overcooking the interior.

pan-roasted greek chicken and vegetables

SAUTÉ & ROAST | GLUTEN-FREE | ONE PAN MEAL

This simple one-pan chicken dish combines savory Greek-inspired ingredients with fresh herbs for a complete dinner solution! The tiny tomatoes are so tender that they burst and mix with the pan drippings, creating a tasty sauce. The clever combination of these dry-heat cooking methods creates a flavorful dish that requires minimal preparation and hands-on time in the kitchen.

SERVES: 4 | **PREP TIME:** 15 minutes | **COOK TIME:** 45 minutes

¾ tsp kosher salt, divided

¼ tsp black pepper, divided

½ tsp paprika

⅛ tsp garlic powder

4 (1½-lb [680-g]) bone-in, skin-on chicken thighs, excess fat and skin trimmed

1 tbsp (15 ml) olive oil

2 cloves garlic, minced

1 lb (454 g) baby red potatoes, quartered

1 cup (149 g) baby tomatoes

2 sprigs rosemary

12 oz (340 g) zucchini, ½-inch (1.3-cm) slices, cut in half

¼ cup (113 g) kalamata olives, sliced in half

2 tbsp (57 g) feta cheese

1 tbsp (3 g) chopped dill

1 lemon, cut into 8 wedges

Adjust the oven rack to the center position and preheat the oven to 400°F (204°C).

Combine ¼ teaspoon of salt, ⅛ teaspoon of black pepper, paprika and garlic powder in a small bowl. Pat the chicken dry with paper towels. Season the chicken with ⅛ teaspoon of the spice mixture on each side.

Heat the olive oil in a 12-inch (30-cm) oven-safe pan over medium-high heat until hot. Place the chicken thighs skin side down in the pan. Cook until the skin is deep golden and crisp, about 7 minutes. Flip the chicken over and turn off the heat. Carefully drain the pan drippings into a heatproof bowl and set aside.

In a large bowl, combine the garlic, potatoes, tomatoes, ¼ teaspoon of salt and 1 tablespoon (15 ml) of pan drippings. Heat the pan containing the chicken over medium heat, add the vegetables and cook for 3 minutes. Turn off the heat and add the rosemary to the pan. Make sure the chicken is not covered by the vegetables to allow the skin to crisp in the oven. Transfer the pan to the oven and bake for 20 minutes.

Meanwhile, combine the zucchini, 1 teaspoon of pan drippings, ¼ teaspoon of salt and ⅛ teaspoon of black pepper in a medium-size bowl.

Remove the pan from the oven and discard the rosemary. Add the zucchini to the pan and bake for 15 minutes, until the zucchini and potatoes are tender and the chicken thighs register 165 to 170°F (74 to 77°C). Season the chicken and the vegetables with salt and pepper to taste. Serve immediately topped with the kalamata olives, crumbled feta cheese, dill and lemon wedges.

COOK'S NOTE:
When taking the internal temperature of the chicken, insert the probe in the thickest part of the thigh. Do not touch the bone or you will get a false high reading.

RECIPE SCIENCE:
Two critical methods are used to achieve tender and juicy chicken with an attractive golden brown appearance. First, a pan-searing technique enables Maillard browning to occur, the reaction responsible for brown pigment and new flavor formation. Second, oven roasting is used to ensure even cooking while retaining the moisture of the chicken.

balsamic roasted pork tenderloin

SAUTÉ & ROAST | GLUTEN-FREE | DAIRY-FREE

Roasted pork tenderloin effortlessly takes on any flavors added to the meat. It's an elegant and hearty weekday meal, and one of my favorites to prepare for my family!

SERVES: 4 | **PREP TIME:** 15 minutes | **COOK TIME:** 40 minutes

1 cup (237 ml) balsamic vinegar

1½ lb (680 g) pork tenderloin, silver skin removed

¼ tsp kosher salt, plus more for seasoning

¼ tsp black pepper, plus more for seasoning

1 tbsp (15 ml) vegetable oil

1½ cups (209 g) sliced zucchini, 1 inch (2.5 cm) thick, cut in half

1½ cups (209 g) sliced yellow squash, 1 inch (2.5 cm) thick, cut in half

2 cups (118 g) brown mushrooms, cut in half

1 cup (149 g) baby tomatoes

1 cup (150 g) diced red onions, 1-inch (2.5-cm) pieces

2 cloves garlic, roughly chopped

1 tbsp (15 ml) olive oil

1 tsp chopped thyme

Adjust the oven rack to the center position and preheat the oven to 400°F (204°C).

In a small saucepan, add the balsamic vinegar. Heat until the vinegar begins to boil, then lower to a simmer with small amounts of bubbles breaking the surface, 185 to 206°F (85 to 96°C). Cook until the vinegar reduces by half to about ½ cup (120 ml), about 20 to 25 minutes. This helps to concentrate the vinegar into a thickened sauce, without over-reducing and burning the sauce. Transfer to a bowl and cool in the refrigerator while you prepare the pork and vegetables.

Trim the pork loin of any excess fat or silver skin. Pat dry the pork with paper towels, pressing out as much surface moisture as possible. Season both sides of the pork with salt and pepper.

The meat is first seared in a small amount of oil that cooks the surface through conduction. In a 12-inch (30-cm) oven-safe skillet, heat the oil over medium-high heat until just beginning to smoke. Carefully add the pork and sear until browned, about 1½ to 2 minutes on each side, 6 to 8 minutes total. Turn off heat and transfer the pork to a plate.

In a large bowl, combine the zucchini, yellow squash, mushrooms, tomatoes, onion, garlic, ¼ teaspoon of salt, ¼ teaspoon of pepper and olive oil. Transfer the vegetables to the skillet and add the seared pork on top.

Use a brush to glaze the tops and sides of the pork with the balsamic vinegar reduction, and roast in the oven for 10 minutes. Remove the skillet and glaze the pork again, cooking for 10 more minutes. Remove the skillet one last time, glaze the pork and cook 5 to 10 minutes, or until thickest part of the pork registers 140 to 145°F (60 to 63°C).

Transfer the pork to a cutting board and glaze with balsamic reduction. Allow the pork to rest for 10 minutes before slicing. Season the vegetables with more salt and pepper to taste. Slice the pork, serve with the vegetables and garnish with the chopped thyme. Serve with the balsamic reduction on the side.

COOK'S NOTE:
The pork is first seared in a small amount of oil that cooks the surface through conduction. It then finishes cooking in the oven with the circulated hot air cooking and internal heat transfer in the meat through convection. The result is a crust that develops multiple new flavors and colors, and a juicy fork-tender slice that has been delicately cooked on the inside.

RECIPE SCIENCE:
When proteins cook, the water stored in the muscle fiber called myofibrils gets squeezed out to the adjacent spaces between as the proteins compress and contract. The proteins shrink when heated and some even dissolve. Resting gives the muscles time to relax, drawing moisture back into where it was originally held in the myofibrils. Instead of all over the cutting board, the juices stay in the meat, making for a more tender and moist slice.

oven-roasted rack of lamb with mint gremolata

SAUTÉ & ROAST | GLUTEN-FREE | DAIRY-FREE

The hot searing temperature helps the unique rich flavors of the fat from the lamb to render and flavor the rest of the roast. A simple fresh herb topping of chopped garlic, parsley, mint and lemon balances the richness of the tender lamb.

SERVES: 2 | PREP TIME: 15 minutes | COOK TIME: 40 minutes

RACK OF LAMB
1¾ to 2 lb (794 to 907 g) frenched rack of lamb, 8 ribs

Kosher salt, for seasoning

Black pepper, for seasoning

2 tbsp (30 ml) olive or vegetable oil

MINT GREMOLATA
2 cloves garlic, minced

1 cup (60 g) parsley, chopped

1 cup (60 g) mint leaves, chopped

Zest from one lemon

2 tbsp (15 ml) extra-virgin olive oil

Adjust the oven rack to the center position and preheat the oven to 350°F (177°C). Prepare a baking sheet with foil.

A frenched rack of lamb is used, meaning part the layer of muscle and fat that extends to the end of the rib bones is taken off so each rib is exposed. Look for about 1 inch (2.5 cm) of fat from the top of the small eye of the meat, trimming more fat as needed. Dry the lamb with paper towels. Season both sides generously with salt and pepper.

Heat the olive oil in a large 12-inch (30-cm) skillet over medium-high heat. Once the oil is hot, add the lamb fat side down, and cook until both sides are browned, about 3 to 4 minutes per side. Sear the bottoms and sides for 30 to 60 seconds each until browned, 8 to 10 minutes total for searing all sides.

Place the lamb fat side up in a foil-lined sheet pan. Transfer the skillet to the oven and roast the lamb until the center of the meat reaches 120 to 125°F (49 to 52°C) for medium rare (about 10 to 20 minutes), and 130 to 135°F (54 to 57°C) for medium (about 20 to 30 minutes). Allow the meat to rest for 10 minutes before slicing. Resting the lamb chops will help retain the moisture inside of the meat that you worked so diligently to retain; between 5 to 10 minutes is the optimal time. Meanwhile, make the gremolata.

For the gremolata, combine the minced garlic, chopped parsley and mint, lemon zest and olive oil in a medium-size bowl. Season with salt and pepper to taste. Serve with the lamb.

COOK'S NOTE:
When purchasing rack of lamb, you may be presented with two options. Smaller-size racks from New Zealand or Australia have a more gamey flavor due to a more grass-based diet. American lamb mainly originating from Colorado or the Midwest is typically larger in size and has a more mild flavor due to the grain-based diet. American lamb is higher in price and considered better in quality and consistency. Adjust cooking times for the smaller racks.

RECIPE SCIENCE:
The temperatures of a stove-top pan can reach 400°F (204°C) easily within minutes, which is great for searing the lamb but not for nailing a nice warm medium-rare center. The heat transfer is not as controlled or consistent on the stove top compared to an oven over long periods of cook time. In order to avoid ruining a pricier cut of meat, the lamb finishes cooking by roasting in the oven so that the moisture is retained. The oven is not as efficient at conducting heat, therefore the pan holding the lamb will stay cooler for a less harsh cook, yielding a juicier roast.

crispy vegetable fritters

PAN-FRY | VEGETARIAN

One clever way to get your daily serving of vegetables is to pack them into vegetable fritters! Each golden brown patty has a blend of sweet potatoes, carrots, zucchini and kale for a wholesome and tasty appetizer or side dish. Savory Parmesan cheese, cumin and garlic powder infuses flavors on the inside of each fritter. Lightly frying the mixture creates a crisp exterior and soft center. To complement the golden fritters, a cool and creamy honey yogurt sauce with fresh dill and mint makes for a tasty dip!

MAKES 6 fritters | **PREP TIME:** 15 minutes | **COOK TIME:** 20 minutes

1 quart (1 L) water

1 cup (106 g) thinly sliced sweet potatoes, ⅛ x ⅛ x 2 inches (3 mm x 3 mm x 5 cm)

1 cup (87 g) thinly sliced carrots, ⅛ x ⅛ x 2 inches (3 mm x 3 mm x 5 cm)

1 cup (116 g) thinly sliced zucchini, ⅛ x ⅛ x 2 inches (3 mm x 3 mm x 5 cm)

1 cup (39 g) thinly sliced kale leaves, ⅛ inch (3 mm)

½ cup (71 g) all-purpose flour

⅓ cup (23 g) grated Parmesan cheese

½ tsp kosher salt

⅛ tsp black pepper

1 tsp cumin

¼ tsp garlic powder

1 large egg, whisked

2 tbsp (30 ml) vegetable oil, add more as needed

YOGURT SAUCE

¼ cup (68 g) plain Greek yogurt

1 tsp chopped dill

1 tsp sliced mint leaves

½ tsp honey

The vegetables are blanched in boiling water to soften the cellular matrices, so they can easily be formed together in a ball. In a medium-size saucepan, bring 1 quart (1 L) water to a boil. Add the sweet potatoes, carrots and zucchini, and cook for 2 minutes. Add the kale to the pan with the vegetables and cook for 2 minutes. Drain the vegetables and pat the mixture dry in between paper towels.

Roughly chop the vegetable mixture so the fritters will hold together when formed. Place the chopped vegetables in a medium-size bowl. Add the flour, Parmesan cheese, salt, pepper, cumin and garlic powder to the vegetables, and stir to combine. Add the whisked egg to the vegetable mixture and combine.

Heat a large 10-inch (25-cm) nonstick skillet over medium heat. Add the vegetable oil to the pan and swirl to coat.

To promote more effective browning on the fritters, working in batches is ideal. The vegetables still contain a lot of moisture; adding too many fritters into the oil at one time will immediately drop the temperature of the cooking oil. This results in greasy fritters with uneven color, due to the buildup of too much steam in the pan. Form ¼ cup (73 g) of the vegetable mixture with your hands into a ball. Add 3 balls into the pan and flatten slightly into ½-inch (1.3-cm) thick fritters with a spatula. Cook each fritter 3 to 4 minutes on each side, until golden brown, 6 to 8 minutes total. Transfer the fritters to a plate lined with a paper towel to drain any excess oil. Repeat this procedure for the remaining fritters.

For the yogurt sauce, whisk together the yogurt, dill, mint and honey in a small bowl. Season the sauce with salt and pepper to taste.

Serve the fritters hot with the yogurt sauce.

COOK'S NOTE:
When frying for a longer period of time, choose a vegetable oil like peanut, corn, canola or a vegetable oil blend (see page 204). These oils have higher smoke points (400°F [204°C] or above). A high-smoke-point oil allows the temperature to be maintained around 325°F (163°C) for a crisp and well-cooked product.

RECIPE SCIENCE:
When the flour in the fritters is exposed to the hot oil in the pan, the flour proteins harden to give a nice contrast of texture for an outside crunch and softer, tender center. This pan-fry method requires a moderately high oil temperature between 325 and 375°F (163 and 191°C). This allows for even browning and thorough cooking of each fritter.

pan-seared halibut with tomato basil couscous

PAN-FRY | DAIRY-FREE

The tender yet hearty texture of the white fish yields nicely to the pan-frying method, creating the lovely contrast of crunchy exterior with a light buttery interior flesh. There still is a lot of good fish flavor left in the pan after frying the halibut, so the tangy tomato compote is made in the same skillet.

SERVES: 2 | **PREP TIME:** 20 minutes | **COOK TIME:** 30 minutes

2 (8-oz [227-g]) halibut fillets, about 2 inches (5 cm) thick

½ cup (80 g) pearl Israeli couscous

¾ cup (180 ml) water

¼ tsp kosher salt, plus more for seasoning

Black pepper, for seasoning

¼ cup (60 ml) grapeseed oil or vegetable oil

2 cups (298 g) baby tomatoes, cut in half

¼ cup (50 g) pitted kalamata olives, sliced

¼ cup (36 g) minced shallots

1 garlic clove, minced

1 tbsp (15 ml) red wine vinegar

2 tbsp (30 ml) olive oil

1 tbsp (4 g) minced parsley

1 tbsp (2 g) thinly sliced basil

2 lemon wedges

Remove the fish from the refrigerator and transfer to paper towel–lined plate. Let stand for 15 minutes at room temperature.

Before frying, make sure the surface of the fish is very dry. Use paper towels to wick up any additional moisture, so that immediate browning can occur. Cooking a wet piece of fish will cause excess oil splattering and steam from the pan, which delays browning and can be dangerous.

Prepare the couscous by adding the water in a medium saucepan fitted with a lid, and bring to a boil. Add the couscous, cover and turn down to simmer. Cook until the couscous is tender, about 10 minutes. Set aside.

Season both sides of the fish with salt and pepper. Heat the grapeseed oil in a large 12-inch (30-cm) sauté pan over high heat, until the oil starts to shimmer and is very hot. Carefully add each fillet into the pan presentation side down, pressing down on the fish for a few seconds with a spatula to create direct contact with the oil.

Reduce the heat to medium-high and cook until the fish is golden brown, about 5 minutes; do not move the fish. Carefully flip the fish and reduce the heat to medium, and cook until the internal temperature reaches 135 to 140°F (57 to 60°C), about 4 to 6 minutes. During this time, you can tilt the pan and baste the sides of the fish with the hot oil to help with cooking. Turn off the heat and transfer the fish to a paper towel–lined plate to remove some of the excess cooking oil. Drain the oil from the pan and return to the stove.

In a medium-size bowl, combine the tomatoes, olives, shallots, garlic, red wine vinegar and ¼ teaspoon of salt. Heat the pan over medium heat and add the olive oil. When the oil is hot, add the tomato mixture. Cook until the tomatoes are softened and a light sauce forms, about 6 minutes. Add the couscous, parsley and basil to the pan, and mix to combine. Season with salt and pepper as desired.

Divide the tomato basil couscous in two bowls and top with the halibut. Serve with lemon wedges.

COOK'S NOTE:

The pan-frying technique uses a very high temperature during cooking, so a grapeseed or vegetable oil is selected. These oils have a neutral flavor and have a high smoke point (above 390°F [199°C]) compared to extra virgin olive oil and are therefore safer to use. See page 204 for more information on the smoke points of cooking oils.

RECIPE SCIENCE:

Halibut can dry out very quickly so you don't want a lot of residence time in the pan, but you do want that sought-after super-crisp crust. Typically, frying creates flavorful browned bits of fond, concentrated juices, drippings and cooked bits on the bottom of the pan; however, halibut fillets do not contain a large amount of natural glucose compared to beef.

sticky asian chicken wings

DEEP-FRY | DAIRY-FREE

Deep-fried chicken wings are incredibly hard to resist, especially with a golden brown crispy skin and tossed in a sweet and savory sauce. These sticky Asian wings have a simple and thin flour dredge that has been seasoned with salt, pepper and garlic so that each bite has layers of flavor and crunch. The wings are tossed in a sweet and savory sauce mixture to give a bold Asian flavor. A small amount of cornstarch is used to thicken the sauce so that it coats the chicken without causing the crispy skin to get instantly soggy when they're tossed together.

MAKES 20 pieces | **PREP TIME:** 15 minutes | **COOK TIME:** 30 minutes

SAUCE

¼ cup (60 ml) honey

¼ cup (60 ml) soy sauce

¼ cup (60 ml) hoisin sauce

2 cloves garlic, minced

1 tsp minced ginger

¼ tsp rice vinegar

¼ tsp sesame oil

¼ tsp red chili pepper flakes

1 tsp cornstarch

CHICKEN

64 oz (2 L) canola oil or peanut oil, more as needed for frying

2 lb (908 g) chicken drumettes and wings

2 tsp (12 g) kosher salt, plus more for seasoning

¾ tsp black pepper, plus more for seasoning

1 cup (120 g) all-purpose flour

½ tsp garlic powder

1 tsp sesame seeds

1 tsp sliced green onion, cut on the bias

For the sauce, add the honey, soy sauce, hoisin sauce, garlic, ginger, rice vinegar, sesame oil, red chili pepper flakes and cornstarch to a medium-size saucepan and whisk to combine. Turn the heat to medium-high, and when the sauce just comes to a boil, cook for 30 to 60 seconds, continuously whisking, until the sauce slightly thickens. Turn off the heat and prepare the chicken.

In a large pot or Dutch oven, heat the oil until it reaches 375°F (191°C). You want about 3 inches (8 cm) of oil; add more if needed.

Thoroughly dry the chicken pieces between paper towels. Season the chicken with salt and pepper. In a medium-size bowl, combine the flour, salt, black pepper and garlic powder. Coat the chicken in flour mixture, shaking off any excess.

Place a sheet pan lined with paper towels near the oil. Working in batches of about 5 pieces at a time, fry the chicken until browned and crisp, about 7 to 8 minutes. Make sure to keep moving the chicken pieces with a wire-mesh spider, tongs or wooden chopsticks so that it's constantly exposed to fresh hot oil for even cooking and browning. Otherwise, pockets of cooler oil will surround the chicken and reduce the overall effectiveness of the frying method.

Transfer the hot chicken to the sheet pan to drain any excess oil, and season immediately with salt. Fry the rest of the chicken.

Add the chicken to a medium-size bowl. Add enough sauce to coat the wings, and toss to combine.

Transfer to a plate and top with the sesame seeds and green onions.

COOK'S NOTE:
Other frying oils can be used for this recipe such as sunflower oil, corn oil and soybean oil. They all have smoke points above 440°F (227°C) with varying amounts of low saturated fats (page 204).

RECIPE SCIENCE:
In order to achieve golden color and a nice crust, deep-frying is used to completely submerge the chicken into hot oil at 375°F (191°C). When tackling any deep-frying method, an instant-read thermometer is essential. Canola oil and peanut oil were selected because they have a smoke point between 400 and 450°F (204 and 232°C), at least 25 degrees above the targeted oil temperature. Canola oil has a low amount of saturated fat (around 7 percent), for a clean mouthfeel after eating.

roasted root vegetables

A huge tray of roasted vegetables is always a delight! Cooking vegetables at high temperatures transforms raw vegetables into caramelized and tender pieces. This recipe combines a variety of vibrant root vegetables, each offering their own unique flavor. Roasting carrots intensifies their flavor and brings out their natural sweetness. The licorice notes in fennel add depth in flavor to the vegetables. The Brussels sprouts can have a very sulfurous aroma; however, the high heat of roasting and time unleash their natural sweetness and reduce those undesirable aromas. Beets are naturally packed with sugar and earthy flavor roasting accentuates those notes. This tray of aromatic and tasty roasted vegetables will give you even more reason to eat your produce every day!

SERVES: 8 | **PREP TIME:** 15 minutes | **COOK TIME:** 35 minutes

¼ cup (60 ml) olive oil, divided, plus more for greasing

1 lb (454 g) whole carrots, peeled and cut in half lengthwise

1 fennel bulb (291 g) cut into ½-inch (1.3-cm) slices, reserve green fennel tops

12 oz (347 g) Brussels sprouts, cut in half

2 shallots, peeled and cut into quarters through the root

4 cloves garlic, peeled and cut in half

1 tsp kosher salt, divided

¼ tsp black pepper

6 baby beets (558 g) 2 inches (5 cm) in diameter, peeled and quartered

4 sprigs rosemary

4 sprigs thyme

¼ cup (16 g) parsley, chopped

Adjust the oven rack to the center position and preheat the oven to 400°F (204°C). Lightly drizzle a large sheet pan with olive oil or cooking spray.

In a large bowl, add the carrots, fennel, Brussels sprouts, shallots and garlic. Drizzle with 3 tablespoons (45 ml) of olive oil, ¾ teaspoon salt and the pepper, and toss to coat the vegetables. Spread evenly on the sheet pan.

In the same bowl, toss the beets with 1 tablespoon (15 ml) of olive oil and ¼ teaspoon of salt. Spread out evenly on the tray. Season the vegetables with more pepper. Evenly distribute the rosemary and thyme in different areas of the sheet tray on top of the vegetables.

Roast the vegetables for 20 minutes and then gently stir. Cook for an additional 10 to 15 minutes, or until the vegetables are tender. Discard the rosemary and thyme. Serve the vegetables warm, garnished with parsley and green fennel tops.

COOK'S NOTE:
Cut the same vegetables into similar sizes for consistent cooking time and caramelization. It also helps to roast the Brussels sprouts cut side down on the pan for more flavor and browning.

RECIPE SCIENCE:
Vegetables naturally contain a lot of moisture, and the pectin network in the cell walls breaks down over time in the presence of heat, releasing the moisture through evaporation. This moisture loss allows the vegetables to begin browning for added flavor and texture. The vegetables are roasted at 400°F (204°C) to kick-start cooking. The surface temperature of the vegetables will eventually reach caramelization, beginning at 230°F (110°C) for fructose-containing vegetables. Many vegetables contain a variety of sugars like fructose, glucose and sucrose, which affects the degree of caramelization and how quickly it occurs. You will notice that the beets and carrots will caramelize the most compared to the other vegetables because they have the highest amount of sugars.

mexican quinoa-stuffed sweet potatoes

BAKE | VEGETARIAN

To make this dish a complete meal, each potato is filled with a satisfying Mexican-inspired quinoa and packed with protein, vegetables and spices. An easy chipotle sauce is drizzled on top to add creamy, spicy and smoky flavors.

SERVES: 4 | **PREP TIME:** 20 minutes | **COOK TIME:** 1 hour 15 minutes

SWEET POTATOES

4 (15 oz [425 g] each) large sweet potatoes

1 tbsp (15 ml) olive oil

1 clove garlic, minced

¼ cup (44 g) diced red onion, ¼-inch (6-mm) dice

¾ cup (145 g) quinoa, rinsed with cold water

1 tbsp (12 g) minced jalapeño

½ cup (69 g) diced zucchini, ¼-inch (6-mm) dice

1 cup (178 g) diced tomato, ¼-inch (6-mm) dice

¾ cup (119 g) corn kernels

½ cup (83 g) canned black beans, drained

¼ tsp chili powder

½ tsp cumin

½ tsp kosher salt

¼ tsp black pepper

1¼ cups (300 ml) vegetable broth

¾ cup (116 g) diced red bell pepper, ¼-inch (6-mm) dice

¼ cup (4 g) cilantro, for garnish

CHIPOTLE SAUCE

¼ cup (68 g) plain Greek yogurt

Zest of one lime

2 tbsp (30 ml) lime juice

¼ tsp ground chipotle pepper

½ tsp cumin

1 tbsp (15 ml) olive oil

¼ tsp kosher salt

Black pepper, to taste

Clean, dry and wrap each sweet potato with foil. Preheat the oven to 375°F (191°C). Line a baking sheet with foil and place the potatoes on top, and then transfer to the oven in the center rack position.

Bake the potatoes for 60 to 75 minutes, or until soft to the touch and a knife can easily pierce the flesh.

To prepare the quinoa, heat the olive oil over medium heat in a medium pot fitted with a lid. Add the garlic and red onion, stir to cook until fragrant, 1 minute. Add the quinoa, jalapeño, zucchini, tomato, corn, black beans, chili powder, cumin, salt, pepper and vegetable broth.

Bring to a boil, cover, reduce the heat to low and simmer until the quinoa is cooked and the liquid is absorbed, about 25 to 30 minutes. Turn off the heat and allow to sit covered for at least 10 minutes before stirring. The water should be absorbed and the quinoa will be tender and fluffy. Stir in the bell pepper right before stuffing.

For the chipotle sauce, whisk together the yogurt, lime zest, lime juice, chipotle pepper, cumin and olive oil in a small bowl. Season with ¼ teaspoon of kosher salt and black pepper to taste. Refrigerate until ready to use.

Unwrap the sweet potatoes and make a cut lengthwise ¾ of the way through the center of the potato. Use a fork to fluff up some of the potatoes so it looks mashed. Fill each potato with Mexican quinoa, drizzle with the chipotle sauce and garnish with cilantro leaves.

> **COOK'S NOTE:**
> Select sweet potatoes of similar size so that the cook time won't vary greatly. Wrapping the potatoes in the foil protects the outside from getting too hot. The foil stops any moisture from escaping, giving a more evenly roasted, tasty spud.

> **RECIPE SCIENCE:**
> Potatoes contain starches called polysaccharides, which are composed of sugar molecules called glucose. Roasting sweet potatoes causes enzymes in the potato to convert the starches into maltose, which we taste as sweet. This starts happening when the potatoes' internal temperature reaches 135°F (57°C). The starch-to-sugar conversion stops at 170°F (77°C) when the enzymes can no longer perform. It helps to start the potatoes in a cold oven before it heats up to enhance the sweetness.

tempura shrimp and vegetables

DEEP-FRY | DAIRY-FREE

Light, crunchy and irresistible, tempura is a must-order at any Japanese restaurant. There are many mixing methods, batter combinations and frying temperatures to try. I have finally found a recipe that yields restaurant-quality tempura, so you can enjoy this dish any time you get the craving. The batter is a combination of flour and cornstarch for crisp texture development. If only flour is used, the batter becomes too thick, and with just cornstarch, the batter is very tough. A combination gives just the right structure balance. The high frying temperature yields a light golden color with super-crispy coating, which only takes a few minutes to fry each item. The tempura is served with a light sweet and savory dipping sauce for the ultimate tempura experience.

SERVES: 4 | **PREP TIME:** 30 minutes | **COOK TIME:** 30 minutes

DIPPING SAUCE

2 tbsp (15 ml) soy sauce

1½ tsp (7 ml) honey

1 tbsp (15 ml) mirin rice wine

½ tsp rice vinegar

¼ tsp sesame oil

3 tbsp (45 ml) water

TEMPURA

2 quarts (2 L) vegetable or peanut oil

½ lb (267 g) jumbo shrimp, 16 to 20 per pound, peeled and deveined, tails left on

¾ cup (104 g) all-purpose flour

¼ cup (35 g) cornstarch

½ cup (120 ml) vodka

1 large egg

½ cup (120 ml) cold seltzer water or club soda

Kosher salt, for seasoning

½ cup (31 g) broccoli florets

½ cup (100 g) sweet potatoes, peeled and sliced into ¼-inch (6-mm) thick rounds

½ cup (68 g) zucchini, ½-inch (1.3-cm) thick slices

½ cup (45 g) yellow onion, ½-inch (1.3-cm) thick slices

1 cup (59 g) green beans, ends trimmed

For the dipping sauce, whisk together the soy sauce, honey, mirin rice wine, rice vinegar, sesame oil and water in a small bowl. Transfer to a serving bowl and set aside.

Adjust the oven rack to the center position and preheat the oven to 200°F (93°C).

Heat the oil in a large pot or Dutch oven over medium heat to 385°F (196°C). Use an instant-read thermometer to check the temperature. Line a sheet pan with paper towels and place a wire rack on a separate large sheet pan.

While the oil heats, prepare the tempura shrimp by making two shallow ¼-inch (6-mm) deep cuts on the underside of each shrimp about ½ inch (1.3 cm) apart. Gently use your fingers to pull the shrimp flat so it's not as curled. This will help prevent the shrimp from completely curling up when fried.

In a large bowl, whisk together the flour and cornstarch. In a medium-size bowl, whisk together the vodka and egg. Whisk the seltzer water into the egg mixture and set aside.

As the oil reaches 385°F (196°C), immediately pour the liquid egg mixture into the bowl with the flour mixture. Gently whisk until just combined, just a few stirs; you want a batter that is bubbly and slightly lumpy to give it more texture.

When the oil reaches about 400°F (204°C), immediately add all of the shrimp to the batter, using your fingers to coat. Remove the shrimp one at a time from the batter, allowing excess batter to drip into the bowl. Carefully hold the shrimp close to the surface of the oil and drop it in. Add as much shrimp as will fit; you may have to work in batches. Cook the shrimp until lightly golden in color and crunchy, 1½ to 2 minutes. Transfer the fried shrimp to the paper towel–lined sheet pan and season with salt. Once the excess oil has been absorbed, transfer the shrimp to the wire rack–lined sheet pan and transfer to the oven to keep warm.

(continued)

The frying temperature of the oil needs to be held around 400°F (204°C). Allow the oil to get back up to near 400°F (204°C), about 4 minutes, and repeat with the remaining shrimp and vegetables, working in batches and allowing the heat to get back up to temperature. Fry the broccoli for about 2 to 3 minutes. Fry the sweet potatoes, zucchini and onion for about 2 minutes. Fry green beans for about 1 to 1½ minutes. Drain the tempura on a paper towel and season with salt.

Transfer the tempura to the warm oven until ready to consume. Serve the tempura with dipping sauce.

COOK'S NOTE:

To prevent too much oil from being absorbed into the crisp coating in between frying batches, transfer the fried items to a paper towel–lined sheet pan for a few minutes. Instead of staying on the surface, the oil will be absorbed by the paper towel. You can then transfer the tempura to a wire rack so that the underside doesn't get soggy.

RECIPE SCIENCE:

Seltzer water or club soda is used because the bubbles create a delicate and webbed coating when fried. The pH of the seltzer is around 4, creating a more acidic batter which slows down gluten formation, just what you need in between frying batches. When the fizzy water combines with the flour, the proteins in the flour glutenin and gliadin form gluten, which gives the fried batter structure. However, if the batter is overmixed, too much gluten is formed, creating heavier coating. A neat trick to reduce some of the gluten formation is adding some vodka to replace half of the water in the batter. Only 60 percent of vodka is water, so the remaining 40 percent alcohol portion does not participate in gluten formation. The advantage is a light and crunchy batter throughout the coating process, whereas typically the coating gets thicker and less crisp over time.

cedar-planked mahi mahi with pineapple salsa

GRILL | GLUTEN-FREE | DAIRY-FREE

Did you know you can add even more layers of flavor just by cooking seafood on a wooden plank? The earthy aromas from a charred cedar plank create a different depth of flavor that is infused right into fish. For quick-cooking fish like mahi mahi, this is a great way to maximize flavor transfer since it's indirectly cooking on the grill for under 20 minutes. To complement the natural smoldering flavors of the cedar, a sweet and smoky dry spice blend is generously coated on both sides of the fish.

SERVES: 2 | PREP TIME: 1 hour 30 minutes | COOK TIME: 15 minutes

1 cedar plank (large enough to hold 2 pieces of fish)

2 (8-oz [226-g]) mahi mahi fillets

1 tsp kosher salt

⅛ tsp black pepper

½ tsp garlic powder

½ tsp paprika

⅛ tsp chipotle chili powder

¼ tsp dried thyme

1 tsp brown sugar

6 sprigs of thyme

PINEAPPLE SALSA

1 cup (208 g) diced pineapple, ¼-inch (6-mm) dice

1 cup (160 g) diced tomato, ¼-inch (6-mm) dice

¼ cup (39 g) finely diced red onion

2 tsp (9 g) minced jalapeño

Zest of 1 lime

2 tbsp (30 ml) lime juice

½ cup (8 g) cilantro, chopped

Place a cedar plank on a sheet pan, cover completely with water and place a heavy bottle on top of the board to keep it submerged. Soak the plank for 1 hour.

Dry the mahi mahi fillets with a paper towel, and set aside.

In a small bowl, combine the salt, pepper, garlic powder, paprika, chipotle pepper, dried thyme and brown sugar. Evenly coat both sides of the fish with seasoning mix, about ¾ teaspoon on each side.

Heat the grill to medium-high heat, allowing it to become very hot before adding the cedar plank. Remove the soaked plank from the water and place it on the cooking grate and close the lid. When the plank begins to smoke and just char, about 7 to 10 minutes, turn the plank over.

Place the seasoned fish on the charred side of the plank, spreading the 6 sprigs of thyme across the board. Cook the fish with the lid closed for about 10 to 15 minutes, or until opaque in the center, or the internal temperature reaches 140°F (60°C). Transfer the plank with the mahi mahi to a heatproof surface, and then place the fish on a clean plate.

For the pineapple salsa, stir the pineapples, tomatoes, red onion, jalapeño, lime zest, lime juice and cilantro together in a medium-size bowl until combined. Serve on top of the fish.

COOK'S NOTE:
Any fish can be used for cedar planking. Salmon, halibut, swordfish, snapper and even delicate tilapia are some great choices. The cooking times will differ, so just check with a thermometer for doneness. Typically 125°F (52°C) for salmon and 140°F (60°C) for white-fleshed fish. When cooking a larger whole fillet, use the same internal cooking temperatures to gauge doneness, as it will require more time.

RECIPE SCIENCE:
Planking creates a dry heat environment, similar to roasting by convection in the oven. There are many kinds of planks that can be used, including cedar, alder, maple, apple, oak and hickory. The plank should be soaked for an hour in water to help prevent it from catching fire. To impart a deeper wood flavor to the fish, the cedar plank gets a precook treatment on the grill. This allows a smoky flavor to be generated, and then the fish is cooked on the slightly charred side.

fish katsu with asian slaw

DEEP-FRY | DAIRY-FREE

Katsu is a lighter Japanese style of breaded and fried cutlet of meat or seafood. The secret to the super-crunchy and golden fish katsu is the bread-crumb-coating method and ingredient selection. Panko bread crumbs are large, long irregular-shaped particles with porous structures. When coated on the outside of the fish, the large and bumpy surface creates more depth and intensity to the crunch factor when fried. The result is an elevated crispy and light experience that is extremely addicting.

SERVES: 4 | **PREP TIME:** 30 minutes | **COOK TIME:** 15 minutes

ASIAN SLAW

2 cups (200 g) thinly sliced red cabbage

1 cup (100 g) thinly sliced napa cabbage

1 cup (77 g) shredded carrots

2 cups (190 g) thinly sliced seeded cucumbers

½ cup (64 g) thinly sliced red bell pepper

2 tbsp (30 ml) honey

1 tbsp (15 ml) mirin rice wine

2 tbsp (45 ml) rice vinegar

Kosher salt, as needed for seasoning

Black pepper, as needed for seasoning

CREAMY MISO SAUCE

½ cup (123 g) mayonnaise

1 tbsp (18 g) yellow miso paste

1 tsp honey

Black pepper, as needed for seasoning

FISH KATSU

2 large eggs

½ cup (92 g) rice flour

1 cup (80 g) panko bread crumbs

4 (6-oz [170-g]) catfish, orange roughy or swai fillets

Kosher salt, as needed for seasoning

Black pepper, as needed for seasoning

⅔ cup (160 ml) vegetable oil, divided

For the Asian slaw, combine the red and napa cabbage, carrots, cucumber and bell pepper in a medium-size bowl. In a small bowl, whisk together the honey, mirin rice wine and rice vinegar. Add the honey dressing to the vegetables and stir to combine. Marinate, stirring occasionally, for at least 10 minutes. Season with salt and pepper to taste.

For the creamy miso sauce, whisk together the mayonnaise, miso and honey in a small bowl. Season with pepper to taste.

For the fish katsu, add the eggs into a shallow bowl and whisk until smooth. Place the rice flour and bread crumbs in their own separate shallow bowls or plates.

Dry the catfish fillets in between paper towels. Season both sides of the fillets with salt and pepper. Take one fillet and place into the flour, flip to evenly coat and shake off any excess flour. Dip the fillet in the egg and coat evenly, letting any excess drip off. Last, place fish in the bread crumbs, pressing to ensure they adhere evenly to the fish. Transfer to a clean plate and repeat with the remaining fillets.

Heat a medium nonstick pan over medium-high heat. Add ⅓ cup (80 ml) of vegetable oil to the pan, or enough oil to cover ⅛ of the fish. Once the oil is very hot, add two of the breaded catfish fillets and cook until golden brown and cooked through, 3 to 4 minutes per side. Transfer the fish to a paper towel–lined plate, and immediately season with salt and pepper. Discard the oil and wipe the pan. Reheat and add the remaining ⅓ cup (80 ml) of oil, repeating the frying procedure with the last two breaded fillets. Serve the fish with the Asian slaw and some miso sauce.

COOK'S NOTE:
Rice flour is used instead of all-purpose wheat flour because of its lack of gluten formation. Gluten formation from the wheat flour with the moisture in the egg will create a tougher crust. Since the fish has a more delicate texture when cooked, using rice flour and panko bread crumbs keeps the breading light and crispy.

RECIPE SCIENCE:
Dipping the fish fillets in rice flour helps wick up any additional moisture from the flesh. The hydrated starches in the rice create a gel, giving the beaten egg something to stick to. The egg is necessary because it acts like a sticky glue to attach all of the panko bread crumbs to the surface of the fish. When the egg proteins cook and solidify, the bread crumbs are secured onto the fish, instead of tragically falling off. The crust browning process is relatively quick due to the extra surface area for the oil to come in contact with from the jagged bread crumb coating. Bread crumbs act as an insulator to prevent the fish from drying out.

crispy roasted potatoes

ROAST | VEGETARIAN | GLUTEN-FREE | DAIRY-FREE

For the crunchiest and creamiest potatoes every time, try my go-to oven-roasting technique! Yukon Gold potatoes are waxy potatoes, which means they have less starch content and higher sugar, yielding a creamier flesh. They give a balance of crisp exterior and flavorful interior. What takes these potatoes to the next level is the garlic- and rosemary-infused oil used to coat the potatoes before roasting. The fat-soluble flavor compounds in the aromatics transfer to the oil, for incredible herbaceous flavors with each bite!

SERVES: 4 | **PREP TIME:** 10 minutes | **COOK TIME:** 35 minutes

1 quart (1 L) water

4 tsp (24 g) kosher salt, divided

¼ tsp baking soda

2 lb (908 g) Yukon Gold potatoes, 2 inches (5 cm) in diameter, quartered

¼ cup (60 ml) olive oil

1½ tsp (5 g) minced garlic

2 tsp (1 g) rosemary, chopped

¼ tsp black pepper

2 tsp (2 g) minced parsley

Adjust the oven rack to the center position and preheat the oven to 450°F (232°C).

Heat the water in a large pot over high heat until boiling. Add 1 tablespoon (5 g) of kosher salt, baking soda and potatoes, and stir to combine. When the water comes back to a boil, reduce the heat to a simmer. Cook until the potatoes give little resistance to a knife or fork inserted into the flesh, about 10 to 15 minutes. Drain the potatoes, then return to the hot pot to allow excess moisture to evaporate, 5 minutes.

Meanwhile, heat the olive oil, garlic and rosemary in a small frying pan over medium heat. Cook, shaking the pan constantly until the garlic begins to turn just golden in color, about 2 to 3 minutes. Immediately strain the oil through a metal fine-mesh strainer set in a large-size bowl. Reserve the fried garlic and rosemary to add to the potatoes after roasting.

Transfer the cooked potatoes to the garlic-infused olive oil. Add 1 teaspoon of salt and ¼ teaspoon of black pepper. Use a large spoon to vigorously toss and stir the potatoes until a thick layer of potato paste coats the potatoes.

Transfer the potatoes to a rimmed baking sheet and spread into a single layer. Roast for 10 to 15 minutes.

Place the roasted potatoes in a serving bowl and top with reserved garlic and rosemary, and then garnish with minced parsley. Serve the potatoes hot.

COOK'S NOTE:
Different potatoes such as the starchy Russet type can be used for this recipe. Make sure you keep the pieces of the potatoes large, at least 1 inch (2.5 cm) in diameter, so they do not easily fall apart when parboiling.

RECIPE SCIENCE:
Adding baking soda to the cooking water of the potatoes creates an alkaline environment. This breaks down and releases the starches on the surface allowing for more crunch potential once roasted. It degrades the structural molecule pectin, a soluble fiber that binds the cells in vegetables together. Pectin breaks down at 183°F (84°C); therefore, adding the potatoes to rapidly boiling alkaline water encourages the potatoes' surface structure to come apart more easily. The parboiled potatoes are vigorously stirred to create a visible layer of potato slurry on the surface right before roasting. High oven temperature of 450°F (232°C) allows for gorgeous golden browning and crust formation on the creamy potatoes.

herb-roasted chicken with vegetables

ROAST | GLUTEN-FREE

A crispy whole roasted chicken is the ultimate comfort food to feed a crowd. This recipe is unique because it gives a one-pan meal solution. As the chicken slowly cooks and browns due to the high oven temperatures, the carrots, onions, celery and potatoes also cook and caramelize. Any extra juices can be used to create a delicious pan sauce (page 148).

SERVES: 4 | **PREP TIME:** 2 hours | **COOK TIME:** 65 minutes

5 lb (2.3 kg) whole chicken

6 tbsp (86 g) unsalted butter, softened

1¾ tsp (9 g) kosher salt, divided

1 tsp lemon zest

1 tsp chopped rosemary

1 tsp chopped thyme

1 red onion, peeled and cut into 8 wedges

3 cups (300 g) celery stalks, cut into 2-inch (5-cm) pieces

4 cups (664 g) carrot pieces, peeled and cut into 2-inch (5-cm) pieces

1 lb (454 g) baby red potatoes, quartered

3 tbsp (45 ml) olive oil

12 cloves garlic, peeled and crushed, divided

10 sprigs thyme, divided

3 sprigs rosemary

¼ tsp black pepper

1 lemon, cut into 8 wedges

Remove the chicken from the refrigerator and allow it to come to room temperature, about 1½ to 2 hours.

Adjust the oven rack to the lower third position and preheat the oven to 475°F (246°C).

In a small bowl, combine the butter, ½ teaspoon of kosher salt, lemon zest, chopped rosemary and chopped thyme, and set aside.

In a large bowl, combine the onion, celery, carrot, red potatoes, olive oil, ¾ teaspoon of kosher salt and 8 cloves of garlic. Transfer to a large roasting pan or baking dish, at least 13 x 9 x 2.5 inches (33 x 23 x 6 cm) in size. Scatter 5 sprigs of thyme and the rosemary over the vegetables.

Prepare the chicken by removing the neck and innards, then dry the inside and outside of the chicken with paper towels to remove as much moisture as possible. Season the cavity with ½ teaspoon of kosher salt and the black pepper, and add the 4 remaining cloves of garlic and the 5 remaining sprigs of thyme. Massage the inside cavity to infuse it with the flavors. Carefully add 1 tablespoon (15 g) of the butter mixture beneath the skin to cover the breast, and repeat with the other side. If desired, truss the chicken with butcher's twine. Use the remaining butter to coat the outside of the chicken.

Make a nest in the center of the vegetables and place the chicken breast side down on top. Roast the chicken for 30 minutes. Remove the tray from the oven and, using paper towels and oven mitts, carefully turn the chicken over, breast side up. Roast 30 to 35 minutes, or until the juices run clear and temperature in the thickest part of the breast reaches 160°F (71°C). If needed, return the chicken to the oven for more roasting, checking every 5 minutes for doneness. Transfer the chicken to a cutting board and rest for 20 minutes.

Just before serving, set the roasting pan of vegetables over medium heat and reheat the vegetables, turning and glazing with pan juice; season with salt and pepper as needed.

Cut the chicken and arrange over the vegetables. Serve with a pan sauce if desired (page 148).

COOK'S NOTE:

Make sure that the thickest part of the chicken reaches the proper temperature, about 160°F (71°C) for the breast and 170°F (77°C) for the thighs, before stopping the cooking process. Whole chickens are not affected by carryover cooking, the heat transfer that continues happening after cooking stops (page 203). This is because the hollow cavity allows heat and steam to leave, which keeps the chicken from retaining the heat.

RECIPE SCIENCE:

Cooking the chicken breast side down first protects the chicken breast from overcooking and drying out. This also enables the back and thighs of the chicken to cook first, as the thighs require longer cooking to reach higher internal temperatures of about 170°F (77°C). Halfway through cooking the chicken is turned over so that the chicken breast can roast and become crispy brown.

caramelized asparagus wrapped in bacon

ROAST | GLUTEN-FREE

Bacon-wrapped asparagus is indulgent, savory and, in my husband's opinion, probably the tastiest way to enjoy your vegetables. To promote the caramelization of the bacon and asparagus, a black pepper maple syrup mixture is generously glazed onto the vegetable bundles at the beginning and a few times throughout the oven-roasting process. This seasons the asparagus and browns the tips for more flavor. The bacon gets a sticky candy-like coating for the ultimate crispiness and flavor.

SERVES: 5 | **PREP TIME:** 10 minutes | **COOK TIME:** 30 minutes

3 tbsp (45 ml) olive oil

¼ cup (60 ml) pure maple syrup

½ tsp black pepper, plus more for seasoning

5 slices thick-cut bacon

1 lb (454 g) asparagus, trimmed to 7-inch (18-cm) long spears

Kosher salt, as needed for seasoning

Adjust the oven rack to the center position and preheat the oven to 400°F (204°C).

In a small bowl, whisk together the olive oil, maple syrup and black pepper. Set aside.

Line a sheet pan with foil and place a wire rack on top. Spray the rack with nonstick cooking spray.

Place 5 slices of bacon spaced evenly apart on the pan. Roast until the bacon just begins to shrink and turns a slightly red color, but is still flexible, about 5 minutes, depending on thickness. You don't want the bacon to be completely crispy, because it will break when wrapping around the asparagus.

Remove the bacon from the oven and brush with the maple syrup mixture on both sides. Roast the bacon for 3 more minutes. Allow the bacon to cool until it's easy to handle with your fingers.

Divide the asparagus into five even-size bundles. On a cutting board, wrap one slice of the parcooked bacon overlapping over the length of the asparagus spears. Secure the bacon with a toothpick. Carefully place the bundles on the baking rack. Generously brush the maple syrup mixture over the bacon-wrapped asparagus spears on both sides. Lightly season each bundle with salt and pepper.

Roast the asparagus bundles for 10 minutes, remove from the oven and brush the maple mixture over just the bacon. Roast for 5 minutes, or until the bacon is browned and crispy, and the asparagus is tender.

COOK'S NOTE:

The thickness of the bacon you choose will impact roasting time. I selected a thick-cut bacon so it was easier to handle when precooking, did not crisp too quickly and could be easily wrapped around the asparagus spears.

RECIPE SCIENCE:

There are two common issues when wrapping vegetables in bacon. First, the bacon never gets crispy enough on both sides. Second, the asparagus shrinks to tiny sticks. To tackle these issues, the bacon is roasted on a rack at 400°F (204°C), just until both sides begin to brown but are not crisp. The goal is to have a parcooked piece of flexible bacon that's easy to wrap around the spears but isn't raw. Typically, it would take over 30 minutes to crisp the raw bacon, which leads to overcooked asparagus. Pre-cooking the bacon cuts down that oven time so the asparagus gets a little crisp on the edges but remains tender and green.

moroccan-spiced chicken skewers with apricot glaze

GRILL | GLUTEN-FREE | DAIRY-FREE

Fire up the grill because these chicken skewers are loaded with flavor and ready to sizzle! The chicken is marinated in a mixture of pungent spices then glazed with a sweet apricot sauce to deliver the flavors of Morocco to each skewer. These savory sweet chicken skewers have an explosion of spices and aromatics, taking your taste buds on a culinary journey.

MAKES: 10 skewers | **PREP TIME:** 40 minutes | **COOK TIME:** 10 minutes

1½ lb (680 g) boneless skinless chicken breasts

¼ cup (60 ml) honey

¼ cup (60 ml) olive oil, plus more for greasing

½ tsp lemon zest

3 tbsp (45 ml) lemon juice

2 tsp (8 g) minced ginger

1 garlic clove, minced

1 tsp ground cumin

½ tsp ground coriander

½ tsp ground cinnamon

½ tsp smoked paprika

⅛ tsp cayenne pepper

1 tsp kosher salt

¼ tsp black pepper

10 skewers, soaked in water for 15 minutes if wooden

APRICOT GLAZE
½ cup (94 g) apricot preserves

1 tsp lemon zest

2 tbsp (30 ml) lemon juice

1 tbsp (1 g) sliced mint leaves, divided

Slice each chicken breast into ¾- to 1-inch (2- to 2.5-cm) thick strips. Be sure to slice with the grain so it yields a long piece. Each breast should yield about 4 to 6 strips depending on size.

In a medium-size bowl, whisk together the honey, olive oil, lemon zest, lemon juice, ginger, garlic, cumin, coriander, cinnamon, smoked paprika, cayenne pepper, salt and black pepper. Transfer to a large resealable plastic bag or baking dish. Add the chicken and marinate at least 30 minutes to 1 hour. Thread the chicken onto the skewers and set aside.

To prepare the apricot glaze, whisk together the apricot preserves, lemon zest and lemon juice in a small bowl. Microwave for 30 seconds, and stir to combine. Cook for an additional 30 seconds if needed until the glaze is smooth. Add 2 teaspoons of the mint and stir to combine. Set aside.

Heat the grill to medium heat. Add a small amount of oil to a folded piece of paper towel, and carefully grease the grill with the oil. Once the grill is very hot, add the chicken skewers. Cook the first side for 5 minutes, flip over and brush with the apricot glaze. Close the lid and cook 4 to 5 minutes, or until the chicken is no longer pink, and the internal temperature reaches 160 to 165°F (71 to 74°C). Coat the other side of the chicken with the apricot glaze. Garnish with 1 teaspoon of sliced mint. Transfer to a clean plate and serve hot.

COOK'S NOTE:
Too much time in the acidic lemon marinade can change the chicken's protein charge and cause it to become dry. The acidic environment makes the protein reach an isoelectric point of pH 5.2. The proteins come closer together and squeeze out any liquid in between.

RECIPE SCIENCE:
By increasing the surface area of the chicken, there is more opportunity for the water-soluble flavor compounds like garlic and ginger to be infused into the meat, while fat-soluble compounds like spices stick to the surface and hit your tongue first. The salt plays a huge role in not only seasoning the chicken, but when diffused in liquid, restructures the proteins in the meat to allow for gaps that fill with water to create a more juicy piece of meat. When marinating chicken breasts, allow for 30 minutes at minimum and up to 1 hour. A brief marinating time prevents dry chicken and mushy texture from the acids in the lemon juice. The grill is an excellent quick-cooking dry-heat method, rapidly creating flavors through Maillard browning when the surface temperature of the food reaches 300°F (149°C).

grilled salmon burgers

GRILL | QUICK (30 MINUTES OR LESS) | DAIRY-FREE

When grilling season hits, these salmon burgers are the first to get thrown on the barbecue! The special blend of fresh fish, capers, mustard, sun-dried tomatoes and bread crumbs creates a hearty, mouthwatering patty. This recipe creates a tender salmon burger with little bursts of flavor from the pungent and sweet add-ins. I always make some Lemon Basil Aioli (page 142) to spread on my burgers. Be bold with your toppings to create your own irresistible salmon dish!

SERVES: 4 | **PREP TIME:** 20 minutes | **COOK TIME:** 7 minutes

1½ lb (684 g) skinless salmon fillet, cut into 1-inch (2.5-cm) pieces

2 tbsp (30 ml) Dijon mustard

¼ cup (54 g) minced shallots

2 tbsp (30 g) capers, drained

1 tsp chopped dill

½ tsp kosher salt

¼ cup (45 g) sun-dried tomatoes, oil drained

½ cup (67 g) bread crumbs or ½ cup (36 g) panko bread crumbs

Olive oil, as needed for greasing

4 Whole Wheat Hamburger Buns (page 188)

Suggested toppings: lettuce, tomato, avocado, red onions, Lemon Basil Aioli (page 142)

In a food processor or blender, add the cut salmon pieces, Dijon mustard, shallots, capers, dill, salt and sun-dried tomatoes. Pulse and scrape down the sides of the machine until the salmon is coarsely ground with some small chunks.

Transfer the salmon patty mixture to a medium-size bowl and add the bread crumbs, and mix together until combined. Evenly divide the mixture into 4 portions, about 7 ounces (171 g) each. Shape into 4-inch (11-cm) wide, ¾-inch (2-cm) thick patties. Lightly brush each side of the patties with olive oil.

Heat the grill to medium heat. Clean and oil the grill grates. Grill the patties for 3 minutes covered, flip over and close the lid, and cook 2 to 4 minutes. The internal temperature should be about 130°F (54°C); do not overcook!

Grill the buns for a few minutes until warm and toasted. Serve the salmon burgers with your choice of toppings.

COOK'S NOTE:
To prevent the salmon burgers from drying out on the grill, make sure to have an instant-read thermometer handy. Once the internal temperature reaches 130°F (54°C), the patty is done cooking. Fish does not need additional time to rest to get to the desired doneness as it is not as affected by carryover cooking.

RECIPE SCIENCE:
Salmon is packed with a high amount of healthy oils from omega-3 fatty acids, which help to prevent the burgers from getting dried out when on the grill. Adding the bread crumbs helps bind the ground ingredients together when formed, and prevents the patties from shrinking on the grill. The bread crumbs also absorb liquid from the patty mixture, helping to trap and keep the moisture in instead of running out into the hot barbecue. When the patties are placed on the grill, the radiant heat coming from the bottom heat source quickly heats the grates to instantly encourage browning where it comes into contact with the salmon. Closing the lid on the grill helps the patties cook quickly like an oven, creating a consistent environment of hot air.

grilled corn salad with cilantro lime dressing

GRILL | VEGETARIAN | DAIRY-FREE | GLUTEN-FREE

Grilling fresh sweet cobs of corn right on the hot barbecue imparts the most flavor in just a short period of time. While corn adds a naturally sweet and slightly charred flavor, freshly diced onions, bell pepper, cucumber, tomatoes, avocado, jalapeño, garlic and cilantro bring pungent, creamy and crunchy flavors to the salad. The salad is drizzled with an emulsified tangy cilantro lime dressing to balance the sweetness of the corn and spiciness of the jalapeño.

SERVES: 4 | PREP TIME: 20 minutes | COOK TIME: 12 minutes

4 ears of corn, husk removed

1 tbsp (15 ml) olive oil

Kosher salt, for seasoning, plus more for greasing

Black pepper, for seasoning

½ cup (75 g) diced red onion, ¼-inch (6-mm) dice

½ cup (90 g) diced red bell pepper, ¼-inch (6-mm) dice

¾ cup (123 g) diced English cucumber, ¼-inch (6-mm) dice

½ cup (75 g) baby tomatoes, quartered

½ cup (82 g) avocado, ¼-inch (6-mm) dice

1 clove garlic, minced

1 tbsp (12 g) minced jalapeño

1 tbsp (1 g) cilantro, plus more for garnish

2 tbsp (21 g) roasted sunflower seeds

CILANTRO LIME DRESSING

¼ cup (60 ml) extra-virgin olive oil

2 tbsp (1 g) chopped mint

¼ cup (4 g) chopped cilantro

2 tbsp (30 ml) apple cider vinegar

1 tbsp (15 ml) lime juice

Zest of 1 lime

1 tsp (8 ml) honey

1 clove garlic, minced

⅛ tsp kosher salt

Black pepper, as needed for seasoning

Lightly brush each ear of corn with the olive oil, and sprinkle each side with salt and pepper.

Heat the grill to high heat. Add a small amount of oil on a folded piece of towel, and then carefully grease the grill with the oiled paper towel using tongs. Once the grill is hot, add the corn.

Close the lid and cook 2 to 3 minutes on each side, rotating the corn until all of the sides are lightly charred, about 10 to 12 minutes total. Set the corn aside and allow to cool enough to handle. Cut the kernels off the cob and transfer to a large bowl.

Add the onion, bell pepper, cucumber, tomatoes, avocado, garlic, jalapeño and cilantro to the bowl with the grilled corn.

For the cilantro lime dressing, add the olive oil, mint, cilantro, vinegar, lime juice, lime zest, honey, garlic and salt to a blender. Blend on medium-high speed until the dressing becomes thickened and an opaque light green color with cilantro speckles, 30 seconds. Season the dressing with salt and pepper to taste.

Drizzle the dressing onto the corn salad and combine. Season with salt and pepper to taste, then top with the sunflower seeds and cilantro leaves.

COOK'S NOTE:
Try to pick the freshest corn possible. Once the corn is cut from the stalks, the sugars slowly go through an enzymatic process to convert to more starch. The result is that over time the corn becomes less sweet, so the fresher the better!

RECIPE SCIENCE:
There are three basic ways to grill corn: wrapped in foil, in the husk or directly on the grill without the husks. I like adding them uncovered straight on the grill with just a little bit of olive oil, salt and pepper. This allows the most flavor compounds developed from Maillard browning due to the high radiant heat coming from the bottom heat source of the grill. Within just a few minutes you'll see the kernels begin to deepen in color, which equals smoky, succulent, sweet corn flavor. To make a creamy dressing without the added dairy, using a high-speed blender has the sheer power to create a thickened emulsion within seconds. The droplets of olive oil get separated into tiny fat droplets that are suspended in the lime juice and vinegar to create a temporary emulsion. The blender creates a more finely dispersed emulsion compared to whisking the dressing, so it will stay stable for longer .

soy marinated flank steak

GRILL | GLUTEN-FREE | DAIRY-FREE

If you want to turn a relatively uninteresting piece of steak into a mouthwatering masterpiece, marinating is your answer! Flank steak is a wonderful candidate for marinating in a flavorful Asian-style sauce. It is a lean primal cut from the underbelly of the cow, providing a strong beefy flavor that's tender in texture with a nice chew. Grilling the marinated flank steak adds another layer of flavor from the high energy transmitted through radiant heat from the grill plates, generating those glorious grill marks full of brown flavor compounds.

SERVES: 4 | **PREP TIME:** 1 hour 30 minutes | **COOK TIME:** 10 minutes

½ cup (120 ml) soy sauce or tamari (for gluten-free option)

¼ cup (60 ml) honey

¼ cup (60 ml) vegetable oil, plus more for greasing

1 tsp sesame oil

4 cloves garlic, minced

2 tsp (10 g) minced ginger

½ tsp black pepper

¼ tsp red chili pepper flakes

2 tbsp (6 g) thinly sliced green onion, plus more for garnish

¾ tsp rice vinegar

2 lb (907 g) flank steak

In a medium-size bowl, combine the soy sauce, honey, vegetable oil, sesame oil, garlic, ginger, black pepper, red chili pepper and green onions. Remove ¼ cup (60 ml) of the marinade and combine with the rice vinegar in a small bowl. Cover and refrigerate.

Place the remaining marinade and steak in a 1-gallon (3.6-L) resealable bag. Remove as much air as possible and seal the bag. Refrigerate for at least 1 hour by laying the steak flat, and flipping the bag after 30 minutes. The steak can be marinated in the refrigerator for up to 12 hours.

Remove the steak from the marinade, drain any excess liquid and transfer to a pan. Discard the marinating bag.

Set the grill to high. Add a small amount of oil on a folded piece of paper towel, carefully greasing the grill with the oil. Allow the grill to preheat for 15 minutes, and once the grill is very hot, add the steak. Cover and cook the steak until well browned, about 4 to 5 minutes, then flip and cook until desired doneness, about 3 to 4 minutes. For medium rare, cook the steak until the internal temperature reaches between 120 and 125°F (49 and 52°C). For medium, cook between 130 and 135°F (54 and 57°C).

Transfer the steak to a cutting board and allow to rest for 10 minutes. Slice the steak against the grain into ¼-inch (6-mm) thick slices. Pour the reserved marinade on top and serve hot.

COOK'S NOTE:

When marinating meat, the aromatic compounds in the marinade will never fully penetrate into the very center. I've found with this recipe at least 8 hours gives great flavors, so marinate in the morning and it will be ready for dinner. Any longer than 12 hours won't add much more benefit.

RECIPE SCIENCE:

The marinade adds flavor to the inside and surface of the meat, while salt makes the meat juicier. Water-soluble flavor compounds come from the garlic, ginger, green onions, and sodium chloride and glutamates from the soy sauce to provide an umami flavor, and are all able to enter the meat for flavor penetration. The oil allows the fat-soluble flavors from capsaicin from the pepper flakes and black pepper to infuse the oil and stick to the surface of the meat so there is tremendous flavor transferred on the outside as well. The honey in the marinade aids in promoting quicker browning to solidify intense smoky, charred flavors on the meat. Around 200°F (93°C), the fructose in the honey caramelizes into visible brown pigments on the surface of the beef.

moist-heat cooking

LET THE WATER DO THE WORK

Water is not just an ingredient. It's a fascinating molecule that is essential to the structure of foods, and a way to change the appearance, taste and texture. Let's explore how water can be used in a moist-heat cooking method to quickly poach, simmer, boil and steam ingredients to naturally elevate their flavors.

the simple science

Water is one of the most interesting and important tools in cooking. Understanding how to change the properties of water by manipulating temperature provides the knowledge to create desired culinary outcomes. This is where using your senses and some scientific tools will help you nail moist-heat cooking. Do you love popsicles? Then you know that freezing the liquid to below 32°F (0°C) will give you a nice, solid chilly treat. Between 160 and 212°F (71 and 100°C) is where you can have fun poaching, simmering and boiling your ingredients. If you keep the liquid at a consistent boiling temperature of 212°F (100°C) over time, the conversion of the liquid to gas allows you to use the steam to quickly cook food.

moist-heat cooking basics

Poaching: This is the most gentle moist-heat cooking method, which tenderizes the food in a relatively short time. Poaching temperature ranges between 160 and 180°F (71 and 82°C), which must be carefully maintained to keep the food intact and tender. Some minimal movement on the surface of the poaching liquid is seen, but you don't want bubble development. There are two ways to poach: submersion or shallow poaching. Submersion poaching completely covers the food, while shallow poaching reaches about halfway up the ingredient, which may be covered with parchment paper or a lid to prevent drying of the food's surface. Broths, stocks, vegetables, herbs, spices or sweeteners can be added to heighten the taste after cooking. Poaching is great for delicate foods such as fish like salmon, lean chicken breast, fruit like apples and pears and, most famously, eggs. Who doesn't love an oozy, runny egg yolk for breakfast?

Simmering: Simmering helps to tenderize tougher cuts of meat like chuck, shank, shoulder and brisket over a longer period of time with a relatively gentle moist-heat process. Temperatures range between 185 and 205°F (85 and 96°C). Look for some bubbles to break the surface, but not an excessive appearance. As the food cooks, there will be an exchange of flavors over time, so make sure your cooking liquid is loaded with aromatic and tasty flavors.

Boiling: This method uses rapidly boiling liquid with an abundance of bubbles to quickly cook the food at a sea-level temperature of 212°F (100°C). The most important thing is to have enough water to sufficiently cover the amount of food being cooked. The food entering the water instantly reduces the temperature of the liquid. The more boiling water in the pot, the quicker the temperature can recover to properly cook the food. This is key when blanching foods such as beans for just a few minutes to get bright green color and crisp texture. Some things that can increase the boiling point and cook the food faster are sugar and salt. They not only pleasantly flavor the food, they can also cut down on the cook time. On the other hand, alcohol and higher altitude lower the boiling point of water, so it takes longer to cook the ingredients.

Steaming: The hot steam in an enclosed pot provides maximum heat transfer in a short time. The goal is to get the steam circulating around the food so convection cooking occurs, transferring the heat from the steam to the food. Since the food never touches the boiling water at the bottom of the pot, more nutrients are retained in foods like vegetables, because they do not leech into the water. Steaming is an effective method for fast-cooking items like chicken, fish and vegetables.

KEEP IT GREEN

Everyone dreads mushy, unattractive, overcooked vegetables. Luckily, there are a few simple steps to prevent a vegetable disaster. In order to achieve tender and vibrant-colored green vegetables, just blanch and shock. Blanching submerges the vegetables in boiling salted water for just a few minutes to soften the vegetables' cell walls. As this occurs, the dull green chlorophyll transforms into a bright green color, due to the air between the cells bubbling off in the hot environment and the tissue of the plant becoming more transparent. If the cooking process is not halted immediately, the bright green can change to a dreary dull olive green. This is because as the chlorophyll molecule becomes heated, the magnesium ion contained in the center releases, and if not swiftly managed, causes the unpleasant color change. Shocking vegetables in a large ice water bath right after blanching stops any further change in color. The result? Crisp, tender, gorgeous green vegetables. This method is great for green vegetables like broccoli, snow and snap peas, asparagus and green beans.

moist-heat cooking methods

METHOD	HEAT TRANSFER	TEMPERATURE	EQUIPMENT	FOOD
Poaching	Convection	160–180°F (71–82°C). No bubbles on surface	Shallow or deep pot	Eggs, chicken, fish
Simmering	Convection	185–205°F (85–96°C). Small amount of bubbles	Shallow or deep pot	Eggs, tough cuts of meat
Boiling	Convection	212°F (100°C). Big bubbles on surface	Deep pot	Pasta, potatoes, blanch vegetables
Steaming	Convection	212°F (100°C) or above	Deep pot, lid and basket	Fish, chicken, vegetables, dumplings

eggs benedict

POACH | VEGETARIAN

This popular breakfast can be recreated at home with ease and a little practice. This version of eggs benedict layers fresh sautéed greens, ripe tomatoes, a stunning poached egg and velvety Blender Hollandaise Sauce (page 139) for an unforgettable breakfast that you can make any day of the week.

SERVES: 4 | **PREP TIME:** 10 minutes | **COOK TIME:** 30 minutes

SPINACH AND KALE TOPPING
1 tbsp (15 ml) olive oil

1 garlic clove, minced

2 cups (62 g) packed baby spinach leaves

2 cups (58 g) packed baby kale

1 tsp lemon juice

Kosher salt, as needed for seasoning

Black pepper, as needed for seasoning

POACHED EGGS
2 quarts (2 L) water

2 tbsp (30 ml) vinegar, optional

8 large eggs, cold

EGGS BENEDICT
4 English muffins, sliced, or biscuits (page 163)

4 slices ripe tomato

½ cup (120 ml) Blender Hollandaise Sauce (page 139)

Paprika, as needed, for garnish

1 tbsp (3 g) chopped chives

For the spinach and kale topping, heat a large sauté pan over medium heat. Add the olive oil and, once hot, add the garlic and cook for 30 seconds. Add the spinach and kale to the pan, and cook until wilted, about 2 minutes. Add the lemon juice and stir to combine. Season the vegetables with salt and pepper to taste. Set aside, and cover with a lid to keep warm.

Fresh eggs should be used when poaching because the whites start to thin as they age, giving a more misshapen appearance. For the poached eggs, add 2 quarts (2 L) of water, or enough to reach about 3 inches (8 cm) of water, to a medium-size pot. Add the vinegar, if using. Bring the water to barely a simmer and hold at a temperature between 180 and 190°F (82 and 88°F), adjusting the heat as needed. The water should be held at this constant temperature range to create minimal agitation for a better-formed poached egg. This temperature also allows the proteins in the whites to begin setting without becoming tough and rubbery.

Crack one egg into a small bowl or ramekin. Carefully slide the egg into the simmering water, and then slowly stir the water at the edges of the pot for 10 seconds. Cook until the whites are set, 3 to 5 minutes. Use a slotted spoon to remove the egg and trim any ragged edges with a small knife or kitchen scissors, if desired. Place the egg in a small, clean bowl and repeat the process for the remaining eggs.

Toast the English muffins, and top each muffin half with a slice of tomato, warmed spinach mixture, poached egg, hollandaise sauce, paprika and chopped chives.

COOK'S NOTE:
Egg whites are naturally divided into a thick layer closer to the yolk, and a thinner layer surrounding the egg. Some separation when poaching is inevitable because of the distinct thickness differences of the white, which looks like wispy fringes of whites when cooked. To achieve a more rounded and tighter egg white appearance, use the strainer method. Add the cracked egg into a small fine mesh strainer and allow the thinner egg white layer to strain, leaving the thicker white, no more than 5 seconds. Quickly transfer the strained egg to the hot water, lightly shaking and then tilting to release the egg.

RECIPE SCIENCE:
The key to foolproof poached eggs is understanding egg structure and coagulation temperatures. The egg white, or albumin, is composed of protein and water and thickens and sets between 140 and 150°F (60 and 66°F). The yolk contains fat, protein, vitamins, mineral and lecithin, and cooks between 150 and 160°F (66 and 71°F). A small amount of vinegar can be added to the poaching water as extra insurance for a quicker onset of coagulation. The whites become more tender with the vinegar because it breaks the bonds that keep the proteins twisted together, causing them to unravel and loosely bond back together.

chicken udon soup

POACH | DAIRY-FREE

When you need a hot and soothing meal on chilly days, warm up with this Japanese-style chicken udon soup. Each bowl is brimming with tender chicken, vegetables and thick, chewy wheat noodles in a savory soy ginger broth. Grab some chopsticks and a spoon because you're going to want to dive into this light and tasty bowl of chicken udon soup!

SERVES: 4 | **PREP TIME:** 15 minutes | **COOK TIME:** 45 minutes

POACHED CHICKEN

2½ cups (115 g) fresh shiitake mushrooms

5 cups (1.2 L) unsalted chicken broth

6 slices peeled fresh ginger, ¼ inch (6 mm) slices

2 cloves garlic, crushed

1 green onion, cut into 2-inch (5-cm) pieces

1 lb (454 g) boneless skinless chicken breasts

UDON SOUP

1 tbsp (15 ml) vegetable oil

½ cup (65 g) sliced carrots, ⅛ inch (3 mm) thick

2 tsp (7 g) minced ginger

1 clove garlic, minced

¼ cup (60 ml) sake or dry white white, optional

2 tsp (10 ml) soy sauce

⅛ tsp black pepper

Kosher salt, as needed

1½ cups (172 g) sliced zucchini, ⅛ inch (3 mm) thick

30 oz (851 g) udon noodles

¼ cup (10 g) sliced green onion, cut on the bias

TOPPING SUGGESTIONS

Soft- or hard-boiled egg, enoki mushrooms, hot chili sauce or tempura (page 47)

For the poached chicken, wash the mushrooms, remove and reserve stems. Slice the mushrooms to ¼-inch (6-mm) thick pieces.

In a large pot, add the mushroom stems, broth, ginger slices, crushed garlic and green onions. Bring the soup to poaching temperatures, between 160 and 180°F (71 and 82°C). No bubbles should break the surface of the soup. Add the chicken and cook until it's no longer raw and the internal temperature reaches 160°F (71°C), about 30 to 35 minutes. Turn off the heat and transfer the chicken to a plate, covering with foil. Shred or slice chicken once cool enough to handle. Strain the broth into a large bowl, reserving the liquid.

For the udon soup, place the empty pot on the stove and turn the heat to medium-high. Add the vegetable oil, and once hot, add the sliced mushrooms and carrots, and cook for 2 minutes. Add the minced ginger and garlic, and sauté until fragrant, about 30 seconds.

Add the sake and cook for 2 minutes until mostly evaporated, scraping any browned bits from the bottom of the pan. Add the strained chicken broth to the pot and bring to a boil, then reduce to a simmer over medium-low heat. Add the soy sauce and black pepper. Taste and season with salt as needed. Add the zucchini and simmer for 4 minutes, until just tender, and turn off the heat.

In a separate pot, cook the udon noodles in boiling water until tender, according to package directions. Drain the noodles and divide evenly amongst four bowls. Add the soup, vegetables and shredded chicken to each bowl. Garnish with the green onions and serve with additional toppings as desired.

COOK'S NOTE:

Delicate and lean proteins benefit from a gentle moist-heat cooking process to ensure the food stays intact and tender. Frequently check to see that no bubbles break the surface during the poaching process and temperature maintains between 160 and 180°F (71 and 82°C). Otherwise the chicken will simmer or boil, yielding a tough and dry product.

RECIPE SCIENCE:

The aromatic ingredients and their water-soluble flavor compounds help to season the chicken as it poaches so the chicken does not taste bland. The poaching liquid is then used as the broth base for the soup, as it contains so many new, rich flavors. The fermented rice beverage sake adds depth and a bright acidity to the broth. To reduce the alcohol taste, the alcohol in the sake is mostly evaporated before adding any other liquid ingredients to the pan. Sautéing minced ginger and garlic adds full and rounded notes, with a slight pungent flavor to the soup. However, be careful not to brown the garlic, as it can turn bitter between 300 and 350°F (149 and 177°C).

orange-glazed almond green beans

BOIL | **VEGETARIAN** | **DAIRY-FREE** | **GLUTEN-FREE**

Fresh crisp citrus green beans topped with crunchy roasted almonds are a fast and healthy side dish. Knowing how to properly cook green beans is an essential technique that can be used any time to create endless dishes and flavor combinations. A foolproof way to achieve tender, radiant green vegetables is to use a blanch and shock method.

SERVES: 4 | **PREP TIME:** 10 minutes | **COOK TIME:** 25 minutes

1 cup (240 ml) orange juice

Zest of one orange

¼ tsp soy sauce or tamari (for gluten-free option)

4½ quarts (4.4 L) water, divided

1½ tsp (9 g) kosher salt, plus more for seasoning

4 cups (946 g) ice

1 lb (454 g) green beans or haricot verts

1 tbsp (15 ml) olive oil

½ cup (60 g) thinly sliced shallots, ⅛ inch (3 mm) thick

2 cloves garlic, thinly sliced

Black pepper, for seasoning

1 tbsp (9 g) sliced almonds

In a small saucepan, add the orange juice, orange zest and soy sauce. Heat the juice over medium-high heat, and the liquid should be gently bubbling. Lower the heat to medium if the juice starts boiling too rapidly. Reduce the orange juice to ⅓ cup (80 ml), about 15 to 20 minutes. Set aside.

In a large pot, heat 2 quarts (2 L) of water and salt over high heat until rapidly boiling.

Make an ice water bath by adding 6 cups (1.4 L) water and the ice to a large bowl, and set aside.

Once the water is boiling, add the green beans and blanch for 2 minutes, until crisp yet tender. Quickly transfer the blanched beans to the ice water bath. Cool for 5 minutes, then drain well.

Heat a large sauté pan over medium heat and add the olive oil. Once the oil is hot, add the shallots and garlic, stir and sauté until fragrant and tender, 3 minutes. Add the beans, stir and cook until beans are warm, about 2 minutes.

Pour the orange glaze over the beans and cook for 2 minutes, until the beans are coated with the sauce. Season with salt and pepper to taste. Transfer the beans to a bowl and top with almonds.

COOK'S NOTE:

A quick blanch will brighten the green hue of the vegetable and softens the texture, but to retain the appearance and crispness, the cooking process needs to be halted as quickly as possible using an ice bath.

RECIPE SCIENCE:

Using rapidly boiling water allows the cell walls in the beans to release some of their internal moisture for a more pliable structure, and breaks down the pectin which helps to soften the structure. Green beans are bright in color due to chlorophyll, a complex molecule key to photosynthesis. There are magnesium ions present in chlorophyll; the cooking process can strip away this ion, leaving a dull darker green appearance if not properly regulated. Using an ice bath causes chlorophyll conversion to stop, resulting in crunchy and bright green beans. An undesirable color change can be further accelerated in the presence of acids, which donate hydrogen ions to replace the released magnesium ion. To prevent this from occurring, the acidic orange juice is reduced to a thicker sauce separately, then warmed and coated with the precooked green beans for just a few minutes before serving.

minestrone soup

SIMMER | VEGETARIAN | ONE-POT MEAL | FREEZER-FRIENDLY

A hot bowl of minestrone soup delivers wholesome and nutrient-rich ingredients full of protein and fiber. Cooking dried beans from scratch is simple and inexpensive, but time consuming. A quick-soaking method of combining the dried beans with hot salted water miraculously cuts the soaking time to just 1 hour! To build the flavor of the soup base, onions, celery, carrots and squash are caramelized in the pan to create sweet and savory notes. Staggering the cooking time of the pasta and vegetables ensures that the noodles are tender and the vegetables are vibrant right before serving.

SERVES: 8 | PREP TIME: 1 hour 15 minutes | COOK TIME: 1 hour 45 minutes

4 quarts (4 L) water, divided

1½ tbsp (24 g) kosher salt, plus for seasoning

8 oz (227 g) dried red kidney beans

2 tbsp (15 ml) olive oil

1 cup (100 g) diced celery, ½-inch (1.3-cm) dice

1 cup (150 g) diced carrots, ½-inch (1.3-cm) dice

2 cups (300 g) diced yellow onion, ½-inch (1.3-cm) dice

1 cup (127 g) diced zucchini, ½-inch (1.3-cm) dice

1 cup (114 g) yellow summer squash, ½-inch (1.3-cm) dice

3 cloves garlic, minced

4 cups (1 L) vegetable broth

1 sprig rosemary

1 dried bay leaf

1 lb (454 g) roma tomatoes or canned whole tomatoes, peeled and chopped into ¼-inch (6-mm) dice

1 cup (128 g) dried ditalini pasta

1 cup (124 g) cut green beans, ½-inch (1.3-cm) pieces

Kosher salt, to taste

¼ tsp black pepper, plus more to taste

1 tbsp (4 g) chopped parsley

¼ cup (46 g) freshly grated Parmesan cheese, for garnish

In a 4-quart (4.78 L) stock pot or Dutch oven, add 2 quarts (2 L) of water, salt and beans, and stir to combine. Bring to a boil over high heat, then turn off the heat and cover. Allow the beans to stand for 1 hour. Drain and rinse the beans, transfer to a medium-size bowl and set aside. Dry the stock pot and return to the stove.

Heat the stock pot over medium-high heat and add the olive oil. Once the oil is hot, add the celery, carrots and onions. Cook, stirring frequently, for 5 minutes. Add the zucchini and squash; cook until all of the vegetables are softened and lightly brown in color, 5 minutes. Add the garlic and sauté for 30 seconds, until fragrant. Transfer the vegetables to a sheet pan to cool and spread into an even layer. This prevents overcooking before adding back into the soup.

Add the soaked beans, vegetable broth, 4 cups (1 L) of water, rosemary and bay leaf. Bring the liquid to a boil, then reduce to a simmer at 206°F (96°C). Cook and stir occasionally, until the beans are tender and liquid begins to thicken, for 45 minutes to 1 hour. Remove and discard the rosemary and bay leaf.

Add the tomatoes to the beans and simmer for 10 to 15 minutes. Turn the heat to medium and bring the liquid to a vigorous simmer. Add the pasta and cook until al dente and tender, about 10 minutes.

Add the reserved vegetables and green beans to the pot, and cook until the beans are tender, about 3 to 5 minutes. Add more broth or water as needed to thin out the soup, about 2 to 3 cups (480 to 720 ml).

Taste the soup broth and season with salt and pepper as desired. Garnish the soup with parsley and Parmesan cheese.

COOK'S NOTE:

A long, gentle simmer of the beans not only changes the internal texture, but also helps to add some thickness to the soup. Some of the starches from the bean slowly infuse into the broth, through the outer seed coat called the hilum. The released starches interact with the hot water, absorbing, swelling and then rupturing to release the starch molecule amylose.

RECIPE SCIENCE:

The bean skins start tough because of the strong bonds created by the calcium and magnesium ions with pectin molecules in the beans' cell walls, creating a protective barrier. When salt ions are introduced, it displaces some of the calcium and magnesium ions, weakening the pectin structure and allowing the skins to soften.

mushroom risotto

A traditional aromatic flavor base for the risotto, rich in flavor-enhancing glutamates, is sautéed onions, garlic, Parmesan cheese and dry white wine for brightening the dish. They add earthy, comforting aromas you would expect in Italian cuisine infused into the risotto. Two types of fungi are used to add a savory and hearty flavor: porcini and brown mushrooms loaded with umami taste. Making a big comforting pot of risotto takes a little bit of time and care, but sharing the tasty results with your loved ones makes it all worthwhile!

SERVES: 4 | **PREP TIME:** 20 minutes | **COOK TIME:** 40 minutes

8 cups (2 L) unsalted vegetable stock

0.7 oz (20 g) dried porcini mushrooms

¼ cup (60 ml) olive oil, divided

8 oz (227 g) brown mushrooms, ¼-inch (6-mm) slices

1 tsp kosher salt, divided

1 cup (150 g) diced yellow onion, ¼-inch (6-mm) dice

6 cloves garlic, minced

2 cups (390 g) arborio rice

½ cup (120 ml) dry white wine

1 cup (39 g) freshly grated Parmesan cheese, plus more for garnish

⅛ tsp black pepper

¼ cup (16 g) chopped parsley

In a large pot, add the vegetable stock and heat over medium-low heat until warmed.

Soak the dried porcini mushrooms in warm water until softened, 20 minutes. Drain and roughly chop the mushrooms.

In a separate Dutch oven, or a large sauté pan with high sides, add 2 tablespoons (30 ml) of olive oil and heat over medium-high heat. Once the oil is hot, add the sliced mushrooms and porcini mushrooms, and sauté until tender, about 3 minutes. Add ½ teaspoon of salt, stir and cook 1 minute. Transfer the mushrooms to a plate and reserve.

Heat the pan over medium heat and add 2 tablespoons (30 ml) of oil and heat until hot. Add the onions and garlic, and cook until soft and translucent, about 3 minutes. Add the rice and stir until the grains are coated with oil, and cook for 2 minutes. Add the wine to the pan, stirring until the wine has evaporated.

Add the warm stock, ½ cup (120 ml) at a time, stirring frequently. Add more stock once the liquid has been almost entirely absorbed by the rice. Repeat adding the stock in ½ cup (120 ml) additions as the liquid is absorbed, frequently stirring, until rice is tender yet slightly chewy, about 25 to 30 minutes. The desired result is a nice pudding or oatmeal consistency that is loose and not a big clump of rice.

Add the mushrooms and cook for 2 minutes. Turn off the heat and add the Parmesan cheese, ½ teaspoon of salt and the black pepper. Taste and season more as needed.

Immediately serve the risotto in bowls and garnish with more cheese and parsley.

COOK'S NOTE:
Do not rinse the rice before cooking. Rice naturally contains starch on the exterior of each grain. There are times to rinse the rice first before cooking to wash away excess starch, like for long grain rice or pilafs, so the grains stay separate. However, for risotto, you want a creamy texture, which those starches will help you achieve.

RECIPE SCIENCE:
Risotto is made with arborio rice, an Italian grain high in starch content (19 to 21 percent amylose). The chubby round shape of the grains and starch provides a rich texture, yet the rice stays separate and a tiny bit chewy when cooked. Sautéing the rice in olive oil before adding the liquid helps to lightly toast the grains for a nutty flavor. The fat also coats the rice to prevent an immediate release of the starches, which would cause the grains to stick together during cooking. Frequent stirring of the rice during cooking releases the starch, allowing the granules to separate and efficiently thicken the cooking liquid, creating a creamy sauce for the rice.

chinese sticky rice

BOIL | DAIRY-FREE

My grandparents Bing Chow and Kam Kwei Yee used to make this Cantonese-style rice for our family and friends on special occasions. The glutinous rice grains stick together, providing an addictive, soft and chewy texture, and readily soak up the savory sauce. A mixture of chopped tender Asian mushrooms, sweet dried sausage and pork are stirred into the rice to add elevated flavors and texture with each bite. Sticky rice is the ultimate comfort food and Chinese families have their own traditional version passed down to each generation. I cannot wait to teach my children how to make this soul-satisfying rice dish!

SERVES: 4 | **PREP TIME:** 35 minutes | **COOK TIME:** 25 minutes

1 cup (217 g) Japanese sweet rice

½ cup (106 g) jasmine rice

1½ cups (360 ml) water, plus more for rinsing

6 dried Chinese black or shiitake mushrooms

1 tbsp (15 ml) vegetable oil

1 cup (227 g) ground pork or chopped cooked barbecue pork (char siu), ¼-inch (6-mm) dice

¾ cup (93 g) Chinese sausages (lap chong), ¼-inch (6-mm) dice

2 tbsp (30 ml) soy sauce

2 tbsp (30 ml) oyster sauce

1 tsp sesame oil

2 tbsp (26 g) roasted peanuts, roughly chopped with some whole pieces

1 tbsp (4 g) sliced green onion

Mix the Japanese sweet rice and jasmine rice together in a medium-size bowl. Cover the rice with cool water and use your hands to rub the grains together, washing the rice. Drain and repeat until the water runs clear, about 3 to 4 washes total.

Transfer the rice to a medium-size pot fitted with a lid. Add 1½ cups (360 ml) of water to the rice. Allow to soak for about 30 minutes. Soaking allows the grains to begin absorbing the water so the starches quickly swell once the heat is applied.

Soak the mushrooms in hot water until rehydrated and tender, about 15 to 20 minutes. Drain and squeeze out excess moisture, then roughly chop.

Heat a wok or medium-size sauté pan over high heat. Add the vegetable oil, and once hot, add the ground pork. Stir-fry and break the pork into smaller chunks and cook until no longer pink, 1 minute. Skip this step if adding pre-cooked barbecue pork.

Add the Chinese sausage and cook for 1 minute. Add the mushrooms and cook for 1 minute. Add the soy sauce, oyster sauce and sesame oil, stir to combine and turn off the heat. Transfer the mixture to a medium-size bowl.

Once the rice is done soaking, turn the heat to high and bring the rice to a boil, then reduce to a simmer. Cook the rice until the grains are tender, 20 minutes.

Add the meat mixture on top of the rice, then cover the pot. Allow the mixture to sit for 5 minutes to absorb some of the sauce. Stir to combine the rice and meat, taste the mixture and adjust seasonings as desired.

Serve the rice topped with chopped peanuts and green onions.

COOK'S NOTE:

To control the starch levels in the rice before cooking, the grains are thoroughly washed in cool water, until the liquid becomes clear. This helps to remove excess surface starch on the rice so it cooks up more fluffy and light.

RECIPE SCIENCE:

The protein and amylose starch molecules present in the different types of rice affect the texture. This recipe uses a ratio of 2:1 short-grain Japanese sweet rice (about 15 percent amylose, 6 percent protein) and long-grain jasmine rice (about 22 percent amylose, 8.5 percent protein). A higher ratio of glutinous rice is used because it creates moist grains that cling together after cooking due to their lower levels of protein and amylose starch molecules. The jasmine rice is higher in amylose and protein content, cooking up into soft and fluffy separate pieces. The rice combination adds variety in texture and prevents the rice from becoming overly sticky and mushy.

chicken carbonara pasta

A simple yet luscious Italian pasta dish to master is carbonara. The rich pieces of smoky sautéed bacon, tender peas and creamy sauce make each bite of this pasta irresistible. The only tricky part is making sure that the eggs thicken while staying smooth and velvety, and don't curdle up into scrambled eggs. The trick is using a gentle water-bath method for cooking the sauce. Once a creamy sauce is formed and clings nicely to the pasta, it's time to eat! I like to add sautéed chicken breast for extra protein to the dish, and to create an entrée-size portion for two.

SERVES: 4 | **PREP TIME:** 15 minutes | **COOK TIME:** 30 minutes

4 quarts (4 L) water

1 tbsp (18 g) kosher salt, plus more for seasoning chicken and pasta

1 lb (454 g) boneless skinless chicken breast, pounded to even ¾-inch (2-cm) thickness

Black pepper, for seasoning

Paprika, for seasoning chicken

1 tbsp (15 ml) olive oil

8 oz (227 g) dried spaghetti or gluten-free pasta

6 slices thick-cut bacon, cut into 1-inch (2.5-cm) pieces

6 cloves garlic, minced

½ cup (73 g) peas, fresh or frozen (defrosted)

2 large eggs

1 cup (60 g) freshly grated Parmesan cheese, plus more for garnish

1 tbsp (4 g) minced parsley

Bring the water plus 1 tablespoon (18 g) of salt to a boil.

Season both sides of the chicken with salt, pepper and paprika. Heat a large skillet over medium-high heat and add the olive oil. Once the oil is hot, carefully add the chicken and cook for 4 minutes. Reduce the heat to medium, flip the chicken and cook for 5 to 7 minutes, or until the internal temperature of chicken reaches 165°F (74°C). Reserve the pan drippings.

Transfer the chicken to a clean cutting board and allow to cool slightly. Chop the chicken into ½-inch (1.3-cm) cubes, transfer to a bowl and set aside.

Add the pasta to the boiling water and cook until al dente, according to package directions. Reserve the hot pasta water.

Heat the same pan used to cook the chicken over medium-high heat. Add the chopped bacon and sauté until crispy, stirring every minute, about 6 to 7 minutes. Drain off most of the excess bacon grease, reserving 2 tablespoons (30 ml) of grease in the pan. Add the garlic and sauté until fragrant, 1 minute. Add the peas to the pan and cook for 30 seconds. Add the chicken and stir to combine. Turn off the heat and set the pan aside until the pasta is ready.

In a large metal mixing bowl, whisk together the eggs and Parmesan cheese. Add the pasta straight from the boiling water into the bowl, reserving the pasta water.

Stir the pasta to combine the noodles with the sauce. Gradually add and mix ¼ cup (60 ml) of pasta water to the noodles. Stir constantly to combine, until a lightly-thickened sauce that coats the pasta is created.

(continued)

> **COOK'S NOTE:**
> Pasta releases some starch from the noodles into the cooking liquid, making it opaque in color. Adding some of this liquid to the egg sauce not only thickens the sauce with the starches and heat, but also helps to keep the eggs from curdling. When the proteins in the egg and starch granules are stirred together, amylose strands of starch coat the proteins, making it difficult for the proteins to link together and coagulate into firm curds.

Sauté the chicken breast.

Whisk the egg and Parmesan cheese mixture together for the sauce.

Toss the pasta with the egg mixture over a bain-marie.

Place the bowl of pasta over the pot with boiling pasta water. Make sure that the bowl does not touch the water. Toss and stir the pasta frequently until the sauce tightens up, looks creamy and leaves clear trails behind as you stir it, about 1 to 2 minutes. Add up to an additional ¼ cup (60 ml) of pasta water to loosen the sauce if needed, stirring to combine.

Taste the pasta and season with salt and pepper as desired. Add the chicken and bacon mixture to the pasta. Serve the hot pasta topped with parsley, Parmesan cheese and freshly cracked black pepper.

RECIPE SCIENCE:

This recipe uses a water-bath method to create a cheesy egg sauce. It's a balance between cooking the egg sauce enough, so it's safe to eat (above 140°F [60°C] so bacteria is destroyed), yet still creamy like a custard. For the most gentle cooking of the egg sauce without curdling the proteins, the pasta and sauce mixture is cooked and constantly stirred in a large bowl over a pot of boiling water (bain-marie). The steam elevates the temperature of the bottom of the bowl just enough to cook the sauce, without a direct flame that could potentially scramble the eggs if not carefully watched and stirred. The pasta and egg sauce are vigorously stirred together to distribute heat. This helps thicken the sauce with the proteins from the eggs and starches from the pasta. The starches also increase the coagulation temperature of the eggs to help stabilize the egg proteins when heated, and prevent quick curdling. However, if the sauce is allowed to sit, the hot pan will solidify the egg sauce instead of keeping it smooth. Whole eggs set between 144 and 158°F (62 and 70°C).

mediterranean steamed mussels

STEAM | DAIRY-FREE | ONE POT MEAL

Steamed mussels with red wine and garlic is an easy Mediterranean-style recipe. Aromatic vegetables are cooked with fresh mussels for a light appetizer or served with pasta for a heartier entrée. The complex flavor developed in the steaming liquid is perfect for dipping and soaks up nicely with the crunchy croutons to enjoy with the bowl of mussels.

SERVES: 4 | **PREP TIME:** 15 minutes | **COOK TIME:** 25 minutes

1 loaf baguette, ½-inch (1.3-cm) sliced on the bias

1 tbsp (15 ml) extra-virgin olive oil

½ tsp kosher salt, more for seasoning

Black pepper, for seasoning

1 lb (454 g) fresh mussels

1 tbsp (14 g) unsalted butter

⅓ cup (82 g) minced shallots

2 cloves garlic, minced

¼ cup (25 g) diced celery, ⅛-inch (3-mm) dice

1 cup (160 g) diced roma tomatoes, ¼-inch (6-mm) dice

1 dried bay leaf

⅓ cup (80 ml) red wine, merlot recommended

1 tbsp (15 ml) lemon juice

2 tbsp (8 g) chopped parsley

4 lemon wedges

Adjust the oven rack to the center position and preheat the oven to 375°F (191°C).

To make the croutons, lightly brush each side of the bread with the olive oil and sprinkle with salt and pepper. Place on a baking sheet and bake for 10 minutes. Flip the bread over and cook another 2 minutes, until golden brown on each side. Cool and reserve. Alternatively, grill the bread over medium heat for a few minutes on each side until grill lines appear and the bread is crunchy.

Wash the mussels under cool running water, scrubbing the outside and debearding the mussels if necessary. To debeard, simply pull the fibrous beard to remove and discard.

In a large shallow stock pot, heat the butter over medium-high heat. When the butter starts to foam, add the shallots, garlic and celery. Stir and cook until the shallots are transparent and the garlic is soft, about 3 minutes. Add the tomatoes, stir and cook, about 2 minutes. Add the bay leaf, wine, lemon juice and ½ teaspoon of salt. Stir to combine.

Quickly add the cleaned mussels to the pot, cover and steam for 3 minutes. Carefully open the lid and stir. Cover and steam until mussels are open and cooked, about 2 to 3 minutes.

Top the mussels with parsley and serve with lemon wedges and croutons.

COOK'S NOTE:
Mussels should be purchased fresh and alive. Properly store mussels by immediately removing them from the plastic bag, transferring to a bowl and covering with a damp paper towel or cloth. Do not soak mussels before cooking as the fresh water will kill them. They can be kept for a few days and still smell like salt water from the ocean. When you're ready to cook, make sure to drain any water that collects at the bottom of the bowl. Discard any mussels that do not open after cooking; this indicates they were not fresh.

RECIPE SCIENCE:
The cooking liquid used for steaming the mussels should be extremely flavorful, so that each bite is pleasing to the palate. Lightly caramelizing the butter, shallots, garlic and celery adds a natural sweetness to the liquid. The savory flavors of the broth are enhanced by cooking glutamate-containing ingredients like garlic, shallots, tomatoes and red wine with nucleotides found in the mussels for a heightened umami flavor. The mussels require high heat, generated from the steam of the closed vessel above 212 °F (100°C), to quickly cook, open and release their flavorful juices. The high heat also allows the volatile alcohol in the wine to vaporize by almost 95 percent, so that the oaky and fruity flavors come through in the broth.

creamy macaroni and cheese

An elevated twist on a classic macaroni and cheese recipe with three types of cheese and topped with crunchy rosemary bread crumbs. Learning how to make a traditional béchamel cream sauce allows you the versatility to experiment with different cheese varieties, each adding its own unique flavor and texture.

SERVES: 8 | **PREP TIME:** 15 minutes | **COOK TIME:** 25 minutes

5 tbsp (71 g) unsalted butter

6 tbsp (51 g) all-purpose flour

1 tbsp plus 1¼ tsp (25 g) kosher salt, divided

⅛ tsp ground nutmeg

1 tsp Dijon mustard

5 cups (1.25 L) whole milk

8 oz (228 g) sharp white cheddar cheese, grated

8 oz (228 g) Monterey Jack cheese, grated

2 oz (60 g) cream cheese

4 quarts (4 L) water

1 lb (454 g) cavatappi pasta (corkscrew shaped)

½ cup (37 g) panko bread crumbs

1 tsp (1 g) chopped rosemary

Black pepper, as needed for seasoning

1 tbsp (4 g) chopped parsley

In a large pot or wide saucepan with high sides, heat the butter over medium-high heat until melted. Add the flour, 1 teaspoon of salt and nutmeg. Cook the flour mixture, constantly whisking until fragrant and blond in color, 1 minute. Add the Dijon mustard and whisk to combine.

Gradually add the milk to the hot flour mixture, whisking constantly, and bring to a boil. Once the liquid comes to a boil, reduce to a simmer over medium heat. Occasionally whisk sauce until it is thickened and coats the back of a spoon with no raw flour taste, 7 minutes.

Turn off the heat and slowly whisk in the cheddar, Monterey Jack and cream cheese until completely melted and combined. In a large pot, bring 4 quarts (4 L) of water to a boil. Add 1 tablespoon (17 g) of salt and the pasta, stir to combine. Cook the pasta according to the manufacturer's directions, stirring often until the pasta is tender, just past al dente (firm but tender). Drain the pasta and reserve the cooking liquid. Add the hot pasta to a large bowl, stir in enough sauce to coat the noodles and keep warm.

Heat a medium-size sauté pan over medium heat. Add the bread crumbs and toast, shaking the pan until bread crumbs are evenly golden brown in color, about 3 to 5 minutes. Keep a close eye as the bread crumbs can burn quickly. Transfer the toasted panko to a bowl, add ¼ teaspoon of salt and the chopped rosemary, and stir to combine.

Serve the macaroni and cheese topped with freshly cracked black pepper, parsley and toasted bread crumbs.

COOK'S NOTE:

The cheese sauce starts with making a white roux using butter and flour that is briefly cooked, then milk is whisked in to help thicken and disperse the starch into the sauce base. A combination of cheeses is used. Sharp cheddar cheese has a longer aging and ripening process, providing savory flavor compounds. Monterey Jack is a softer young cheese, creating a super-creamy consistency due to its higher moisture level. Cream cheese is incorporated for an extra layer of velvety texture, due to its high fat content and moisture, adding a pleasing light sweetness and tartness to the sauce.

RECIPE SCIENCE:

Incorporating a starch component into the cheese sauce prevents the proteins in the cheese from clumping together and tasting gritty. This is because when the cheese appears to melt during heating, what is actually happening is the bonded casein proteins break apart, then the molecules separate and flow. That's when the incorporated starch granules in the flour release elongated threads of amylose, a soluble polysaccharide in starch. The starch wraps around the casein proteins in the cheese and prevents fat from releasing and proteins from forming back together into undesirable broken clumps.

fluffy roasted garlic mashed potatoes

BOIL | GLUTEN-FREE

Knowing how to make smooth and creamy mashed potatoes is an essential culinary technique that can be seamlessly mastered. This recipe infuses the sweet and earthy flavors of roasted garlic to elevate the taste of the potatoes. To ensure the potato mixture stays light, room temperature butter is folded into the potatoes before adding the milk. The warmed milk mixed with the softened garlic is slowly folded into the potatoes, creating a silky and airy purée.

SERVES: 4 | **PREP TIME:** 15 minutes | **COOK TIME:** 60 minutes

1 head of garlic

1 tsp olive oil

4 quarts (4 L) water

2 tsp (12 g) kosher salt, divided

2 lb (910 g) russet potatoes

6 tbsp (84 g) unsalted butter, cut into 6 slices, room temperature

1 cup (240 ml) whole milk

Black pepper

1 tbsp (3 g) chopped chives

Adjust the oven rack to the middle position and preheat the oven to 400°F (204°C).

Cut about ¼ inch (6 mm) off of the top of the head of garlic, making sure to expose all of the cloves. Place on a piece of foil large enough to wrap the garlic, and drizzle the cut cloves with olive oil. Wrap the garlic in foil and place on a sheet pan. Roast for 40 to 50 minutes, until the center cloves are tender and lightly golden in color. Once cooled, squeeze out the cloves of garlic and chop into a paste, then set aside.

In a large pot, add 4 quarts (4 L) of water and 1 teaspoon of salt, and bring to a boil. Peel the potatoes and cut into 1-inch (2.5-cm) pieces. Add the potatoes to a bowl and rinse under cool water, removing the starchy water until the water is clear, about two to three additional times. Drain the potatoes and add to the boiling water.

Cook until the potatoes are fork-tender, about 15 minutes. Drain the potatoes in a colander and rinse the potatoes with hot water to remove any residual potato starches, 30 seconds.

Set a food mill, ricer or fine-mesh strainer over the pot used to cook the potatoes. Pass the potatoes through into the pot. Add the butter and gently fold into the potatoes. This allows the fat to coat the starch granules, hindering the interaction of water in the milk with the starches, preventing a gluey texture.

Microwave the milk for 1 minute or heat in a small pan until warmed, about 120°F (49°C). Whisk together the milk, 1 teaspoon of salt and roasted garlic. Gradually fold the milk mixture into the potatoes in three equal additions, until the liquid is absorbed. If needed, rewarm the potatoes over medium heat, stirring occasionally. Season the potatoes with salt and pepper to taste. Garnish with the black pepper and chives.

COOK'S NOTE:

Roasting garlic cloves removes the sharp and sulfurous flavor notes of raw garlic. When garlic is heated to about 150°F (67°C), the enzymes that produce new pungent flavors are destroyed. The heat then transforms the existing flavor compounds to a sweet and caramel-tasting product.

RECIPE SCIENCE:

Russet potatoes are used for their high starch content and mealy texture, perfect for readily absorbing the milk and butter to add richness. However, the amount of starch incorporated into the dish needs to be controlled. To regulate the level of starch released and cooked with the potatoes, the skin is removed and the potato is cut into 1-inch (2.5-cm) pieces. The size of the potatoes allows greater surface area to cook the potatoes efficiently and soften the pectin in the cell walls. The potatoes are rinsed twice, once before cooking with cold water and then after cooking with hot water. This allows excess starch to be removed from the potatoes to ensure the fluffiness factor. Pressing the cooked potato through a fine-mesh sieve or food mill is a more gentle process to reduce starch release from rough shearing of the potatoes' cell structure. The small individual holes in the mill also separate the potato particles so they do not become dense and heavy.

lobster sliders

STEAM | QUICK (30 MINUTES OR LESS)

Lobster always seems to be reserved for special occasions; however, why not enjoy the ocean delicacy any time the craving hits? It can be intimidating to prepare lobster at home. With a higher price tag, you want to make sure to cook the seafood so it stays sweet and succulent, rather than becoming tough and rubbery. A brief steaming and roasting method is used to enhance the flavor of the lobster.

SERVES: 8 | **PREP TIME:** 15 minutes | **COOK TIME:** 15 minutes

5 (3-oz [85-g]) lobster tails, about 8 oz (227 g) meat

1 tbsp (16 g) plain Greek yogurt

1 tbsp (14 g) mayonnaise

1 tbsp (10 g) minced shallots

2 tbsp (15 g) chopped celery

1 tsp chopped tarragon

1 tsp chopped parsley

1 tsp chopped chives

Zest of 1 lemon

1 tsp lemon juice

¼ tsp kosher salt

Black pepper to taste

Whole Wheat Hamburger Buns (page 188)

4 butter lettuce leaves

Adjust the oven rack to the middle position and preheat the oven to 350°F (177°C). Line a large sheet pan with foil and place a wire rack on top.

In large pot, add 1 inch (2.5 cm) of water. Place a steamer insert on top, cover and bring water to a boil over high heat. Once the water is steaming, carefully remove the lid and add a single layer of lobster tails to cover, working in batches. Cover and steam the lobster for 2 minutes, then transfer to the rack set in the baking sheet. Repeat steaming with the remaining lobster tails.

Transfer the sheet pan with the steamed lobster tails to the oven and roast until the tails reach an internal temperature of 135 to 140°F (57 to 60°C), about 4 to 6 minutes. Remove from the oven and allow to cool just enough to handle.

Use kitchen shears to cut through the underside of the lobster. Pull the sides apart and carefully remove the meat from the tail. Place the meat on a clean plate lined with a paper towel. Once dried, cut into ½-inch (1.3-cm) pieces.

Add the lobster to a medium-size bowl and combine with yogurt, mayonnaise, shallots, celery, tarragon, parsley, chives, lemon zest, lemon juice, salt and pepper. Taste the mixture and adjust seasoning as desired.

Toast the rolls and fill with 2 to 3 tablespoons (20 to 30 g) of lobster filling, or as it fits with bun. Top with a small piece of the lettuce.

COOK'S NOTE:
To achieve tender lobster, use an instant-read thermometer to track the doneness. The internal temperature should be between 135 and 140°F (57 and 60°C) after roasting in the oven. Lobster meat yield is about 30 to 40 percent of the total weight.

RECIPE SCIENCE:
The traditional method of boiling the lobsters for several minutes does the job of cooking the meat; however, a lot of the characteristic flavor compounds can be lost in the cooking liquid. I learned a different way to quickly cook lobster by steaming. An enormous amount of energy stored in the steam helps to quickly cook just the exterior flesh of the lobster tails so that the proteins constrict and pull away from the shell, making it easier to remove. If this process does not happen fast enough, the proteins will instead chemically bond and stick to the surface of the shell, making it hard to extract the meat. To further intensify the flavor of the lobster, it finishes cooking in the oven until tender. The dry-heat environment allows the lobster to cook evenly and dries some of the residual surface moisture from steaming, resulting in a more concentrated seafood flavor and sweeter taste.

shumai chinese steamed dumplings

STEAM | DAIRY-FREE

Recreating my favorite childhood dishes is the best part of being in the kitchen, as it brings so many fond memories. Each weekend we would meet at the popular local Cantonese Chinese restaurant. We would sit around the table with the lazy Susan spinning and filling up with steamer baskets filled with dim sum delicacies. My absolute must-have item was shumai (or siu mai), steamed juicy pork and shrimp dumplings bundled in thin wheat wrappers.

MAKES: 30 dumplings | **PREP TIME:** 1 hour | **COOK TIME:** 7 minutes

1½ cups (343 g) ground pork

1 tsp honey

½ tsp black or white pepper

1 tsp cornstarch

1 tbsp (15 ml) Shaoxing wine or dry sherry

4 tsp (20 ml) soy sauce

1 tbsp (15 ml) water

1½ tsp (22 ml) sesame oil, divided

½ lb (227 g) large shrimp, peeled, deveined, chopped into ¼-inch (6-mm) pieces

¼ tsp kosher salt

4 (8 g) dried shiitake mushrooms, soaked in hot water for 20 minutes, finely chopped

1 tsp finely minced ginger

1 tbsp (3 g) finely minced green onions

1 tsp oyster sauce

30 to 40 round pot sticker dumpling skins or wonton wrappers, 3½-inch (9-cm) diameter

30 to 40 fresh or frozen peas

¼ cup (57 g) diced carrots, cut into ¼-inch (6-mm) squares

Soy sauce or chili sauce, for serving

In a medium-size bowl, add the pork, honey, pepper, cornstarch, Shaoxing wine, soy sauce, water and 1 teaspoon of sesame oil. Vigorously stir for 3 minutes until mixture resembles a paste.

In a second medium-size bowl, combine the chopped shrimp, salt and ½ teaspoon of sesame oil, and mix for 1 minute. Add the shrimp mixture to the pork mixture.

Add the chopped mushrooms, ginger, green onions and oyster sauce to the filling. Mix until well combined, 3 minutes. Refrigerate the filling for 30 minutes before wrapping.

To form the dumpling, place the wrapper in the palm of your hand. Have a small bowl of water ready on the side. Brush or use your finger to place a small amount of water along the edges of the wrapper. Add 2 to 3 teaspoons (6 to 9 g) of the filling in the center of the wrapper. Bring up the two opposite sides of the wrapper, pressing them gently against the filling to adhere. Fold up the other two corners to form a cup, lightly squeeze in your fist to hold the wrapper in place. The top edges should stick together. Add a little more water on the edges and press or pinch together as needed so it does not fall apart as it steams. Lightly brush the outsides of the dumpling with water as needed to help the pleats stick together. While holding the dumpling in your hand, use your other hand to flatten the bottom of the dumpling so it can be placed flat in the steamer. Top each dumpling with one pea and one piece of cut carrot in the center.

In a large pot, add water to the bottom and a steamer insert on top. Bring the water to a boil until it begins to steam, then turn heat down to medium-high. Oil the bottom of a bamboo steamer or line it with a piece of round parchment paper. It also helps to lightly brush vegetable oil on the parchment paper as well to ensure the dumplings do not stick. Place enough dumplings that fit into the bamboo steamer, about 1 inch (2.5 cm) apart. Carefully add the dumplings into a steamer with tongs, cover and steam for 7 minutes. Turn off the heat and slowly open the cover.

Transfer the cooked dumplings to a sheet pan. Work in batches, steaming about 5 dumplings at a time, or as many as can fit in your steamer. Enjoy the dumplings hot with soy sauce or chili sauce.

COOK'S NOTE:
Adding some cornstarch to the dumpling filling helps prevent it from becoming tough, preventing the proteins from binding too closely as it's mixed and cooked.

RECIPE SCIENCE:
When the meat and seafood proteins are ground or cut into smaller pieces, the muscle fibers and connective tissues become smaller in size. This process releases sticky soluble proteins to help keep the filling together during steaming.

braising & stewing

WHEN TWO TECHNIQUES ARE BETTER THAN ONE

Learn how to combine dry-heat and moist-heat techniques to master the art of braising and stewing to intensify flavors and tenderize tougher pieces of meat.

the simple science

Braises and stews can be the most comforting meals made in just one cooking vessel. The combination of dry-heat and moist-heat techniques transforms affordable and tough meats into tender and flavorful meals. The process starts with browning the proteins first to add depth, then simmering to finish cooking the dish. Slowly cooking tougher cuts of meat in the presence of water and low heat helps to break down the connective tissue collagen into gelatin to create a rich and tasty product. The main difference between braising and stewing is the size of the cuts of meat and cook time. Braising does wonders for chuck or shoulder cuts like pot roast, brisket or round cuts. Also, portions of meat like chicken thighs that contain more fat do well when braised. Stewing utilizes smaller pieces of meat and vegetables cut into uniform sizes for even cooking time. Utilizing both techniques can create irresistible dishes for those who are not in a rush!

braising and stewing basics

Braising: This method is great for tenderizing and infusing tons of flavor into larger cuts of meat. The idea is to start by using dry heat in a pan by cooking the meat in a small quantity of hot oil using conduction to promote browning of the surface for additional texture and flavor from the Maillard reaction. Vegetables, spices and herbs can be added to the pan to introduce more layers of flavor to the dish. A braising liquid is added to cover half of the meat so that moist-heat cooking through simmering and steaming the meat in the covered pot can occur. The goal is to slowly cook the food in the oven or on the stove top at consistent simmering temperatures of about 250 to 300°F (120 to 150°C). The meat cooks by conduction of the braising liquid and convection of the hot air in the closed pot. The result is a fork-tender meat and braising liquid exploding with flavor. The liquid can easily be thickened into a sauce by either adding cornstarch, a butter and flour roux or even reducing the sauce.

Stewing: If you are looking for a slightly quicker path from cook time to first bite, and want to create a wholesome one-pot meal, stewing is a fantastic option. The protein is cut into smaller pieces and browned in fat for dry-heat cooking and browning, just like braising. Sometimes the meat is tossed in flour first to create a thin coating for additional texture. A roux or other thickening agent is added to the pot before the liquid so that it can be evenly dispersed and mixed in when the liquid is added. This allows the starches in the flour to gradually swell and thicken over time in simmering liquid for a rich sauce. The liquid completely covers the stew ingredients to promote steady and even cooking. The stew is cooked in a covered pot in either the oven or on the stove at simmering temperatures; however, the smaller cuts of meat need less time for overall cooking.

ADD A LITTLE TENDERNESS

It may seem a little puzzling why you should cook some meats longer, even past well-done, for them to become extremely tender. Those cuts contain more connective tissue collagen, membranous cells and protein filaments that surround muscle fibers. It requires an elevated temperature of 160 to 180°F (70 to 82°C) and a longer cooking time to convert to the highly desirable gelatin. This conversion begins to happen above temperatures of 140°F (60°C), and the triple-helix strands of the collagen unwind, revealing a single-stranded protein gelatin. This breakdown is crucial because it allows the collagen to absorb moisture back into the meat from the cooking environment. This adds a luscious thickness to the liquid, and tender and flavorful meat. You want to use this method on tough cuts like beef brisket and pork shoulder, and not on lean cuts like filet mignon or pork tenderloin.

braising and stewing cooking methods

METHOD	HEAT TRANSFER	TEMPERATURE	EQUIPMENT	FOOD
Braising	Conduction/ (Sauté & Convection Simmer)	160–180°F (70–82°C). Small amount of bubbles, deep pot	Dutch oven	Beef, pork, lamb, chicken thighs, vegetables, tougher cuts of meat, large cuts of meat (shoulder, chuck, round)
Stewing	Conduction/ (Sauté & Convection Simmer)	160–180°F (70–82°C). Small amount of bubbles, deep pot	Dutch oven	Lamb, chicken, vegetables, legumes, smaller cuts of meat

thai green curry with shrimp

STEW | DAIRY-FREE | QUICK (30 MINUTES OR LESS) | GLUTEN-FREE

When you are craving a Thai-inspired dish, spicy green curry delivers robust exotic flavors in just minutes. During culinary school, I got the chance to make the most intense and delicious curry paste. It was a labor of love, grinding the ingredients with a mortar and pestle, but the taste was unforgettable! Purchasing pre-made curry pastes is a time-saver that won't lack flavor. Many high-quality green curry pastes combine aromatic elements like lemongrass, galangal (Thai ginger) and fresh green chilis for a spicy kick. These concentrated ingredients are balanced with sweet coconut milk, brown sugar and fermented fish sauce. This seafood stew with tender vegetables highlights the complex and palate-pleasing flavors of Southeast Asian cuisine.

SERVES: 4 | PREP TIME: 10 minutes | COOK TIME: 20 minutes

1 tbsp (15 ml) vegetable oil

3 tbsp (39 g) green curry paste

14 oz (414 ml) unsweetened coconut milk

1 tbsp (10 g) light brown sugar

1 tsp minced lemongrass, optional

½ cup (77 g) thinly sliced red bell pepper, ⅛-inch (3-mm) thick slices

½ cup (77 g) thinly sliced green bell pepper, ⅛-inch (3-mm) thick slices

1 cup (83 g) sliced Japanese or Chinese eggplant, ¼-inch (6-mm) thick slices

1 cup (125 g) sliced zucchini, ¼-inch (6-mm) thick slices

⅓ cup (57 g) bamboo shoots

1 lb (454 g) jumbo peeled and deveined shrimp, 16/20 count

1 tsp fish sauce

Salt, for seasoning

Pepper, for seasoning

¼ cup (3 g) basil, Thai if available

¼ cup (4 g) cilantro leaves

Heat a large high-side skillet over medium heat. Add the oil, and once hot, add the curry paste and stir until fragrant, 30 seconds. Add the coconut milk, brown sugar and lemongrass, and whisk to combine. Bring to a boil, then lower to a simmer for 5 minutes.

Add the bell peppers, eggplant, zucchini and bamboo shoots. Simmer for 5 minutes, increasing the heat if needed.

Add the shrimp and cook until no longer translucent, stirring as needed, 3 to 5 minutes. Turn off the heat, add the fish sauce and stir to combine. Season with salt and pepper to taste. Garnish the curry with basil and cilantro.

COOK'S NOTE:

Shrimp can overcook quickly but there are some easy visual cues to keep them succulent and tender. When shrimp is raw, the flesh is a whitish-gray color. As it cooks, the protein turns to an opaque whitish-pink color. The shrimp should curl up into a loose C shape when properly cooked. If they have curled up into a tight O shape, then you may have overcooked them.

RECIPE SCIENCE:

Do not skip the fish sauce! Just a little bit of the strong umami flavor adds depth to the curry. The fish sauce contains glutamates, a type of salt form of the amino acid glutamic acid known to give a savory and meaty flavor to foods. The umami flavor is even more potent in fish sauce because the fermented anchovies in the sauce contain compounds called nucleotides, and are found in shrimp as well. These compounds synergistically affect the perception of glutamate, heightening umami flavor by 20 to 30 times! This is caused by the nucleotides changing the shape of the glutamate taste receptor in the tongue, magnifying the savory signals to the brain. The brininess from the fermented anchovies enhances the other flavors in the sauce. However, it should be used in moderation to avoid overpowering the dish.

andouille sausage and shrimp gumbo

STEW | FREEZER-FRIENDLY

Get a taste of New Orleans cuisine right at home with this savory and delicious andouille sausage and shrimp gumbo. Visiting Louisiana allowed me to dine in the Crescent City, where I had my first taste of delicious gumbo. I was instantly hooked! I was in awe of how a simple bowl of stew could dance on the tongue with myriad flavors. The smoky sausage, tender shrimp, vibrant vegetables and touch of sassafras makes this festive recipe perfect for sharing.

SERVES: 6 | **PREP TIME:** 15 minutes | **COOK TIME:** 1 hour 30 minutes

1 lb (454 g) okra, cut into 1-inch (2.5-cm) pieces, use frozen if fresh not available

½ cup (120 ml) water

½ cup (113 g) unsalted butter

½ cup (68 g) all-purpose flour

1 cup (137 g) diced yellow onion, ¼-inch (6-mm) dice

¾ cup (115 g) diced red bell pepper, ¼-inch (6-mm) dice

¾ cup (115 g) diced green bell pepper, ¼-inch (6-mm) dice

½ cup (60 g) diced celery, ¼-inch (6-mm) dice

2 cloves garlic, minced

2 cups (327 g) diced canned tomatoes with juice

12 oz (339 g) andouille sausage, ¼-inch (6-mm) slices

1 dried bay leaf

1 tsp chopped thyme, fresh

1 tsp dried basil

¼ tsp cayenne pepper, plus more for seasoning

½ tsp black pepper, plus more for seasoning

1 tsp kosher salt, plus more for seasoning

4 cups (1 L) unsalted chicken stock

1 lb (454 g) jumbo shrimp, peeled and deveined, 16/20 count

1 tbsp (5 g) gumbo filé

Steamed rice, for serving

In a medium-size saucepan, add the okra and water. Bring the water to a boil, reduce the heat to a simmer and cover the pot. Simmer the okra for 7 to 9 minutes, until tender, stirring occasionally. Transfer the okra to a colander to drain the water, and set the okra aside.

Heat a large pot or Dutch oven over medium heat. Add the butter and flour, frequently whisking to make an amber-brown-colored roux, about 12 to 15 minutes.

Add the onion, bell peppers, celery and garlic. Sauté the vegetables until tender, 8 to 10 minutes.

Add the cooked okra, tomatoes and sausage to the pot. Cook for 5 minutes, stirring occasionally. Add the bay leaf, thyme, basil, cayenne, pepper and salt. Add the chicken stock, and stir to combine. Bring to a boil, then simmer over low heat for 30 minutes, with the pot loosely covered, stirring occasionally.

Add the shrimp and cook until no longer translucent, 3 to 5 minutes. Turn off heat and slowly stir in the gumbo filé. Do not reboil after adding the filé as it tends to make the gumbo stringy. Season with more cayenne, salt or pepper to taste. Serve with steamed rice.

COOK'S NOTE:

Filé is sassafras leaves that have been dried and ground into a fine powder. It's used to lightly thicken gumbo just before serving, and gives the gumbo a characteristic taste. It can be served as a condiment to add to your liking.

RECIPE SCIENCE:

The flavor development begins by creating a brown roux, imparting rich flavors and a deep amber color to the dish. Roux is a classic French technique used as a thickening agent. It's a mixture of equal parts fat (butter) and flour. A general rule of thumb is the lighter the roux, the higher the thickening power, but there will also be less flavor. Therefore more roux is needed due to the reduction of thickening power of the starches, with the longer cooking time of over 10 minutes. An essential element of the stew is using a combination of bell pepper, celery and onion. The sautéed vegetables add beautiful aromatics and flavor to the gumbo. Okra is also added, which is a long, green pod vegetable from the Malvaceae, or mallow, family of plants. It has unique texture and flavor when cooked and, if sliced into smaller pieces, releases a viscous, sticky liquid that can add additional thickness to the soup. For this recipe, it is cooked separately to minimize any slimy texture, and to make sure it is tender before adding to the stew.

red curry lemongrass chicken meatballs

BRAISE | **DAIRY-FREE** | **QUICK (30 MINUTES OR LESS)** | **GLUTEN-FREE**

Thai cuisine embraces savory, pungent, sweet and spicy flavors for an unforgettable culinary experience. Chicken meatballs are an excellent way to capture the bold flavors in small delicious bites. The meatballs are made with a combination of ground chicken, aromatic ginger, garlic, citrusy lemongrass, jalapeño, soy and fish sauce to really enhance the umami notes of the dish. The meatballs are simmered in a flavorful red curry coconut sauce to coat each tender bite of protein.

SERVES: 4 | **PREP TIME:** 10 minutes | **COOK TIME:** 20 minutes

1 lb (454 g) ground chicken

1 cloves garlic, minced

1 tbsp (8 g) ginger

1 tbsp (8 g) minced lemongrass, white parts only

1 tbsp (11 g) minced jalapeño

¼ cup (4 g) cilantro leaves, finely chopped

1½ tsp (8 ml) Thai fish sauce, divided

1 tsp soy sauce or tamari (for gluten-free option)

½ tsp kosher salt, plus more as needed for seasoning

¼ tsp black pepper, plus more as needed for seasoning

1 tsp cornstarch

3 tbsp (45 ml) vegetable oil, divided

2 tbsp (20 g) red curry paste

1¾ cups (420 ml) coconut milk

1 tbsp (24 g) maple syrup or light brown sugar

3 cups (547 g) thinly sliced sweet potato, ⅛-inch (3-mm) slices or spiralized

1 cup (112 g) thinly sliced red bell pepper, ⅛-inch (3-mm) slices

3 cups (222 g) thinly sliced zucchini, ⅛-inch (3-mm) slices or spiralized

Cilantro, for garnish

In a large bowl, combine the chicken, garlic, ginger, lemongrass, jalapeño, cilantro, ½ teaspoon of fish sauce, soy sauce, salt, pepper and cornstarch.

Lightly grease your hands with vegetable oil and form the mixture into 12 evenly shaped meatballs, about 2 tablespoons (28 g) or 1 inch (2.5 cm) in size.

Heat a large high-side pan over medium heat. Add 2 tablespoons (30 ml) of vegetable oil, and once hot, add the meatballs to the pan. Cook the meatballs on all sides until golden in color, turning every minute, about 5 minutes total. Transfer to a clean plate.

In the same pan, add the curry paste and sauté until fragrant, 15 seconds. Add the coconut milk and maple syrup, and whisk to combine. Bring the sauce to a boil, then reduce to a simmer over medium-low heat. Add the meatballs back to the pan and simmer for 10 minutes, stirring the meatballs every few minutes so that they evenly cook. Add 1 teaspoon of fish sauce and stir to combine. While the meatballs simmer, cook the vegetables.

Heat a large sauté pan over medium-high heat. Add 1 tablespoon (15 ml) of oil to the pan, and once hot, add the sweet potatoes and sauté for 2 minutes. Add the bell peppers and sauté for 1 minute. Add the zucchini and sauté for 2 to 3 minutes, until all of the vegetables are crisp-tender. Season with salt and pepper as desired.

Divide the vegetables evenly among bowls, top with the meatballs, sauce and cilantro leaves.

COOK'S NOTE:

A spiralizing tool is a quick and easy way to create long, voluminous, curly vegetable and fruit noodles or ribbons. Handheld or counter models can produce various shapes and sizes of noodles. Food that can be spiralized must have a firm flesh, be void of pits and at least 1½ inches (4 cm) in diameter and 2 inches (5 cm) long. Carrots, zucchini, squash, cucumber and potatoes are some good ingredients to make into noodles.

RECIPE SCIENCE:

To make this dish gluten-free, a small amount of cornstarch is added instead of bread crumbs. The starch helps to bind some of the moisture that is released as the protein in the meatballs contracts and releases its juices, and also prevents them from becoming dry. The ground chicken is very lean with little connective tissue, so braising for long periods of time in the curry sauce like traditional beef meatballs is not recommended. The meatballs are browned first in a hot pan to create a flavorful crust and set the shape of the delicate meatball mixture. The meatballs are briefly simmered in the fragrant red curry sauce until it reaches an internal temperature of 160 to 165°F (71 to 74°C), to keep them tender and moist.

italian seafood stew

STEW | **GLUTEN-FREE** | **DAIRY-FREE**

This Italian-style seafood stew is loaded with fresh mussels, shrimp, scallops and snapper simmered in a savory white wine tomato broth for the ultimate one-pot meal. The sauce is given ample time to simmer and reduce the majority of alcohol in the wine, so only a savory, bright and slightly briny flavor from the clam juice remains before adding the seafood. This hearty seafood stew is meant to be shared!

SERVES: 4 | **PREP TIME:** 15 minutes | **COOK TIME:** 50 minutes

¼ cup plus 2 tbsp (90 ml) olive oil

1 cup (150 g) diced white onion, ¼-inch (6-mm) dice

4 cloves garlic, minced

½ cup (48 g) sliced leeks, white parts only, ⅛-inch (3-mm) slices

½ cup (60 g) diced celery, ¼-inch (6-mm) dice

⅛ tsp red chili flakes

2 tsp (1 g) dried oregano

28 oz (794 g) canned diced tomatoes with juice

2 tbsp (34 g) tomato puree

½ cup (120 ml) dry white wine

Zest of one lemon

1 tbsp (15 ml) lemon juice

2 cups (480 ml) water

¾ cup (180 ml) clam juice

½ tsp kosher salt, plus more for seasoning

¼ tsp black pepper, plus more for seasoning

½ lb (227 g) scallops, about 8 pieces

½ lb (227 g) snapper, 2 x 1 inch (5 x 2.5 cm) pieces

¾ lb (341 g) mussels, cleaned and debearded

½ lb (227 g) jumbo shrimp, peeled and deveined, about 10 pieces

2 tbsp (8 g) chopped Italian parsley

1 tbsp (1 g) thinly sliced basil

4 lemon wedges

Heat a large pot fitted with a lid over medium heat. Add ¼ cup (60 ml) of olive oil, and once hot, add the onion, garlic, leeks, celery, chili flakes and oregano. Sauté until the vegetables are tender, about 10 minutes.

Add the diced tomatoes, tomato puree, wine, lemon zest, lemon juice, water, clam juice, salt and pepper and stir to combine. Bring to a boil then reduce to a simmer over medium-low heat, 25 minutes, stirring occasionally.

Heat a medium-size sauté pan over medium-high heat. Add 2 tablespoons (30 ml) olive oil, and once hot, add the scallops. Cook until the surface is golden brown, about 3 minutes. Flip the scallops and cook until cooked through, about 2 minutes. Transfer to a clean plate. Add the snapper to the pan and cook until golden in color, 2 minutes. Flip and cook until cooked through, 1 minute. Transfer to a plate with the scallops.

Turn the heat to medium-high on the large pot with the stew ingredients. Add the cleaned mussels and shrimp to the pan, cover and cook for 3 minutes. Remove the lid and stir, add the scallops and snapper and cover the pot. Cook, covered, until the mussels have opened and the seafood is cooked, 3 minutes. Season the stew with more salt and pepper to taste.

Serve the stew garnished with parsley and basil and with a side of lemon wedges.

COOK'S NOTE:

The seafood is cooked in phases because the delicate fish proteins require different cooking times, considering the effect of heat on their texture. The shrimp is heartier in texture and cooks alongside the steamed mussels in the liquid broth. The scallops and snapper are sautéed to give a nice color and crust on the seafood before adding to the stew.

RECIPE SCIENCE:

To build a fragrant tomato base for the stew, the oregano and chili flakes are bloomed in the olive oil first instead of added to the liquid to intensify their taste. Oregano is a hearty and potent herb that when cooked with the aromatics (onion, garlic, leeks and celery) softens so that it can permeate the stew. Oregano has a noticeably dominant taste due to the stable non-volatile flavor compounds called phenols, particularly carvacrol and thymol. Cooking the chili flakes in a hot oil solvent intensifies the flavor and kicks up the Scoville heat units (SHU) for greater spiciness perception, which is why only a small amount is added to the stew.

moroccan lamb stew

Making a big pot of piping hot stew is a simple braising cooking technique to make tougher cuts of meat tender and tasty! The fragrant spices gently infuse the bites of lamb with flavor from whole cinnamon sticks, cumin, ginger, coriander, paprika and lemon peel. Green olives add a briny and piquant flavor to the stew to balance the sweet notes from the spices and plump currants.

SERVES: 4 | **PREP TIME:** 15 minutes | **COOK TIME:** 1 hour 30 minutes

1½ lb (680 g) lamb shoulder or leg, cut into 1-inch (2.5-cm) cubes

½ tsp ground cumin

1 tsp ground ginger

1 tsp ground coriander

1 tsp paprika

½ tsp kosher salt, plus more for seasoning

¼ tsp black pepper, plus more for seasoning

¼ cup (60 ml) olive oil, divided

1 cup (150 g) diced yellow onion, ¼-inch (6-mm) dice

2 cloves garlic, minced

1 cup (228 g) thinly sliced carrots, ⅛-inch (3-mm) thick slices

28 oz (794 g) canned diced tomatoes with juice

½ cup (120 ml) orange juice

⅓ cup (57 g) dried currants

1½ cups (360 ml) unsalted beef stock

1 cinnamon stick

1⅓ cups (219 g) canned garbanzo beans

1 cup (139 g) green olives, pitted

Zest of 1 lemon

1 tbsp (15 ml) lemon juice

2 tbsp (8 g) chopped Italian parsley

1 tbsp (3 g) thinly sliced mint

¼ cup (26 g) sliced almonds

COUSCOUS

2 cups (480 ml) unsalted beef stock

1 tbsp (15 ml) olive oil

½ tsp kosher salt

1 cinnamon stick

1½ cups (172 g) couscous

In a medium-size bowl, combine the lamb, cumin, ginger, coriander, paprika, ½ teaspoon of salt, ¼ teaspoon of black pepper and 2 tablespoons (30 ml) of olive oil.

Heat a large pot or high-side pan over medium-high heat. Add 1 tablespoon (15 ml) of oil, and once hot, add the seasoned lamb. Brown the lamb on all sides, 5 minutes. Transfer the lamb to a clean plate and reserve.

Reduce the heat to medium and add 1 tablespoon (15 ml) of oil. Add the onions and garlic, and sauté until softened, 5 minutes. Add the carrots, tomatoes, orange juice, currants, beef stock and cinnamon stick to the pot. Bring the stew to a boil, stir, reduce to low and cover so that the stew simmers for 1 to 1½ hours, until the lamb is very tender.

Add the garbanzo beans and olives, stir to combine, cover and cook 10 minutes. Add the lemon zest and lemon juice. Season the stew with more salt and pepper to taste.

For the couscous, bring the beef stock, olive oil, salt and cinnamon stick to a boil in a 2-quart (2-L) saucepan. Add the couscous, stir, cover and turn off heat. Let the couscous sit for 10 minutes, then fluff with a fork to separate the grains.

Serve the lamb stew with couscous. Garnish with parsley, mint and almonds.

COOK'S NOTE:

Oil-soluble spices like cumin, coriander and paprika benefit from cooking in oil to release and enhance the aromatic flavor compounds for a stronger flavor impact in the stew. The lamb is seasoned with the spices and tossed in olive oil before searing so that they stick to and season the meat. As the lamb sears, the spices bloom in the oil, intensifying the earthy flavors and immediately sending fragrant volatile compounds into the air to make the stew even more enticing.

RECIPE SCIENCE:

A combination method of dry-heat and moist-heat cooking allows layers of flavors to be developed. Searing the pieces of spice-coated lamb kickstarts flavor on the surface, creating new color pigments by Maillard browning this only happens at a temperature above 285°F (141°C). The shoulder and leg of the lamb are surrounded by tough muscle fibers, connective tissues and fat. Simmering the meat in the cooking liquid over low heat for a longer cooking time creates a tender and moist product. The acids from the orange juice and tomatoes help to gently soften the meat, breaking down the firm proteins as the stew simmers.

indian cauliflower curry

STEW | VEGETARIAN | GLUTEN-FREE | FREEZER-FRIENDLY

Delicious and fragrant Indian cauliflower curry is a wholesome and alluring meal designed for the senses. The hallmark of Indian cuisine is the ample use of bold spices to make the vegetables shine. To create an aromatic base, dried curry powder, turmeric, coriander, cayenne pepper and garam masala illuminate the color and flavor of the sauce. The authentic and powerful taste of the spices comes from the volatile compound molecules that are released into the air, which are immediately detected and strengthened during the cooking process. Each spoonful of curried chickpeas, cauliflower, peas, potatoes and spinach will send bursts of flavor for an unforgettable vegetarian dinner experience.

SERVES: 4 | **PREP TIME:** 15 minutes | **COOK TIME:** 60 minutes

1 tbsp (7 g) curry powder

1 tsp garam masala

1 tsp ground turmeric

1 tsp ground coriander

⅛ tsp ground cayenne pepper, plus more for seasoning

2 tbsp (30 ml) vegetable oil

1 cup (153 g) diced yellow onion, ¼-inch (6-mm) dice

3 cloves garlic, minced

1½ tsp (6 g) minced ginger

¾ cup (180 ml) vegetable broth

15 oz (425 g) crushed tomatoes

1 cup (245 g) plain whole milk yogurt

¾ tsp kosher salt, plus more for seasoning

3 cups (322 g) cauliflower florets, 1-inch (2.5-cm) pieces

2 cups (146 g) diced russet potatoes, peeled, 1-inch (2.5-cm) cubes

1 cup (171 g) canned garbanzo beans

½ cup (76 g) green peas, fresh or frozen

2 oz (59 g) baby spinach

Black pepper, as needed for seasoning

1 tbsp (1 g) chopped cilantro

Heat a small skillet over medium-high heat, add the curry powder, garam masala, turmeric, coriander and cayenne pepper. Constantly stir the spices until slightly darkened and fragrant, being careful not to burn the spices, about 30 to 60 seconds. Transfer to a small bowl.

Heat a large pot fitted with a lid over medium heat. Add the vegetable oil, and once hot add the onions, garlic and ginger. Sauté until the onions are tender, 5 minutes. Add the toasted curry powder, garam masala, turmeric, coriander and cayenne pepper. Stir and cook until fragrant, 1 minute. Add the vegetable broth, tomatoes, yogurt and salt, and stir to combine. Add the cauliflower, potatoes and garbanzo beans.

Bring the curry to a boil, then reduce to a simmer. The cauliflower pieces and potatoes need more time to cook and release natural particulates into the curry for extra thickening. Cover and cook until the potatoes and cauliflower are fork tender, 35 to 45 minutes. Add the peas and spinach, cover and cook until peas are bright green and spinach is wilted, 5 minutes.

Taste the curry and adjust salt, pepper and cayenne pepper to taste. Garnish the curry with cilantro and serve hot.

COOK'S NOTE:

To maximize the flavor potential in the sauce, curry powder and garam masala are toasted first in a dry skillet. High direct heat in the pan activates the formation of Maillard browning reaction products like pyrazines and boosts flavors by bringing aromatic oils to the surface of the spices for a more complex and strong aroma.

RECIPE SCIENCE:

Blooming the spices in oil before adding the broth allows the fat-soluble spices in the garam masala (cardamom, cinnamon, black pepper), coriander and cayenne pepper to intensify in flavor as the molecules are quickly released from solid to solution state in the hot oil. When simmered with the tomatoes and yogurt, the acid in the fruit and fermented dairy competes with bitter compounds by reducing their perception and brightening the spices' flavors. The creamy yogurt helps to balance the intensity of the spices, and the fat can help disperse and coat the fat-soluble flavor compounds for prolonged perception while preventing them from tasting too robust.

grandma's ginger beef stew

STEW | DAIRY-FREE | FREEZER-FRIENDLY

There is one dish that I always looked forward to when going to my grandparents' house: Chinese ginger beef stew. Each step from start to finish was prepared with careful attention and love, and I was the luckiest kid to get a piping hot bowl for dinner. Not only was the stewing technique achieved to perfection, the layers of umami taste were enhanced by the precise selection of Asian sauces and seasonings to build on the meaty flavor. In my family, this beef stew with a variety of root vegetables is always served with a bowl of fluffy, white Calrose rice, so that the grains can catch and absorb every drop of the flavorful sauce.

SERVES: 4 | **PREP TIME:** 10 minutes | **COOK TIME:** 45 minutes

1 lb (454 g) boneless beef chuck-eye roast, shoulder or bottom round, cut into 1½-inch (4-cm) cubes

½ tsp kosher salt, plus more for seasoning

¼ tsp black pepper, plus more for seasoning

1 tbsp (15 ml) soy sauce

1 tsp sesame oil

3 cloves garlic, minced

2 tbsp (30 ml) vegetable oil

2 slices peeled ginger, ¼-inch (6-mm) thick

1½ cups (165 g) diced red onions, 1-inch (2.5-cm) dice

1 tbsp (15 ml) oyster sauce

2 cups (343 g) diced russet potatoes, 1-inch (2.5-cm) dice

1 cup (140 g) sliced carrots, ½ inch (1.3 cm) thick

1 cup (137 g) diced butternut squash, ½-inch (1.3-cm) dice

1 cup (137 g) sliced turnip, ½-inch (1.3-cm) slice

3 cups (720 ml) unsalted beef stock

2 tbsp (20 g) cornstarch

¼ cup (60 ml) water

¼ cup (4 g) cilantro leaves

In a medium-size bowl, combine the beef, salt, pepper, soy sauce, sesame oil and garlic.

Heat a large pot or Dutch oven fitted with a lid over medium-high heat. Add the oil, and once hot, carefully add the ginger and beef mixture in a single layer. Sear the meat on one side for 2 minutes, flip and cook another 2 minutes on the other side. The beef will not be fully cooked.

Reduce the heat to medium, add the onions and sauté for 2 minutes. Add the oyster sauce to the pot and stir to combine. Add the potatoes, carrots, butternut squash, turnip and beef stock. Bring the liquid to a boil, then reduce to a simmer over low heat. Cover and cook until the potatoes and butternut squash are tender, 30 to 45 minutes.

In a small bowl, whisk together the cornstarch and water until a slurry forms. Bring the stew to a gentle boil, then gradually add the cornstarch slurry to the center of the pot, whisking to disperse, then stir to combine. Cook, stirring until the liquid is thickened, 60 to 90 seconds.

Garnish the stew with cilantro and serve hot.

COOK'S NOTE:

In Asian cooking, cornstarch slurries are used at the very end of cooking to instantly thicken sauces to create just the right level of cling to the small pieces of food in the dish. The cooked cornstarch gives the sauce an attractive shine to make the stew even more irresistible.

RECIPE SCIENCE:

Before the beef gets cooked, it's marinated in soy sauce, sesame oil and garlic to instantly kick up the beefy notes in the dish. The soy sauce, oyster sauce, garlic and onions are rich in glutamate, a type of salt form of the amino acid glutamic acid known to give a savory and meaty flavor to foods. The beef and stock are rich in nucleotides (mainly inosinate and guanylate), which synergistically heighten umami flavor! A quick sear in the pan gives a flavorful crust and golden color to the beef. The onions are sautéed to develop caramelized flavors, which will add a hint of sweetness to the stew. The beef and vegetables are gently stewed until tender in a covered pot, using the braising method. This time allows the connective tissues to melt down, convert to gelatin and tenderize the beef, while the vegetables soften and absorb the savory flavors of the braising liquid.

beer-braised chicken and vegetables

BRAISE | DAIRY-FREE | ONE-POT MEAL

This hearty one-pot braised chicken is loaded with protein and vegetables and gets a flavor boost from hoppy pale ale beer. Adding the beer to the braise provides a welcoming slight bitterness and earthy notes from the hops plant used during the brewing process. The bitterness is balanced with the natural sweetness of the carrot, sweet potatoes and a hint of brown sugar.

SERVES: 4 | **PREP TIME:** 15 minutes | **COOK TIME:** 1 hour 25 minutes

1½ to 2 lb (681 to 908 g) bone-in chicken thighs with skin

1 tsp kosher salt, plus more for seasoning

¼ tsp black pepper, plus more for seasoning

Paprika, for seasoning

1 tbsp (15 ml) olive oil

1 cup (150 g) diced yellow onion, ½-inch (1.3-cm) dice

1 clove garlic, sliced

2 tbsp (32 g) tomato paste

¼ cup plus 2 tbsp (53 g) all-purpose flour, divided

3 cups (720 ml) unsalted chicken stock

1 cup (240 ml) beer, pale ale recommended

1 tbsp (12 g) dark brown sugar

1 tsp chopped thyme

1 cup (168 g) red potatoes, cut into 1-inch (2.5-cm) pieces

1 cup (164 g) carrots, cut into 1-inch (2.5-cm) pieces

1 cup (146 g) sweet potatoes, cut into 1-inch (2.5-cm) pieces

1 cup (91 g) sliced brown mushrooms, ¼-inch (6-mm) thick slices

2 ears corn, 1 cob cut into 4 pieces, 1 cob kernels removed

¼ cup (15 g) parsley leaves

Adjust the oven rack to the center position and preheat the oven to 300°F (145°C).

Generously season the chicken thighs with salt, pepper and paprika on both sides. Heat a large pot or Dutch oven fitted with a lid over medium-high heat. Add the olive oil, and once hot, add the chicken skin side down. Cook until crispy and golden brown, 5 minutes. Flip the chicken and cook 3 minutes. Turn off the heat and transfer the chicken to a clean plate.

Reserve 1 tablespoon (15 ml) of chicken fat drippings in the pan, then turn the heat to medium. Add the onions and garlic, and sauté until the onions are tender, 3 minutes. Add the tomato paste, stir and cook for 1 minute. Add ¼ cup (36 g) of flour, stir and cook for 1 minute.

Whisk in the chicken stock, beer, brown sugar, thyme, salt and pepper. Use a whisk to scrape and incorporate the browned bits on the bottom of the pot. Bring the liquid to a simmer, with light bubbles breaking the surface, and cook until slightly thickened, 5 minutes.

Add the chicken, potatoes, carrots, sweet potatoes, mushrooms, corn kernels and cut corn cobs to the pot. Cover pot with a lid and transfer to the oven. Cook until the vegetables are tender, 55 to 60 minutes.

Remove the pot from the oven. In a small bowl, combine 2 tablespoons (18 g) of flour and ½ cup (120 ml) of the braising liquid. Whisk to combine, transfer back to the pot. Whisk into the braise until incorporated, cover with a lid and return to the oven for 5 minutes. Season with salt and pepper to taste. Garnish with parsley.

COOK'S NOTE:

Bones consist of a calcium phosphate porous structure, which makes them poor conductors of heat. This can be advantageous for cuts of meat or poultry cooked for long periods of time with the bones attached. The meat residing next to the bone will not cook as quickly and prevents overcooking and moisture loss for a juicier product.

RECIPE SCIENCE:

The slow, yet consistent heat of the oven provides moderate energy transfer on all sides of the pan for even cooking of the food inside. To create a lightly thickened braising liquid, a white roux is made using the fat drippings from searing the chicken and flour to create a paste. The beer and chicken stock disperse the roux into the liquid for braising and are simmered so that the starches in the flour can begin to gelatinize and thicken the sauce. To ensure that the sauce clings to the meat and vegetables, a little more flour is added at the end of cooking for extra viscosity. Wheat starches can lose some of their thickening power when cooked for longer periods of time, especially during the prolonged braising process.

buddha's braised tofu and vegetables

BRAISE | VEGETARIAN | DAIRY-FREE | ONE-POT MEAL

For a luxurious vegetarian dish packed with savory Chinese flavors, the tofu shines as the star of this recipe. The pressed soybean cake is sliced and seared just like any meat or seafood to add a more attractive color and texture before braising. The ingredients simmer in a fragrant soy sauce mixture, which effortlessly gets infused into the tofu and vegetables.

SERVES: 4 | **PREP TIME:** 30 minutes | **COOK TIME:** 25 minutes

6 dried shiitake mushrooms

14 oz (397 g) firm or extra-firm tofu

3 tbsp (45 ml) soy sauce

3 tbsp (45 ml) oyster sauce

¾ cup (180 ml) vegetable broth

¼ tsp honey

2 tbsp (30 ml) vegetable oil

3 cloves garlic, minced

1 tbsp (11 g) sliced white parts of green onion

1 tsp minced ginger

½ cup (68 g) sliced carrots, ⅛ inch (3 mm) thick

1 cup (93 g) Chinese long beans, cut into 2-inch (5-cm) pieces

4 oz (115 g) baby bok choy, cut in half

¼ cup (33 g) bamboo shoots, canned

¼ cup (43 g) sliced water chestnuts, canned

½ cup (77 g) baby corn, canned

½ cup (56 g) sliced red bell pepper, ¼ inch (6 mm) thick

1 cup (45 g) thinly sliced napa cabbage, ¼ inch (6 mm) thick

½ cup (36 g) bean sprouts

2 tsp (6 g) cornstarch

1 tbsp (15 ml) water

Black pepper, as needed for seasoning

1 tbsp (4 g) sliced green onions

Soak the mushrooms in 2 cups (480 ml) of warm water until rehydrated, 20 minutes. Drain and set aside.

Cut the tofu into 1-inch (2.5-cm) thick slices, then cut into squares and then into triangles. Place the tofu in between paper towels, pressing lightly to soak up excess water. Allow to dry for 10 minutes.

In a medium-size bowl, whisk together the soy sauce, oyster sauce, vegetable broth and honey, and set aside.

Heat a large wok or high-side pan fitted with a lid over medium-high heat. Add the oil, and once hot, add the tofu. Allow to sauté until golden brown, not moving the tofu, about 4 minutes. Use a spatula to release the tofu and flip; cook 4 minutes on the other side. Remove the tofu from the pan and transfer to a clean plate.

Turn the heat down to medium and sauté the garlic, whites from green onions and ginger until fragrant, 1 minute. Add the carrots, tofu, drained mushrooms and soy sauce mixture. Bring to a boil, then reduce to a simmer. Cover and braise the tofu for 10 minutes.

Add the beans, bok choy, bamboo shoots and water chestnuts to the pan, stir and cover. Cook for 4 minutes. Add the corn, bell pepper, cabbage and beans sprouts to pan. Stir, cover and cook for 2 minutes.

Whisk the cornstarch and the water in a small bowl. Make a well in the center of the pan and turn heat to high to bring the liquid to a boil. Add the cornstarch slurry mixture and whisk until the sauce is thickened and combined with the vegetables, 30 to 60 seconds. Turn off the heat and season the vegetables with pepper. Garnish with the green onions and serve hot.

COOK'S NOTE:
Soft tofu is good for pureeing into desserts, dressings or soups. Medium is suitable for baking or stir-frying, but may not hold together as well. Firm and extra-firm work well when battering, stir-frying, pan-frying and braising as it holds together with more physical agitation.

RECIPE SCIENCE:
Each tofu piece is dried as much as possible before searing, so that it can brown and form a light crust instead of steam in the pan. Each vegetable in the dish requires different cooking times, as some are more delicate and others more robust. Braising on the stove allows you to easily cook the various vegetables in phases so that the finished dish has just the right textures. To lightly thicken the sauce, a cornstarch slurry is added at the very end of cooking. The gelatinized starch granules add a nice thickness to the sauce, coating the food with a glossy sheen.

pork pappardelle pasta

BRAISE | **GLUTEN-FREE**

A big bowl of savory pork pasta with a built-in sauce is an irresistible one-pot meal. The combination of the tender savory pork, sweet caramelized vegetables and tart apples creates a pleasingly balanced pasta that gets more addictive with every bite.

SERVES: 6 | **PREP TIME:** 30 minutes | **COOK TIME:** 3 hours

1 tbsp (18 g) kosher salt, plus more for seasoning

¼ tsp black pepper, plus more for seasoning

1 tsp smoked paprika

2 lb (908 g) boneless pork shoulder, excess fat trimmed

¼ cup (60 ml) vegetable oil, divided

2 cups (238 g) Granny Smith apples, 1-inch (2.5-cm) dice

1 cup (100 g) celery, 1-inch (2.5-cm) dice

1 cup (152 g) carrots, 1-inch (2.5-cm) dice

1 cup (133 g) yellow onion, 1-inch (2.5-cm) dice

3 cloves garlic, roughly chopped

4 thyme sprigs

½ cup (131 g) tomato paste

1 cup (240 ml) dry white wine, sauvignon blanc or chardonnay

2 cups (480 ml) unsalted chicken stock

⅓ cup (80 ml) apple cider vinegar

3 tbsp (45 ml) pure maple syrup

1 lb (454 g) pappardelle pasta

1 tbsp (4 g) chopped parsley

¼ cup (60 g) freshly grated Parmesan cheese

Adjust the oven rack to the lower third position and preheat the oven to 300°F (149°C).

In a small bowl, combine the salt, pepper and paprika. Evenly season the pork with the seasoning. Heat a large Dutch oven over medium-high heat. Add 2 tablespoons (30 ml) of vegetable oil, and once hot, add the pork to the pan. Brown all sides of the pork, about 10 minutes, then transfer to a clean plate.

Rinse the Dutch oven, dry and return to the stove. Heat the pot over medium heat and add 2 tablespoons (30 ml) of oil. Add the apples, celery, carrots, onion, garlic and thyme. Sauté until the vegetables just begin to brown, 6 minutes. Add the tomato paste, stir and cook until color deepens, 2 minutes. Add the wine, chicken stock, vinegar, maple syrup and browned pork. Stir and bring the liquid to a boil, then reduce to a simmer. Cover, turn off the heat, then transfer the pot to the oven. Braise the pork for 3 hours, turning over once halfway through cooking, until the pork is tender and can be shredded easily with a fork.

Transfer the braised pork to a clean plate. Shred the pork using two forks, removing any large pieces of fat. Remove the thyme sprigs and discard. Use a large spoon to remove any excess fat on top of the liquid and discard. Strain the braising liquid into a large bowl, pushing the vegetable and apple pieces with the back of a spoon to release the flavors and liquid, and then transfer the solids to a blender.

Add ¼ cup (60 ml) of the liquid to the blender and puree until smooth. Transfer the strained liquid back to the pot. Add just enough of the vegetable puree, about ¼ to ½ cup (60 to 120 ml), to lightly thicken the sauce. Stir to combine, and season with salt and pepper. Add the shredded pork, keep warm over low heat and cover.

Bring a large pot of salted water to a boil. Add the pasta and cook according to the package directions. Drain the pasta and toss with the pork and sauce over medium heat until coated and warm. Divide the pasta among bowls and garnish with parsley and Parmesan cheese.

COOK'S NOTE:
For a successful braise, a pot that has a thick bottom and sides with a heavy tight-fitting lid helps with even cooking and locks in moisture.

RECIPE SCIENCE:
During the long three-hour cooking time, the dry exposed parts of the pork even at low temperatures of 160°F (71°C) can initiate Maillard browning to produce more flavor compounds over time. Meanwhile, the braised pork becomes tender, rich and flavorful from the rendered pork fat. Instead of using flour to further thicken the sauce for the pasta, the tender sautéed vegetables and apples in the braise get puréed in a blender with the braising liquid to create a hot coulis. The fine particulates get suspended in the liquid for a smooth yet thickened textured sauce.

red wine–braised short ribs

BRAISE | DAIRY-FREE

Tender beef short ribs are often a dish you would wait to order at a fine dining restaurant, but it's actually quite easy to prepare at home with simple equipment and a braising technique. The rich and meaty ribs are served with a light yet creamy cauliflower purée.

SERVES: 4 | **PREP TIME:** 30 minutes | **COOK TIME:** 3 hours

3 lb (1.4 kg) bone-in beef short ribs, about 2 inches (5 cm) thick, 4- to 6-inch (10- to 15-cm) long pieces, English cut

Kosher salt, as needed for seasoning

Black pepper, as needed for seasoning

2 tbsp (30 ml) olive oil

1½ cups (225 g) diced yellow onions, ¼-inch (6-mm) dice

¾ cup (117 g) diced carrots, ¼-inch (6-mm) dice

¾ cup (75 g) diced celery, ¼-inch (6-mm) dice

3 cloves garlic, roughly chopped

3 tbsp (27 g) all-purpose flour

1 cup (240 ml) red wine, merlot or cabernet sauvignon

1 cup (240 ml) unsalted beef stock

1 tbsp (17 g) tomato paste

2 tsp (3 g) minced rosemary

1 tsp minced thyme

1 bay leaf

8 oz (226 g) brown mushrooms, quartered

1 tbsp (4 g) minced parsley

CAULIFLOWER PURÉE

4 cups (468 g) cauliflower florets

1 cup (118 g) sliced yellow onion

1 clove garlic, sliced

2 tbsp (30 ml) olive oil

½ tsp kosher salt, as needed for seasoning

Adjust the oven rack to the lower third position and preheat the oven to 350°F (177°C).

Generously season the short ribs with salt and pepper on each side. Heat a large Dutch oven over medium-high heat. Add the olive oil, and once hot, add the short ribs. Sear on each side until browned, 8 minutes total, and transfer to a clean plate. Leave about 3 tablespoons (45 ml) of drippings in the pan.

Reduce the heat to medium and add the onions, carrots and celery. Sauté until the vegetables are tender, 5 minutes. Add the garlic; sauté until fragrant, 1 minute. Add the flour and stir to combine. Add the wine, beef stock, tomato paste, rosemary, thyme and bay leaf, and stir to combine. Bring to a boil. Add the mushrooms and short ribs to the pan. Cover, turn off the heat and transfer the pan to the oven.

Braise the short ribs for 2 to 2½ hours, until the meat is tender and just falling off the bone. After 45 minutes of cooking, flip the short ribs over to ensure even cooking in the liquid. Transfer the meat to a clean plate.

Allow the cooking liquid to stand for 5 minutes, then skim off any excess fat on the surface and discard. Bring the cooking liquid to a boil, and reduce by one-fourth of the volume, about 10 minutes. Remove the bay leaf and discard. Season the braising liquid with salt and pepper to taste. Return the short ribs to the pot, turn off the heat and cover until ready to serve.

For the cauliflower purée, add the cauliflower, onions and garlic to a medium-size pot. Cover with enough water to reach 1 inch (2.5 cm) above the vegetables. Bring the water to a boil and cook until the cauliflower is very tender, about 8 to 10 minutes.

Drain the vegetables and add to a blender, reserving the liquid. Blend the vegetables until a purée is formed, and while the blender is running, slowly drizzle in the olive oil. Add more as needed to achieve a smooth purée. If needed, add the reserved cooking liquid 1 tablespoon (15 ml) at a time to thin out the purée. Season the purée with ½ teaspoon of salt, or to taste.

Add the cauliflower purée to each plate, and top with braised short rib. Pour some of the sauce with vegetables on top, and garnish with minced parsley.

> **COOK'S NOTE:**
> English-cut short ribs are long slabs of meat with the bones attached. This cut is used in this recipe because the thicker meat lends itself to longer braising times.

> **RECIPE SCIENCE:**
> Beef short ribs are rich in fat and collagen within the meat and the bones. When kept in a hot moist-heat environment for long periods of time, the collagen in the beef will transform into gelatin, which binds moisture and adds body to the sauce in the braise. The bone marrow also contributes rich flavors as it migrates to the meat during the cooking process.

slow cooking

SAVE TIME WITH A SLOW COOKER

Yes, it might sound contradictory, but with a little upfront prep, patience and imagination, slow cooker meals can be the hero of your busy household. Let's cover the basics, benefits and a few of my favorite recipes to have meals ready when you want them, with little effort and cleanup.

the simple science

Slow cooking is similar to a stovetop or Dutch oven. In a slow cooker, heat begins at the base and works its way up the sides, then into the food. The steam generated from the heat creates a vacuum seal with the lid. Low and consistent temperatures help to retain moisture during cooking. The liquid does not evaporate or become concentrated. The basic cooking techniques achieved in a slow cooker are poaching, braising or stewing. Poaching is best for seafood, fish and lean meats like chicken breast. Braising is great for tougher, inexpensive cuts of meat with marbling, like shoulder cuts from beef or pork. Stewing can be accomplished with smaller cuts of meat. There are new technologies available now that even allow you to sauté and steam. Desserts can also be made in the slow cooker, so there are a variety of uses for one.

slow cooking basics

HOW TO SELECT A SLOW COOKER

There are many brands, shapes (round or oval), sizes (1½ to 7 quarts [1.5 to 6.5 L]) and prices ($20 to $200) available. Depending on the size and brand you use, the results may vary. With a little bit of practice and experimentation, you will find what method works best for your unit. If you are looking to buy your first slow cooker, I recommend at least a programmable 6-quart (5.6-L) size (see page 196) especially if you are cooking for four people or more, or if you like leftovers. Below is a guide to slow cooker sizes based on how many people you're feeding.

RECOMMENDED SLOW COOKER SIZE

SERVING SIZE	COOKER SIZE
1 to 2 people	2 to 3.5 quarts (2 to 3.3 L)
3 to 4 people	3.5 to 4.5 quarts (3.3 to 4.2 L)
4 to 5 people	4.5 to 5 quarts (4.2 to 4.7 L)
6 plus people	5 to 7 quarts (4.7 to 6.6 L)

HOW TO USE A SLOW COOKER

Ingredient temperature: It's best to use thawed or fresh proteins when cooking. Frozen items may not reach safe cooking temperatures.

Fill: A good rule of thumb is that the slow cooker typically needs to be filled at least halfway to operate correctly, but should not be filled more than ⅔ full.

Settings: Typically there are just two cooking settings, "high" or "low." Some cookers even have a "keep warm" setting for when you are entertaining or holding the food over time. What setting you choose depends on the model you have, how fast you want to cook the dish and what kind of ingredients you are using. For large roasts, you can use the low or high setting. Lean proteins like chicken breasts, thighs, bone-in pieces or pork loin work well when cooked on low. Stews and soup can use either the low or high setting.

Time: Most slow cooker recipes have a time range. Different variables like temperature, thickness, type of meat and how full the cooker is affect how much time is needed. Usually the low setting takes twice as long as the high temperature. Give yourself a little extra time before serving, in case you need to cook the dish for a bit longer.

Cooking temperatures: To ensure that your slow cooker is working efficiently, make sure the temperature of the cooking liquid is 185°F (85°C). If it runs too high, you can overcook meat (depending on the cut); if it runs too low, your food will be unsafe to eat. The temperature danger zone of optimal growth for spoilage microorganisms is about 40 to 140°F (4 to 50°C), especially if held for over 3 to 4 hours at this range.

HOW TO PREPARE FOODS FOR SLOW COOKING

Vegetables: Root vegetables like potatoes and carrots cook longer than meat. Cut into smaller even-size pieces and place on the bottom of the cooker with the meat on top. Add more delicate vegetables during the last 15 to 60 minutes. Ingredients like spinach, zucchini, kale, chopped fresh tomatoes, peas, fresh basil and parsley benefit from being added toward the end.

Beans: Canned beans are recommended and can be added in during the last 30 minutes to keep their shape while warming. You can use dried beans, but they are trickier to cook. You must soak overnight if using dried beans, except lentils and split peas. Don't add acids, sugar or salt to dried beans at the beginning of cooking because it prevents them from becoming tender. Add those ingredients at the end.

Dairy: Add milk, cheese, sour cream, cream cheese or others at the end of cooking (last hour) because they tend to break down over long periods of cooking.

Removing fat: Make sure to skim excess fat from stews, braises and chili before serving. This reduces the fat content of the recipe and makes the dish more palatable. You can use a large spoon to remove the fat, or transfer the liquid to a fat separator and allow it to sit until the fat rises to the surface.

Fish and seafood: Add at the end of cooking as these tend to cook very quickly.

Meat: If roasts are larger than 3 pounds (1.4 kg), cut in half for even cooking. Trim excess fat as it retains heat and can cause overcooking. Browning some meats before cooking can add more color and texture to the proteins, which is optional.

Oats: Old-fashioned and steel cut oats hold up better in a slow cooker, but instant can be used as well.

Pasta: It's best to cook separately then add at the end of cooking, as dry pasta gets very sticky in the slow cooker. However, pasta can be cooked in the last 30 to 45 minutes. Smaller pasta like orzo cooks better in the slow cooker, but only in the last hour of cooking to prevent it from becoming mushy.

Rice: Instant rice should be added during the last 30 minutes of cooking. Converted (parboiled) rice works well for all-day cooking.

BOOSTING FLAVORS IN SLOW COOKER MEALS

Fresh aromatics: Onions, garlic, lemon or lime (juice and peel), celery, bell pepper, spicy peppers, cilantro, parsley and basil add fantastic flavor to dishes. If you are meal prepping, chopped and frozen onions, celery, carrots and bell peppers also work well in the slow cooker.

Fresh and dried herbs: Aromas may become muted over the long cooking time. Packing in a good amount of aromatics in the beginning, and then adding some fresh herbs, citrus or other ingredients at the very end of cooking refreshes the flavors and makes the dish extra tasty. Examples are thyme, basil, oregano, rosemary and bay leaf.

Spices: Cinnamon, nutmeg, allspice (Jamaican), Chinese five spice, cloves, ginger, garlic, onion, paprika (smoked too), chili powder, cayenne, cumin and curry are all wonderful in slow cooker dishes.

Convenience products: Soy sauce, tomato paste, chili paste, hoisin sauce, oyster sauce, brown sugar, granulated sugar and honey can be used to boost flavor as well. Tomato paste and soy sauce can enhance meaty flavors, especially when you're not browning foods before cooking in the slow cooker. Vegetable, chicken or beef stock/broth is great for creating a flavorful braising liquid. Cornstarch, flour or instant tapioca starch is perfect for thickening sauces.

ESSENTIAL SLOW COOKER TIPS

Don't open the lid! Try not to be tempted to open the lid repeatedly. A secured lid generates steam, which creates a seal. Each time you lift the lid and lose steam, you may be adding 20 or so minutes to your cooking time, so no peeking unless instructed by the recipe!

Use a thermometer. Check the doneness of food at the beginning of the recommended time for the temperature setting and allow to cook longer as needed. Overcooking meats for braises, stews, chilis and soups is not as much of a concern because well-done meats are desirable. However, if you are making fish, whole pork loins or desserts, getting the internal temperature just right is critical. See page 203 for temperature guidelines.

Serve safe food. To keep food safe, remove the contents of the slow cooker within an hour of completely cooking, and then refrigerate the leftovers. Don't reheat food in the slow cooker; it's better to use the stove or microwave to heat then add back to the slow cooker.

honey hoisin garlic chicken

SLOW COOKER | DAIRY-FREE | GLUTEN-FREE

On busy days, a homemade meal may seem impossible, but not when you use a slow cooker to help make a flavorful Asian-style chicken dish. The honey hoisin sauce gives a savory, sweet and pungent flavor to the chicken. As the chicken slowly cooks, this gives the sauce the opportunity to infuse into the surface of the chicken skin and meat. The result is an intensely flavorful piece of chicken, molasses in color and sticky to the touch.

SERVES: 4 to 6 | **PREP TIME:** 10 minutes | **COOK TIME:** 3 to 6 hours

1½ to 2 lb (681 g to 908 g) bone-in chicken thighs, skin on

Kosher salt, for seasoning

Black pepper, for seasoning

2 tbsp (30 ml) vegetable oil

⅓ cup (160 ml) hoisin sauce

⅓ cup (80 ml) honey

⅓ cup (80 ml) soy sauce or tamari (for gluten-free option)

2 tbsp (30 ml) hot water

1 tsp (4 g) minced ginger

4 cloves garlic, minced

Sesame seeds, as needed for garnish

¼ cup (4 g) cilantro leaves

Season both sides of the chicken with salt and pepper.

Heat a large sauté pan over medium-high heat. Add the vegetable oil, and once hot, carefully add the chicken skin side down. Sauté until golden brown, 5 to 6 minutes. Flip the chicken and cook 2 more minutes. Transfer the chicken to the slow cooker.

In a medium-size bowl, whisk together the hoisin sauce, honey, soy sauce, hot water, ginger and garlic. Add to the slow cooker.

Cover and cook the chicken skin side down on high for 3 to 4 hours, or 5 to 6 hours on low. If possible, flip the chicken halfway through cooking so the sauce infuses the surface of both sides.

Glaze the chicken with the sauce; garnish with sesame seeds and cilantro.

COOK'S NOTE:
Bone-in or boneless skinless chicken breasts may be substituted for this recipe. The cooking time will need to be reduced for chicken breasts to ensure that the chicken does not dry out quickly. Skip the sautéing step and check at the 2-hour mark for the high setting, and the 4-hour mark at the low setting. Use an instant-read thermometer to check the internal temperature for doneness, between 160 and 165°F (71 and 74°C).

RECIPE SCIENCE:
Bone-in chicken thighs are used in the recipe because the heartier dark meat contains more fat, and connective tissue, which provide flavor to the dish and tenderize the meat nicely in the long and moist cooking environment of the slow cooker. The skin gets a nice crisping in the pan before being added to the pot. Keeping the skin on the chicken adds additional texture and extra protection to avoid the meat becoming dry.

turkey chili with quinoa

SLOW COOKER | DAIRY-FREE | GLUTEN-FREE | FREEZER-FRIENDLY

A big pot of chili is a comforting meal that can be made with ease in a slow cooker. Just a little bit of preparation can naturally enhance the flavors of the ingredients even before they are added to the pot. Sautéed ground turkey offers new flavors and textures to the chili. Dried ground spices like cumin, paprika and chili powder are great flavoring agents prized for their aromatic compounds released during cooking. To add some plant-based protein and thickness to the chili, quinoa and beans are added to the soup. This healthy and hearty chili provides protein and tender vegetables all in one cooking vessel. Add your favorite toppings for a personalized bowl!

SERVES: 8 | **PREP TIME:** 10 minutes | **COOK TIME:** 3 to 6 hours

1 cup (152 g) finely chopped yellow onion

1 cup (175 g) diced red bell pepper, ½-inch (1.3-cm) dice

1 cup (175 g) diced green bell pepper, ½-inch (1.3-cm) dice

4 cloves garlic, minced

2 tbsp (22 g) seeded and minced jalapeño

2 tbsp (39 g) tomato paste

1 tbsp (8 g) chili powder

1 tbsp (4 g) ground cumin

1 tsp smoked paprika

1 tsp dried oregano

3 tbsp (45 ml) olive oil, divided

1 lb (454 g) ground turkey

2 tsp (12 g) kosher salt, plus more for seasoning

½ tsp black pepper, plus more for seasoning

1 cup (194 g) uncooked quinoa, rinsed and drained

28 oz (794 g) canned diced tomatoes and juice

2 cups (300 g) diced butternut squash, ¼-inch (6-mm) dice

15 oz (425 g) canned black beans, drained and rinsed

15 oz (425 g) canned pinto beans, drained and rinsed

1 cup (156 g) corn kernels, fresh or canned

3 cups (710 ml) unsalted chicken broth

Suggested toppings: cilantro, green onions, sour cream and jalapeños

In a medium-size microwave-safe bowl, add the onions, bell peppers, garlic, jalapeño, tomato paste, chili powder, cumin, paprika, oregano and 2 tablespoons (30 ml) of olive oil. Stir to combine. Microwave the mixture for 3 minutes, and then stir. Cook for 3 more minutes, then transfer to a 6-quart (5.6-L) slow cooker.

Heat a large sauté pan over medium-high heat. Add 1 tablespoon (15 ml) of olive oil and allow to heat. Once the oil is hot, add the ground turkey, 2 teaspoons (12 g) of salt and ½ teaspoon of black pepper, breaking up the turkey with a spoon (leaving some larger chunks), until the meat is no longer pink, about 5 minutes. Transfer to the slow cooker.

Always rinse the quinoa before cooking. Add the quinoa, tomatoes, squash, black beans, pinto beans, corn, chicken broth, salt and pepper to the slow cooker. Stir to combine.

Cover and cook on the high setting until the squash is tender and quinoa is fully cooked, for 3 to 4 hours, or on the low setting for 5 to 6 hours.

Season the chili with salt and pepper to taste. Garnish the chili with your desired toppings.

COOK'S NOTE:

If you don't wash the quinoa, you may taste a bitter note from a natural coating on the grain called saponin. Place the quinoa grains in a fine-mesh strainer and rinse for about 30 seconds under cool water. Shake off the excess water and transfer the grains to your cooking pot. Just 1 cup (194 g) of dried quinoa can absorb the liquid in the chili and cook up to 3 cups (710 ml) in volume.

RECIPE SCIENCE:

The slow cooker can simmer and steam but won't brown the meat, so it's good to spend a few minutes doing this before adding it to the vessel. Precooking prevents the meat from becoming mushy when cooked only in the slow cooker. Cooking the spices in fat first is called blooming, releasing fat-soluble flavor molecules into the oil, resulting in more complex flavors. This is done in the microwave to quickly bloom the spices and tenderize some of the vegetables.

yucatán-style chicken with pickled onions

SLOW COOKER | DAIRY-FREE | GLUTEN-FREE

This colorful crimson-red Yucatán chicken dish is cooked in a citrus achiote sauce with banana leaves to give a unique tropical flavor. Achiote paste, a combination of ground annatto seeds and seasonings, is popular to use in Latin cuisines to add nutty, earthy and sweet flavors and stunning color to sauces, soups, stews and marinades. The combination of achiote, orange, lime and grapefruit juices creates a bold, bright and comforting flavor in the chicken dish. Homemade, pungent pickled onions served with the chicken balance the rustic flavors with some brightness from the vegetables.

SERVES: 4 | **PREP TIME:** 30 minutes | **COOK TIME:** 3 to 6 hours

PICKLED ONION

1 large red onion, thinly sliced into rings, ⅛ inch (3 mm) thick

1 tbsp (18 g) kosher salt

1 tsp dried oregano

1 tsp whole cumin seeds

1 tsp whole black peppercorns

4 cloves garlic, cut in half lengthwise

1½ cups (360 ml) red wine vinegar

1 tbsp (15 ml) honey

CHICKEN

1 piece of banana leaf, 24 inches (61 cm) long, optional

3 lb (1.4 kg) bone-in chicken thighs and drumsticks

Zest of 1 orange

½ cup (120 ml) orange juice

Zest of 3 limes (2 tsp)

⅓ cup (80 ml) lime juice

½ cup (120 ml) grapefruit juice

2 tbsp (30 ml) white wine vinegar

3.5 oz (100 g) achiote paste

1 tsp kosher salt

1 cup (166 g) diced tomato, ½-inch (1.3-cm) dice

1 cup (150 g) diced red onion, 1-inch (2.5-cm) dice

Optional: tortillas, rice, black beans or plantains

To prepare the pickled onions, add the sliced onion and salt to a bowl, and toss to combine. Allow the excess liquid to be released from the onion, about 15 minutes. Transfer the salted onions to a glass jar. Add the oregano, cumin, peppercorns, garlic, red wine vinegar and honey. Cover and refrigerate at least 4 hours. Pickled onions can be made in advance.

Line the bottom and sides of a 6-quart (5.6-L) slow cooker with torn pieces of the banana leaf, if using. Add the chicken to the slow cooker.

Add the orange zest and juice, lime zest and juice, grapefruit juice, vinegar, achiote paste and salt to a blender. Purée until smooth, then pour the sauce over the chicken. Top with the tomatoes and onions. Place the remaining banana leaves on top of the chicken. If desired, marinate the chicken in the pot at room temperature for 1 hour before cooking to infuse more flavor into the chicken.

Cover and cook the dish on high for 3 to 4 hours, or low for 5 to 6 hours, until the chicken is tender and reaches 165°F (74°C) internal temperature.

Serve the chicken with the sauce, pickled onions, tortillas, rice, black beans or plantains.

COOK'S NOTE:
When purchasing achiote spice, it can come in the form of paste or powder. Use the paste version that is only colored with the natural pigments of the annatto seeds, and not the Red 40 dye, as it is a synthetic color. I prefer El Yucateco brand, sold in 3.5-ounce (100-gram) blocks.

RECIPE SCIENCE:
The acids in the citrus juices also serve to tenderize the chicken as it slowly simmers. Chicken thighs and drumsticks are used because they stay moist, tender and intact during long periods of cooking. If you can find banana leaves at a local Latin market, use them to line the insides of the slow cooker to add a distinctive herbaceous flavor to the meat. While the chicken is cooking, the pickled onions are also marinating. Pickling vegetables creates a liquid brine primarily consisting of salt, vinegar and a sweetener. When the pungent sliced onions are added into the pickling liquid, the vinegar removes some of the harsh sulfurous compounds, softens the exposed cell walls of the onion and infuses an addictive tart flavor and slight saltiness. The onions taste even better when refrigerated for a few days.

kung pao chicken

SLOW COOKER | DAIRY-FREE | GLUTEN-FREE

No need to order Chinese food takeout with this homemade spicy Kung Pao Chicken recipe! When you do not have a wok available, a slow cooker can give tasty results. To add some extra flavor and color to the chicken, the chopped pieces of meat are quickly sautéed in a hot pan before adding to the slow cooker. The chicken is simmered in a sweet and savory sauce for a kick of flavor and heat to each piece. Adding in the fresh bell pepper and mushrooms near the end of cooking ensures that they stay crisp and tender. The dish is garnished with green onions and peanuts for an extra crunch.

SERVES: 4 | **PREP TIME:** 10 minutes | **COOK TIME:** 2 to 4 hours

2 lb (908 g) boneless skinless chicken breast, cut into 1-inch (2.5-cm) cubes

¼ cup plus 2 tsp (44 g) cornstarch, divided

½ cup (120 ml) soy sauce or tamari (for gluten-free option), divided

3 tbsp plus 1 tsp (50 ml) sesame oil, divided

¾ cup plus 2 tbsp (210 ml) water, divided

½ cup (120 ml) rice vinegar

½ cup (120 ml) honey

10 dried red chili peppers or dried guajillo, cut in half lengthwise, seeds removed

2 tbsp (30 ml) vegetable oil

1 cup (175 g) diced red bell pepper, 1-inch (2.5-cm) dice

1 cup (175 g) diced green bell pepper, 1-inch (2.5-cm) dice

4 oz (116 g) brown mushrooms, cut into ¼-inch (6-mm) slices

1 cup (146 g) sliced zucchini, ¼-inch (6-mm) slices

½ tsp sesame seeds

2 tbsp (22 g) peanuts

1 tbsp (1 g) thinly sliced green onion

Rice, optional

In a medium-size bowl, combine the diced chicken, 2 teaspoons (6 g) of cornstarch, 2 tablespoons (30 ml) of soy sauce and 2 teaspoons (10 ml) of sesame oil. Allow the chicken to marinate at room temperature while preparing the sauce.

In a small bowl, whisk together ½ cup (120 ml) of water, 6 tablespoons (90 ml) of soy sauce, vinegar and honey. Add the chili peppers, stir to combine and add the sauce to a slow cooker.

Heat a large sauté pan over medium-high heat. Add the vegetable oil, and once hot, add the marinated chicken in a single layer. Sear until golden brown, about 2 minutes on each side. Transfer the chicken to the slow cooker. Cover and cook the chicken on high for 1½ to 2 hours, or 2½ to 4 hours on low.

Switch the slow cooker setting to high to help raise the temperature of the sauce to almost 203°F (95°C), so that the starch granules can effectively swell, thicken and not leave a raw starch flavor. Whisk together ¼ cup (38 g) of cornstarch and 6 tablespoons (90 ml) of water in a small bowl. Add to the slow cooker and whisk to combine. Cook on high for 30 minutes.

Add the bell peppers, mushrooms and zucchini, and stir to combine. Cook on high until the sauce is thickened and vegetables are tender, 30 minutes.

Garnish the chicken with the sesame seeds, peanuts and green onions. Serve the Kung Pao Chicken with rice, if desired.

COOK'S NOTE:
Dried whole chilis give more complex and concentrated flavors. They are split in half rather than chopped so that the spice doesn't overpower the dish. The seeds are removed to better control the heat, but if you like your food spicy, keep them in the dish!

RECIPE SCIENCE:
Tender chicken breast is first marinated in a soy sauce mixture with cornstarch, which helps the sauce adhere better to the surface of the meat. The light coating of cornstarch also helps to accelerate the browning of the chicken and add a golden crust. The characteristic heat of this Kung Pao Chicken dish comes from the dried red chili peppers. A chemical compound called capsaicin found in the rib or white pith of the chili, gives the peppers the spicy heat and varies in intensity between different varieties measured in Scoville units. The seeds and flesh of the peppers do not contribute as much capsaicin; however, the seeds will absorb some capsaicin from the rib. Dried chilis also tend to be a little sweeter than fresh because they are picked and dried at peak ripeness.

pulled pork with barbecue sauce

SLOW COOKER | **DAIRY-FREE** | **GLUTEN-FREE**

Pulled pork is an extremely popular dish: using an inexpensive, tougher cut and transforming it into fork-tender pieces of meat. It does not take a lot of time to prepare the recipe; however, in order to properly tenderize the pork, a long cooking time is needed. The roast is cooked with a sweet and savory barbecue sauce for an all-in-one dish. The juices from the meat are collected into the sauce, creating an intense pork flavor. The braised pork can literally be shredded with a spoon and is ready to add to a sandwich or serve as an entrée with side dishes.

SERVES: 4 to 6 | **PREP TIME:** 10 minutes | **COOK TIME:** 6 to 10 hours

¾ cup (198 g) tomato paste

¼ cup (50 g) packed dark brown sugar

2 tsp (10 g) garlic powder

1 tsp onion powder

½ tsp kosher salt, plus more for seasoning

1 tbsp (15 ml) Dijon mustard

2 tbsp (30 ml) molasses

2 tsp (10 ml) Asian chili sauce (sambal oelek)

½ cup (73 g) minced yellow onion

¾ cup (180 ml) orange juice

3 tbsp (45 ml) apple cider vinegar

4 to 4½ lb (1.8 to 2 kg) boneless pork shoulder, trimmed and cut into 4 pieces

Black pepper, as needed for seasoning

In a medium-size bowl, whisk together the tomato paste, brown sugar, garlic powder, onion powder, salt, Dijon mustard, molasses, chili sauce, onion, orange juice and vinegar.

Add the pork pieces to the slow cooker and pour the barbecue sauce over the meat. Cover and cook on high for 6 to 7 hours, or 8 to 10 hours on low, until the pork is very tender. Transfer the pork to a plate and use two forks to shred it into pieces.

Skim and remove excess fat from the surface of the sauce, or transfer the sauce to a fat separator. It can also be transferred to a large measuring cup and chilled until the fat solidifies on the surface and can be easily removed. Discard the fat.

Transfer the defatted sauce to a large pan and bring to a boil over medium-high heat. Cook until the sauce is thickened and reduced to 1½ cups (360 ml), about 15 to 18 minutes. Season the sauce with salt and pepper to taste. Reserve ½ cup (120 ml) of the sauce to serve warm on the side.

Transfer the shredded pork to the slow cooker and stir in the remaining sauce to coat. Keep warm until ready to serve.

Serve the pulled pork with sauce on the side as an entrée or on a sandwich.

COOK'S NOTE:
Pork shoulder is also labeled as "pork butt" or "Boston butt," however, these are still from the shoulder region. If the meat is not available boneless, purchase around an 8-pound (3.6-kg) roast to account for the weight of the bone and meat yield once the pork is trimmed.

RECIPE SCIENCE:
Pork shoulder is selected because it is a well-marbled and fatty cut of pork that does not dry out. The shoulder also is abundant in connective tissue, mainly collagen protein that is extremely chewy and difficult to eat when undercooked. The slow cooker works its magic by providing a consistent hot environment for the triple-helix protein structure of the collagen to unwind and break down into gelatin. The ideal temperature is between 160 and 180°F (74 and 82°C), held for a long period of time for this change. The pieces of pork shoulder are braised in a flavorful barbecue sauce, which is further thickened by the gelatin. The pork stays moist due to the water-absorbing properties of the gelatin and higher amounts of fat in the shoulder cut.

hawaiian-style pork ribs

SLOW COOKER | DAIRY-FREE | GLUTEN-FREE

Tender, sticky, fall-off-the bone pork spareribs with a Hawaiian island flavor can be made in a slow cooker.
The ribs are first coated with a brown sugar spice rub for flavor infusion on the surface. A soy and pineapple juice marinade is generously brushed on the ribs, and then broiled in the hot oven to develop a caramelized and lightly charred crust.

SERVES: 4 to 6 | PREP TIME: 20 minutes | COOK TIME: 4 to 5 hours

2 to 2½-lb (0.9 to 1.1-kg) rack pork St. Louis–style spareribs

2 tbsp (16 g) paprika

2 tbsp (20 g) brown sugar

2 tbsp (32 g) kosher salt

2 tsp (6 g) black pepper

1 tsp ground ginger

1 cup (240 ml) soy sauce or tamari (for gluten-free option)

1 cup (240 ml) pineapple juice

¾ cup (149 g) packed dark brown sugar

1 tbsp (15 ml) rice vinegar

1 tsp (8 g) sesame oil

3 cloves garlic, minced

2 tsp (8 g) minced ginger

1 tsp sesame seeds

1 tbsp (3 g) sliced green onions

Dry the pork ribs and place on a sheet pan. In a medium-size bowl, combine the paprika, brown sugar, salt, pepper and ginger. Evenly sprinkle the dry rub mixture on both sides of the ribs.

Arrange the ribs upright in a 6 to 7 quart (5.6 to 6.6 L) oval slow cooker, with the meaty sides facing outward. Cover, making sure that you can completely close the lid. Cook on low for 4 to 5 hours, until the ribs are tender. The longer the ribs cook, the more tender they will be.

In a medium-size saucepan, whisk together the soy sauce, pineapple juice, brown sugar, vinegar, sesame oil, garlic and ginger. Bring to a rapid simmer over medium-high heat, until it has thickened and reduced to 1 cup (240 ml), about 20 minutes.

Transfer the ribs, meaty side up, to a foil-lined sheet pan with a greased wire rack set on top.

Adjust the oven rack to the upper third position, about 10 inches (25 cm) from the broiler. Preheat the oven to broil.

Brush the ribs with some of the sauce and broil until the ribs are browned and sticky, a total of about 10 minutes. Flip and brush each side with sauce every 2 minutes. You should end cooking with the meaty side up. Allow the ribs to rest on a cutting board for 10 minutes.

Slice the ribs, garnish with sesame seeds and green onions. Serve with additional sauce on the side.

COOK'S NOTE:
There are two ways to check for doneness of the ribs. First, you can visually see the meat easily separate from the bone and give it a taste test for tenderness. When the internal temperature reaches between 190 and 200°F (88 and 93°C), the ribs are done!

RECIPE SCIENCE:
In order for two whole racks of ribs to fit in the vessel, St. Louis–style cut spareribs are used. They are trimmed to be smaller and more uniform in size, making them much easier to evenly cook and eat. There is a thin membrane on the underside of the ribs, and if it's not already removed, leave it intact. The membrane helps keep the ribs together, making them easier to handle, since slow cooking will make the rib meat extremely tender. In order to tenderize the rib meat they are placed in a slow cooker for at least 4 hours to allow the moisture from the steam and heat to cook the meat, melt the fat and soften any of the tough connective tissue of the ribs. Once the ribs are done slow cooking, the sweet and smoky flavors are developed in the oven by using a high heat broiling and basting technique. Basting is repeated multiple times on both sides of the ribs so layers of flavor and texture are created.

Evenly sprinkle the dry rub mixture on both sides for a flavorful crust.

Place the meaty sides facing outward in the slow cooker.

Broil the racks in the oven to develop sweet and smoky flavors.

Baste with the sauce to create a sticky caramelized surface.

grandma's italian meatballs

SLOW COOKER | FREEZER-FRIENDLY

Spaghetti and meatballs are my husband Jason's favorite meal. I even promised in our wedding vows to make it for him once a month! This recipe is inspired by his Italian Grandma Rose, and I was lucky enough to have her share her meatball-making secrets with me. I adapted this recipe for the slow cooker so that it is easy to prepare ahead of time and simmer for hours without the need to watch the stove.

SERVES: 4 | **PREP TIME:** 20 minutes | **COOK TIME:** 2 to 5 hours

1 lb (454 g) lean ground beef (80 to 92 percent fat)

1 large egg

½ cup (36 g) panko bread crumbs or traditional bread crumbs

2 tbsp (21 g) minced yellow onions

1 tsp minced garlic

½ cup (20 g) freshly grated Parmesan cheese, divided

2 tbsp (8 g) minced Italian parsley leaves, divided

¼ tsp dried oregano

1¼ tsp (9 g) kosher salt, divided, plus more for seasoning

½ tsp black pepper

TOMATO SAUCE
½ cup (76 g) minced yellow onions

2 tsp (8 g) minced garlic

¼ cup (60 ml) olive oil

6 oz (170 g) tomato paste

56 oz (1.6 kg) crushed tomatoes

½ tsp dried oregano

2 tsp (12 g) kosher salt

Adjust the oven rack to the upper third position and preheat the oven to broil. Line a large sheet pan with foil, grease with cooking spray or olive oil and set aside.

To prepare the meatballs, in a medium-size bowl, combine the beef, egg, bread crumbs, onions, garlic, ¼ cup (10 g) of Parmesan cheese, 1 tablespoon (4 g) of minced parsley, oregano, 1 teaspoon of salt and pepper. Thoroughly mix and roll into 1½ inch (4 cm) meatballs, about 14 meatballs total. Place on the greased sheet pan and broil until lightly browned, 10 minutes.

To prepare the tomato sauce, in a medium-size microwave-safe bowl, add the onions, garlic, olive oil and tomato paste, and stir to combine. Microwave for 2 minutes and stir. Microwave again for 1 minute, and transfer the mixture to the slow cooker. Add the crushed tomatoes, oregano and salt, and stir to combine.

Add the meatballs to the sauce until submerged, then cover and cook on high for 2 to 3 hours, or on low for 4 to 5 hours. Do not uncover until cooking is complete. Season the sauce with salt and pepper to taste.

Garnish the meatballs with the remaining Parmesan cheese and 1 tablespoon (4 g) of parsley. Serve the meatballs hot with pasta or in a sandwich.

COOK'S NOTE:
No peeking under the lid! Once you put the lid on, do not remove it. If the steam and heat are released, the vessel needs more time to get hot again, which means longer cooking time for the meatballs.

RECIPE SCIENCE:
When the beef is ground and combined with the other ingredients, the muscle protein fibers are shortened and release sticky soluble proteins that hold them together. Browning the meatballs first in the oven adds texture, color and flavor to the exterior of the meatball. As the meatballs cook, the proteins shrink and release almost 25 percent internal moisture, which can result in dry meat. To keep the meatballs juicy, the liquid in the eggs adds some additional moisture, and fat from the yolk helps to coat and lubricate the muscle fibers. The starches in the bread crumbs also block some of the meat proteins from connecting as strongly. These starches absorb the moisture from the eggs and form a gel, which encases the meat proteins to reduce shrinking as the meatballs cook and keep them tender. The starches keep working hard as the meatballs simmer in the tomato sauce, absorbing liquid from their surroundings and swelling to thicken the liquid in the meatballs, keeping the moisture locked in.

emulsification & thickening

ELEVATED ADD-ONS

Dressings and sauces are culinary solutions to enhance flavors and complement other ingredients. Explore how emulsification works to create tasty dressings and how starch gelatinization is key to developing delicious sauces. These simple add-ons help to elevate any dish without being the star of the plate.

the simple science

Sauces can help add depth of flavor, texture and moisture to make food more tantalizing. They come in different forms: hot, cold, savory, sweet, textured or smooth. Most commonly, sauces are liquids that have been thickened by whole fruit or vegetables (purées, pestos and coulis) or thickening agents. There are two ways to thicken a sauce: emulsification or starch gelatinization. One key difference is that emulsified sauces can be made hot or cold, and starch-based sauces must be heated to thicken. Let's take a closer look at these two ways to create a rich and flavorful sauce.

emulsification & thickening basics

WHAT IS AN EMULSION?

The first thing I learned in my introductory food science class was that oil and water do not mix . . . well, of course! The discussion led to why and how to make them mix together for food applications. The solution is to create an emulsion, a uniform mixture of two unmixable liquids like oil and water, using agitation and chemistry to create a uniform suspension. Not all emulsions last forever. The ingredient being added to the sauce and when the meal will be enjoyed determine what type of emulsion to create.

LECITHIN: THE SECRET SAUCE!

An emulsifier is an ingredient that can help immiscible ingredients stay suspended, preventing the oil from regrouping immediately and floating to the top of the sauce or dressing. One powerful and effective emulsifier is lecithin, a protein found in egg yolks. The lecithin in one egg yolk has the ability to emulsify about 7 ounces (207 ml) of oil. Any more oil and you will visibly see the emulsion separate and thin out.

TYPES OF EMULSIONS

Temporary: Lasts a short time, usually separates in under an hour since no emulsifier is used, only agitation (whisking, blending). They are brief suspensions like oil and vinegar dressings and vinaigrettes.

Semipermanent: Emulsion lasts hours, like hollandaise sauce, which contains eggs.

Permanent: Lasts multiple days, like mayonnaise-based sauces, which contain eggs.

types of emulsion-based dressings and sauces

Vinaigrette: A temporary emulsion made without an emulsifier. A common ratio of three parts oil to one part acid is used; however, these amounts would need to be adjusted based on the type of oil and acid and/or vinegar.

Mayonnaise-based: A dressing using a mayonnaise for the base with additional flavorings, and liquids like dairy (buttermilk, sour cream, yogurt), acids (vinegar, lemon or lime juice), fruits (tomatoes, olives, berries), vegetables (celery, onions, carrots), condiments (mustard, seasonings, sweeteners, capers) and protein (eggs) for a permanent emulsion.

Emulsified vinaigrette: Oil and vinegar vinaigrette emulsified using whole eggs for a creamy permanent emulsion.

Hollandaise: Warm egg and oil emulsion sauce used on a classic poached egg for benedicts.

Acid: Apple cider, red wine, white wine, rice wine, balsamic, raspberry vinegars; lemon, orange or lime juice

Oils: Canola, corn, grapeseed, soybean, safflower, olive, hazelnut, walnut

Emulsifiers: Lecithin (protein found in egg yolks), mustard and honey are weaker emulsifiers

Flavors and seasoning: Shallots, garlic, mustard, spices, herbs (chives, rosemary, thyme, dill), sweeteners (sugar, honey, maple syrup, agave), fruits (strawberry, raspberry, tomatoes, blueberry), salt, pepper

the swell—thicken sauce with starches

Home cooks and chefs can take advantage of the unique properties of starches in food to transform a thin and volumeless liquid into a luscious sauce within minutes! Plants naturally contain starches as an energy source, which can be extracted and used for adding thickness to food. Grains (corn and rice), cereal grains (wheat, barley, spelt and oat), beans, peas, tubers (potatoes), roots (tapioca and arrowroot) and fruits (green bananas and plantains) are examples of plants that contain starches used in cooking applications.

Starches are polysaccharides, large molecular-weight carbohydrates that interact and form gels or thickened dispersions when in contact with water. The two major polysaccharides in starch responsible for thickening foods are amylose (mostly linear structures with few branches) and amylopectin (a highly branched large molecule with a cluster structure). The structures of these polysaccharides are dependent on the plant source and ratio of amylose to amylopectin, which impact their thickening properties. When comparing amylose content, the higher the percent of amylose the stronger the gels are formed to thicken, and the higher the temperature needed to swell. For example, wheat contains 23 percent amylose compared to 23 percent in corn and 21 percent in rice. However, the branch chain length of the amylopectin impacts overall texture and thickening as well. In general the thickening power, clarity and stickiness of a starch paste is greatest with cereal grains, roots and then tubers.

By applying heat to a starch and water mixture, the viscosity increases due to initial swelling and dissolution. There are two stages of swelling for starches to become thickened in a sauce. The semi-crystalline structure of the uncooked starch granule is irreversibly disrupted by heat. This allows amylose and amylopectin starch granules to solubilize and absorb the water and begin swelling (called starch gelatinization). The temperature needed for gelatinization happens over a range and is starch dependent. To achieve maximum thickness (called pasting), the second stage requires the starch slurry to be heated a few degrees higher than the gelatinization temperature and agitation by whisking the sauce. This allows the starches to swell independently from each other while the heat reaches the end-point cooking temperature for the greatest thickness capability of the sauce. Once the sauce has thickened, there should be no raw flour or starch taste, and it should have a consistency that can coat the back of a spoon so that it will stick to the food. If you hold the starch paste too long at its end-point temperature, you will notice the viscosity start to thin. This is called breakdown or shear thinning, which is why some starches like arrowroot or cornstarch should not be reheated. There are different ingredients that can be used to sufficiently thicken a sauce, the most common in home kitchens and restaurants being flour, cornstarch and arrowroot.

Roux: Equal parts of flour and fat are cooked in a heated vessel, forming different-colored pastes depending on use. The cooking allows the fat to effectively coat the flour to prevent clumping, once whisked into a hot liquid. With more heat and cook time, Maillard browning changes the colors of the roux and the heat breaks down the starch molecules, which reduces gelatinization ability. This impacts the final thickness and flavor of the sauce. To prevent a lumpy sauce, either add cool roux to hot stock, or cool stock to hot roux. Roux are separated into white, blond and brown varieties.

White roux: Cooked for a very short time to keep the color white, and has the most thickening power since the starches are not broken down as much from pre-cooking. Used for cream-type béchamel sauces, like Alfredo or in macaroni and cheese.

Blond roux: Cooked for a few more minutes to take on more color or flavor for chicken- or fish-based velouté-type sauces, and are lighter in body.

Brown roux: Cooked until a notable brown color develops and nutty notes form. Most commonly used in rich gumbo soups or espagnole (brown) sauces made from veal or beef stock. Brown roux has lower thickening power so more is needed to reach a thickness similar to the other sauces.

Cornstarch: Corn naturally contains a thickening powerhouse. The corn endosperm is ground, washed and dried to a fine powder. This gluten-free thickening agent can be used to rapidly give sauces more viscosity and sheen. It has twice the amount of thickening ability compared to flour, but because of shear thinning, if heated too long, can break down and lose some of its thick consistency. The key to incorporating cornstarch into hot or cold liquids is to make a slurry. Typically two parts cold water is mixed with one part cornstarch until an opaque mix is formed. The cold water is essential because it helps to separate starch granules so they can start absorbing the water and begin swelling. When dispersed in a cool liquid mixture, then heated to 144 to 158°F (62 to 70°C), the irreversible process of starch gelatinization begins. The starch molecules swell and burst, then dissolution occurs, releasing amylose into the sauce to form a gel. Heating the sauce to an end-point temperature a few degrees above 203°F (95°C), allows maximum viscosity of the starch.

Arrowroot: Made from the tubers of the arrowroot plant, Maranata arundinacea is cultivated from tropical climates. The starch is a very fine white powder that has similar thickening properties to cornstarch, has no pronounced flavor and does not add opacity to sauces. If you are avoiding corn, potatoes and gluten, arrowroot starch is a good substitute. However, it is not compatible with cream-based sauces as it changes the texture undesirably. When incorporating into a hot sauce, a 2 to 1 water to arrowroot slurry should be made, similarly to cornstarch. One of the key differences is that it's best to add to a simmering liquid at 185 to 206°F (85 to 96°C) at the very end of cooking. This is because it only takes about one minute to thicken a hot liquid and the arrowroot does not keep its thickening power as long as cornstarch or flour. Avoid reheating an arrowroot-based sauce.

blender hollandaise sauce

EMULSION | QUICK (30 MINUTES OR LESS) | VEGETARIAN

Hollandaise is an elegant, warm, smooth and velvety sauce that is a breakfast staple on dishes like eggs benedict. Once you've tried this blender method a few times, it will be the only way you make the sauce, because it is so quick and easy! This luxurious hollandaise is perfect to add on eggs, seafood and vegetables for an unforgettable meal.

MAKES: 1 cup (240 ml) | **PREP TIME:** 5 minutes | **COOK TIME:** 5 minutes

2 large egg yolks

2 tsp (10 ml) water

2 tsp (10 ml) lemon juice

½ tsp kosher salt

16 tbsp (224 g) unsalted butter

Ground cayenne or chipotle pepper, as needed for seasoning

COOK'S NOTE:

It may take a few tries initially to create a successful sauce in the blender. If the sauce is runny with the oil floating on top, instead of light and uniform in appearance, the sauce is broken. To fix a broken blender sauce, transfer the broken sauce to a measuring cup and clean the blender. Add new egg yolks, water, lemon and salt to the blender, and repeat the process. Instead of new butter, very slowly add in the broken sauce a few drops at a time, at first, until it starts to thicken and get emulsified. Then more can be added to finish the thickening process.

Add the egg yolks, water, lemon juice and a pinch of salt to a blender. Blend on high speed until combined, 10 seconds.

Melt the butter in a small saucepan over medium-high heat, swirling the pan constantly, until the foaming subsides. Turn off the heat and transfer the butter to a measuring cup with a spout. Cool the butter to 165 to 175°F (73 to 80°C) so that it can cook the egg yolks but not scramble them. The butter will still be hot and cools down fairly quickly.

Turn the blender on to medium-high speed. The egg mixture should be vigorously swirling in the blender cup in a consistent vortex. Do not process at the highest speed as the butter, once added, will just kick up in the blender and not get properly emulsified; it should instead get sucked into the center blades of the blender.

Gradual incorporation of the butter into the running blender is key to create the silky sauce. You can see the sauce turn lighter in color and greater in volume, as well as hear the motors of the blender start to slow as the sauce gets more viscous. With the blender running, very slowly add a few drops of the butter to allow it to break into smaller particles. Then continue to slowly add the butter in a very thin, steady stream, stopping after ⅓ of the butter is incorporated. Stop and check that the mixture is becoming pale yellow and starting to thicken.

Continue blending and slowly incorporating all of the butter, checking the sauce when ⅔ of the butter is added. Gradually add the rest of the butter. The entire process should take 1½ to 2 minutes, not including stopping the blender. The hollandaise sauce should be warm, creamy, thick, yet pourable.

Add ½ teaspoon of salt and a pinch of cayenne pepper to the blender on low speed to combine, 10 seconds. Taste the sauce and add more salt or cayenne pepper as desired.

Cover the sauce to keep warm until ready to serve. It's best not to reheat the sauce, as it may separate.

RECIPE SCIENCE:

To reduce the time of a traditional hollandaise sauce and chance for separation or curdling, a high speed blender is used to quickly combine and thicken the emulsion. The egg yolks, water, lemon juice and salt are lightly aerated in the blender first, just like they would be if you were making them in a bowl. Instead of gently cooking the eggs first, the butter is heated right before adding to the egg mixture. This helps the egg gently cook and thicken, which happens for egg yolks around 150 to 160°F (66 to 71°C), while reaching safe eating temperatures above 160°F (71°C).

creamy caesar salad dressing

EMULSION | QUICK (30 MINUTES OR LESS)

This classic creamy Caesar dressing highlights the pleasant briny flavor from salt-cured anchovies and should not be skipped. Don't be shy about working with these tiny fillets; they add an incredible flavor and are a key characteristic to a good Caesar dressing. A good emulsion will have all of the flavors of the dressing evenly dispersed for maximum flavor delivery in the salad. Hearty romaine lettuce leaves or kale work best since the dressing will have a velvety consistency and robust flavor to complement the thicker greens.

SERVES: 4 | **PREP TIME:** 15 minutes | **COOK TIME:** 15 minutes

CROUTONS

2 cups (134 g) sliced rustic bread, ¼ inch (6 mm) thick, torn into 1-inch (2.5-cm) pieces

1 tbsp (15 ml) olive oil

¼ tsp kosher salt

⅛ tsp black pepper

CAESAR SALAD

6 (10 g) anchovies or 1 tablespoon (15 g) anchovy paste

1 garlic clove, minced

¾ tsp kosher salt, divided

1 tsp (7 g) Dijon mustard

1 large egg yolk

2 tbsp (30 ml) lemon juice

1 tsp (1 g) lemon zest

½ tsp pepper

½ cup (120 ml) extra-virgin olive oil

¼ cup (8 g) freshly grated Parmesan cheese, divided

8 cups (256 g) cut romaine lettuce, ½-inch (1.3-cm) thick slices

Adjust the oven rack to the center position and preheat the oven to 375°F (191°C).

To prepare the croutons, transfer the bread to a medium-size bowl. Drizzle the bread with the olive oil, sprinkle with the salt and pepper, and toss to combine.

Spread the bread on a baking sheet in a single layer. Bake for 5 minutes, stir and turn over. Bake until the bread is crunchy, 5 to 10 minutes more, depending on the bread used. Allow to cool on the baking sheet.

To prepare the Caesar dressing, chop the anchovies, minced garlic and ¼ teaspoon of salt together on a cutting board. Use the sides of the knife to mash into a paste. Transfer to a medium-size bowl.

Whisk together the anchovy mixture with the mustard, egg yolk, lemon juice and zest, ½ teaspoon of salt and pepper.

Gradually whisk in the olive oil until a creamy and smooth emulsion is created and the dressing is thickened. Whisk in 3 tablespoons (6 g) of Parmesan cheese.

Add the lettuce to a large bowl and add in the dressing ¼ cup (60 ml) at a time, adding more until the salad is dressed to your liking. Top the salad with the croutons and remaining Parmesan cheese. Serve immediately.

COOK'S NOTE:

Pasteurized eggs can be used in the dressing, indicated on the carton label. Pasteurization destroys harmful bacteria like salmonella, thus pasteurized eggs are safer to eat raw than unpasteurized eggs. Liquid or frozen egg substitutes can be used as well. Each country has its own pasteurization requirements; however, the U.S. Department of Agriculture (USDA) requires that whole eggs be treated at a minimum temperature of 140°F (60°C) and held for 3½ minutes, then cooled to help destroy harmful bacteria without cooking the egg.

RECIPE SCIENCE:

The anchovies are chopped into a paste with garlic and salt for a flavor punch, which is surprisingly not fishy in taste. Egg yolks and mustard are added to emulsify the lemon juice and olive oil mixture so that the sauce stays smooth and uniform. The yolks also add richness to the dressing, without being heavy on the lettuce leaves. If you are hesitant to use raw eggs, mayonnaise can be substituted, about 1 tablespoon (14 g) per yolk. The egg can be omitted completely for a more tangy and light dressing, adjusting with more oil to balance the acidity of the lemon juice.

lemon basil aioli

You will not believe how easy it is to make a mayonnaise-based sauce from scratch! One of my first lessons in culinary school was practicing this fundamental technique to demonstrate how emulsions work. The best way to learn is whisking the emulsion together by hand so you can visually see the mayonnaise aerate and change to an ivory color. It's also easier to feel the viscosity change as the oil droplets are being properly broken into smaller sizes for a stable and smooth emulsion. Adding in pungent garlic brings another layer of flavor, transforming it into an aioli (garlic mayonnaise).

MAKES: 1 cup (240 ml) | **PREP TIME:** 10 minutes

1 (17 g) large egg yolk

¼ tsp kosher salt, plus more for seasoning

⅛ tsp cayenne pepper, plus more for seasoning

1 tbsp (15 ml) lemon juice, divided

1 cup (240 ml) olive oil (see Cook's Note)

1 tsp Dijon mustard

2 tbsp (4 g) thinly sliced basil, sliced just before adding to aioli (see Cook's Note)

2 cloves garlic, very finely minced or finely grated

In a medium-size bowl, add the egg yolk and whisk until the yolk becomes slightly thickened and light yellow in color. Add the salt, cayenne pepper and 1 teaspoon of lemon juice. Vigorously whisk until combined.

Very gradually add a few drops of the olive oil to the egg mixture. Whisk until you see the mixture lighten in color and start to thicken. Continue to add small drops at a time, creating an emulsified and thickened sauce. Once ¼ cup (60 ml) of oil has been added and is visibly thickened, add in another 1 teaspoon of lemon juice to the sauce and mix to combine.

Continue to gradually drizzle and whisk in another ¼ cup (60 ml) of olive oil. Add the last teaspoon of lemon juice, and whisk to combine. Slowly drizzle and whisk the remainder of the olive oil into the mayonnaise. The mixture should look pale-yellow and thick.

Whisk in the mustard, basil and garlic until combined. Season the mayonnaise with more salt and cayenne to taste. Refrigerate until ready to use.

(continued)

COOK'S NOTE:

Basil leaves bruise easily and brown in cut areas due to oxidation, exposure of the green pigments in the basil to air. Reduce the amount of browning by rolling the leaves into a cigar shape and use the sharpest part of your knife, typically the back end of the knife, to swiftly slice the basil. Add immediately to the aioli so the fat can coat and create a barrier around the basil as protection from the air in the environment. Any neutral oil can be used instead of olive oil. Canola and grapeseed oil are good alternatives. Other acids like red wine vinegar, apple cider vinegar or white wine vinegar can be substituted for the lemon juice. Fresh herbs like chopped tarragon, chives, parsley or cilantro can be added or substituted for the basil. Start by adding 1 tablespoon (2.5 g) of herbs, then increasing as desired to 2 tablespoons (5 g) total.

Whisk to aerate the egg yolk.

RECIPE SCIENCE:

Egg-based sauces create the most stable permanent emulsions, lasting up to a few days because of the emulsifying power of the lecithin. The lecithin emulsifying agent in the egg yolk allows the immiscible ingredients, lemon juice and oil, to stay suspended. This prevents the oil from regrouping after mixing. The process takes a few minutes to very gradually incorporate the oil, so patience and a little bit of muscle power is required but worth the effort. A strong garlic flavor is desired; however, to reduce the sharp bite and bitterness, make sure that the garlic is as finely minced as possible by using a chef's knife, garlic press or Microplane grater for a smooth infusion into the mayonnaise. Slice and add the fresh basil right before serving so that the herb retains its green color.

Season the egg yolk with salt, cayenne pepper and lemon juice.

Whisk until a homogenous mixture is created.

Add a few drops of olive oil at first, then whisk to break up the droplets.

Whisk until you see the mixture lighten in color and start to thicken.

Add more oil, and whisk to create a thickened emulsified sauce.

Add the basil and garlic before serving to combine.

citrus herb vinaigrette

A classic vinaigrette is always a tasty solution for a quick dressing to accompany a salad. A bright, citrus dressing with lots of fresh herbs makes a boring bed of lettuce much more festive and flavorful. This vinaigrette recipe makes enough to save and use for multiple days, or serve more on the side of the salad. About ¼ cup (60 ml) of dressing can lightly coat about 8 cups (322 g) of lettuce greens.

MAKES: 1 cup (240 ml) | **PREP TIME:** 10 minutes

¼ cup (60 ml) lemon juice

1 tsp lemon zest

2 tbsp (18 g) minced shallot

2 tsp (8 g) mayonnaise

2 tsp (10 ml) Dijon mustard

1 tsp honey

½ tsp salt

¼ tsp pepper

¾ cup (180 ml) extra-virgin olive oil

½ tsp minced chives

½ tsp minced thyme

½ tsp minced parsley

In a medium-size bowl, whisk together the lemon juice, lemon zest, shallots, mayonnaise, mustard, honey, salt and pepper until the dressing looks opaque in appearance.

Slowly add the olive oil in a thin stream into the lemon mixture, whisking vigorously and continuously. Do not add more oil until the oil is combined with the lemon mixture and no pools of oil are visible.

Continue to gradually whisk and incorporate the oil into the dressing, until a thickened and emulsified vinaigrette is achieved. Refrigerate until ready to serve.

Right before serving, whisk in the chives, thyme and parsley. Taste the vinaigrette and adjust the seasoning as desired.

This vinaigrette can be stored in an airtight container and refrigerated for up 2 days, before the addition of the herbs. Make sure to whisk the vinaigrette thoroughly before serving.

COOK'S NOTE:

To prevent the acid from the lemon juice from breaking down the cell walls of tender lettuce, make sure to dress the salad right before serving. To evenly coat the lettuce with dressing, drizzle a small amount of dressing onto the side of the bowl, and then combine with the leaves until the desired amount of coating is reached. Pouring all of the vinaigrette straight onto the lettuce overly drenches some of the leaves and it's harder to gauge how much is actually needed to just flavor the salad.

RECIPE SCIENCE:

To ensure that this dressing stays a smooth and creamy emulsion for hours and even days, two emulsifying agents are used: mustard and mayonnaise. This duo of ingredients imparts a bold, pungent flavor to complement the lemon, while adding a delightful creaminess without being heavy. Egg yolks contain lecithin, a strong emulsifier that can readily attract both water and oil, creating a more stable water-in-oil emulsion with the oil droplets suspended in the acidic lemon juice. The mustard has complex polysaccharide emulsifying elements that help with stabilization, but not as effectively as lecithin. Make sure to slowly incorporate the olive oil into the lemon juice mixture. The more agitation added during whisking to break the coalesced oil apart into tiny droplets, the more seamless and stable the vinaigrette emulsion will be for a longer duration.

strawberry balsamic vinaigrette

EMULSION | **QUICK (30 MINUTES OR LESS)** | **DAIRY-FREE** | **VEGETARIAN**

A fresh healthy salad for warm summer days can be kicked up with simple seasonal ingredients. You can instantly create a homemade dressing in just a few minutes using a blender. This Strawberry Balsamic Vinaigrette highlights the ripeness of whole berries and infuses tangy vinegar, pungent mustard, honey for a subtle boost of sweetness and olive oil for a creamy mouthfeel. Drizzle and top this vinaigrette on a mix of hearty salad greens like baby spinach, kale, romaine or red leaf lettuce for a light meal or side dish.

MAKES: 1½ cups (355 ml) | **PREP TIME:** 5 minutes

1 cup (175 g) sliced strawberries

2 tbsp (30 ml) water

¼ cup (60 ml) balsamic vinegar

1 tbsp (8 g) minced shallot

1 tsp Dijon mustard

1 tsp honey

½ tsp salt

¼ tsp pepper

½ cup (120 ml) extra-virgin olive oil

Add the strawberries, water, balsamic vinegar, shallots, mustard, honey, salt and pepper to a blender. Blend on high until a smooth puree is formed, 10 seconds.

With the blender running on medium speed, slowly add the olive oil in a thin stream. The dressing should be thickened and emulsified as the vinaigrette is achieved. Taste the vinaigrette and adjust the seasoning as desired.

Cover and refrigerate the vinaigrette until ready to serve. It is best to use the dressing the same day. Vinaigrette can be stored in an airtight container and refrigerated for up to 2 days.

COOK'S NOTE:

Strawberries naturally contain pectin in the fruit's cell walls for structure, which is released and dispersed into the dressing when puréed. The pectin is water-soluble and adds viscosity to liquid mixtures, especially in the presence of sugar and acid (fructose from the strawberries, honey and acid from the vinegar), for a thicker dressing.

RECIPE SCIENCE:

To create a semipermanent emulsion for the dressing, shear rapid force from the blades rotating in the blender helps to break the oil into tiny droplets as it is slowly added to the vinegar mixture. The blender also creates superfine strawberry particulates that stay suspended in the mixture to increase the thickness of the dressing. The Dijon mustard acts as an emulsifying agent surrounding the oil droplets to help them stay dispersed for a unified smooth vinaigrette.

easy pan sauce

Pan sauces are a quick and flavorful addition for sautéed meats, whole roasted chickens or delicate seafood. This sauce recipe gives flexibility to add different ingredients tailored to the type of protein being prepared. The type of stock you use (vegetable, seafood, chicken or beef) will change the depth and flavor of the sauce, providing versatility with each dish. Adding herbs at the end of cooking the sauce provides freshness and a nice hit of aroma. Light herbs like tarragon, sage, thyme, dill and chives pair nicely with fish and poultry, whereas chopped rosemary and oregano would complement beef. The sauce should lightly coat the back of a spoon, so that when it's poured on the food it's flowable but clings for elevated flavor. The pan sauce is a perfect complement to Herb Roasted Chicken with Vegetables (page 54) or Oven Roasted Rack of Lamb (page 37).

MAKES: 1 cup (240 ml) | **PREP TIME:** 5 minutes | **COOK TIME:** 15 minutes

¼ cup (60 ml) dry white wine (see Cook's Note)

1 tbsp (10 g) minced shallots

1 clove minced garlic

1 tbsp (14 g) unsalted butter

1 tbsp (9 g) flour

1 cup (240 ml) unsalted stock (beef, chicken, fish or vegetable) room temperature or cold

Kosher salt, for seasoning

Black pepper, for seasoning

½ tsp tarragon, optional (see Cook's Note)

½ tsp chopped thyme, optional

Heat a medium-size sauté pan over medium-high heat. Add the wine, shallot and garlic. Bring to a boil and reduce until no more than 1 tablespoon (15 ml) of wine is remaining, about 5 minutes.

Reduce the heat to medium and add the butter to the pan. Once the butter is melted, add the flour, whisking constantly to form a paste until the bubbling subsides, 1 minute. The roux should be pale yellow in color.

Gradually add the stock ¼ cup (60 ml) at a time to the roux, whisking constantly to prevent lumps. Bring the sauce to a boil, then reduce to a simmer.

Simmer the sauce until it has thickened and there is no flour taste, 5 to 7 minutes. Season with salt and pepper as desired. Stir in the herbs right before serving.

COOK'S NOTE:

When sautéing a piece of steak, chicken, pork or fish, it will likely leave golden bits of fond, concentrated juices, drippings and cooked bits on the bottom of the pan. The crusty pieces are full of natural flavor. Drain any fat and use the fond to make the pan sauce. Just add the wine, shallots and garlic to the pan, and whisk to scrape and release the fond to incorporate it into the sauce. It will complement the flavor of the sauce very nicely since it's from the protein being served. Substitute red wine instead of white wine. Other herbs to add are chopped rosemary, dill, sage, oregano or chives.

RECIPE SCIENCE:

The pan sauce begins with layering aromatics like shallots and garlic. Then it's reduced with wine for depth and a hint of acidity. Red wine like merlot can be used instead of white wine for a stronger flavored sauce for beef and game. To thicken the sauce, a basic roux is made with equal parts butter and flour. The butter adds richness to the sauce, but also coats the flour to prevent clumping as the starches in the flour cook and thicken in the liquid. The longer the roux is cooked, the more the starches break down which lowers the amount of gelatinization and thickness of the sauce. A white to blond roux is good for most seafood, poultry, pork and lean beef, whereas a brown roux would work nicely for lamb and heartier meats. The key to a smooth sauce is adding room temperature or cool stock to the hot roux, and vigorously whisking to keep the starches separate as they cook. The sauce will thicken once the liquid reaches a boil.

stir-fry sauce

THICKENING | **QUICK (30 MINUTES OR LESS)** | **DAIRY-FREE** | **VEGETARIAN**

A quick stir-fry is a great one-pan dinner option when you want a combination of healthy protein and vegetables tossed together in a savory sauce. Asian-inspired meals will be ready in a snap with the right combination of umami flavors, a hint of sweetness for balance and a quick-cooking thickening agent for the sauce. The stir-fry sauce recipe will cover about 1 pound (454 g) of meat and 3 cups (540 g) of vegetables. This versatile sauce can be added towards the end of cooking right in the pan along with the other ingredients, or in a separate pan and tossed before serving.

MAKES: 1 cup (240 ml) | **PREP TIME:** 5 minutes | **COOK TIME:** 1 minute

¼ cup (60 ml) soy sauce

¼ cup (60 ml) oyster or hoisin sauce

½ cup (120 ml) unsalted chicken, beef or vegetable stock

1 tbsp (15 ml) Shaoxing wine, dry sherry or grape juice for non-alcoholic version

1 tsp sesame oil

1 tbsp (15 ml) honey, brown sugar or maple syrup

1½ tsp (5 g) cornstarch or arrowroot

In a medium-size bowl, whisk together the soy sauce, oyster sauce, chicken stock, cooking wine, sesame oil, honey and cornstarch. Make sure that there are barely any clumps of cornstarch in the sauce.

Add the sauce to the center of a hot pan. Whisk the sauce constantly and bring to a boil, cooking until the sauce is thickened, 30 to 60 seconds.

For vegetarian or vegan sauce options, substitute hoisin sauce for the oyster sauce. Hoisin sauce will add more of an Asian five spice flavor to the stir-fry. Use brown sugar, granulated sugar or pure maple syrup to make it a vegan sauce.

COOK'S NOTE:

If using arrowroot, it requires a lower heat for maximum thickening power, simmering between 185 and 206°F (85 and 96°C). The sauce thickened with arrowroot should be added at the very end of cooking, if placing in the same pan as the food.

RECIPE SCIENCE:

Cornstarch or arrowroot is used to add body and glossiness to the sauce. Both need to disperse in a cool- to room-temperature liquid to create a slurry before adding to a hot pan. If added directly to heat, the starch or arrowroot will swell too fast and form clumps. Once the sauce is cooked, it will thicken just enough to lightly coat and cling to the stir-fry ingredients, without being too heavy and lumpy. Use chicken or vegetable stock for seafood, poultry or pork and beef stock for beef or lamb dishes.

five-minute teriyaki sauce

THICKENING | QUICK (30 MINUTES OR LESS) | DAIRY-FREE | VEGETARIAN | GLUTEN-FREE

A classic restaurant-style Japanese teriyaki sauce can be made at home in just five minutes. The combination of savory, sweet and pungent flavors strikes just the right balance to generously add on top of poultry, meat, fish, tofu or vegetables. The shiny and luxurious teriyaki sauce can be brushed or drizzled on top of proteins, or served alongside for dipping.

MAKES: 1 cup (240 ml) | **PREP TIME:** 3 minutes | **COOK TIME:** 2 minutes

⅓ cup (80 ml) soy sauce or tamari (for gluten-free option)

¾ cup plus 2 tbsp (230 ml) water, divided

6 tbsp (90 ml) honey

1 tbsp (15 ml) rice vinegar

1 tbsp (15 ml) mirin rice wine

½ tsp sesame oil

1 tsp minced ginger

1½ tsp (6 g) minced garlic

1 tbsp (10 g) cornstarch

In a medium-size saucepan, whisk together the soy sauce, ¾ cup (80 ml) of water, honey, rice vinegar, mirin rice wine, sesame oil, ginger and garlic. Bring the sauce to a boil over medium-high heat and cook for 1 minute.

In a small bowl, whisk together the cornstarch and 2 tablespoons (30 ml) of water. Add the cornstarch slurry into the boiling sauce, and whisk to combine. Continuously stir until the sauce is thickened and coats the back of a spoon, 30 to 60 seconds. Serve the hot teriyaki sauce with your favorite protein and vegetables.

COOK'S NOTE:

In order for the cornstarch slurry to properly thicken the sauce, heat to an end-point temperature above 203°F (95°C), near boiling of the liquids, for optimum viscosity. It is best not to reheat the sauce as the cornstarch can break down and lose some of its thickness due to shear thinning when heated too long.

RECIPE SCIENCE:

The sauce ingredients are first mixed together and briefly cooked with ginger and garlic to infuse the aromatics into the base. It only takes 15 to 20 seconds for the ginger and garlic to release their fragrant aromas. The secret to making a quickly thickened sauce is adding a cornstarch slurry. At least double the amount of cold water to cornstarch should be used for dispersing, and then whisked together until no powder is visible. Always add cool slurry to hot liquid to prevent clumping. Continuously whisking the cornstarch slurry into the sauce helps to separate the starch granules so it can efficiently swell and thicken, and stay lump-free.

chemical leavening

SPEED UP BAKING WITH QUICK SHORTCUTS

Baking is the beautiful art of science in motion. In each stage, ingredients are measured, combined, heated and molecularly changed to create an edible masterpiece. Understanding chemical leavening ingredients and what's happening during the process will help you produce the best textures and flavors in quick breads and cookies.

the simple science

When you need a freshly baked good in a short period of time, modern science has thankfully provided the fastest solution in the form of chemical leavening agents. Using the proper mixing techniques paired with the right selection of ingredients can create irresistible oven-baked products like scones, biscuits, muffins, loaf breads, cakes, cookies and brownies. There are three key ingredients to help make dough or batter rise: baking soda, baking powder and baking ammonia.

chemical leavening basics

Baking soda: That little orange box sitting in your pantry or refrigerator is filled with sodium bicarbonate ($NaHCO_3$, for my science geeks out there). It's an alkaline compound (base) that reacts with an acid and moisture to release carbon dioxide gas (CO_2). Common ingredients containing acids used in baking are lemon juice, sour cream, buttermilk, citrus fruits, honey and molasses. The unique thing about baking soda is that it doesn't need heat to create bubbles, so once it's mixed with the wet ingredients the mixture needs to be baked immediately. This maximizes gas retention in the baked good for a good rise. The amount of baking soda used correlates to the quantity of acid in the recipe. The goal is to have enough base to neutralize the acids.

Baking powder: This handy baking ingredient is a mixture of baking soda (sodium bicarbonate) and a dried acid like cream of tartar and/or sodium aluminum sulfate. This means that you do not have to add an acid to the recipe to create gas; it's all combined in one convenient ingredient. Starch is also added to balance the acid and base chemical reaction. Once the moisture is added, gas formation can occur. There are two types of baking powder: single-acting and double-acting. Single-acting requires moisture from ingredients in the recipe to create gas and needs to be baked immediately. Double-acting is more commonly used because when mixed with liquid, there is an initial release of gas, then once heat from the oven is applied, a stronger secondary gas reaction occurs. This gives the baker a little bit more insurance for proper rise, and the recipe does not need to be baked right away. Sometimes baking powder is added in addition to baking soda to provide extra leavening capability.

Baking ammonia: When you want to add crispness to crackers, cookies or biscotti, ammonium bicarbonate (NH_4HCO_3) will do the trick. It serves as a leavening agent and adds that crisp factor. High-temperature baking and large surface area products best utilize this ingredient. You will notice a strong odor coming from the quick release of ammonia and carbon dioxide. Once the internal temperature of the baked good reaches 140°F (60°C), the smell will eventually go away.

mix it up! select the right method for texture success

Weighing and properly measuring ingredients for a baked good is just the beginning of the process to ensure a soft crumb success. When you are looking for a specific texture, the temperature and how you mix the fat into the batter or dough is key. The three major mixing techniques are the creaming, muffin and biscuit methods. Cookies use the high-fat creaming method to give tender products. Muffins, quick breads and cakes use liquid fat for super soft and moist structures. Biscuits, scones and shortcakes utilize cold fats that are broken up into small chunks to create flaky products. Oftentimes when the baked good doesn't come out right, either cookies spread, muffins are tough or biscuits are not layered, we can examine our mixing technique. One important thing to remember is when using wheat flour, overmixing can cause an undesirable increase in gluten bonding from the proteins in flour (glutenin and gliadin) that form when combined with water. It's beneficial for some formation to assist in structure; however, if the batter or dough is overworked you can taste the difference in a more tough texture. Adding fat and sugar helps to tenderize and prevent some gluten formation for tender products, but it's good to keep an eye on technique throughout the baking process.

QUICK BREAD MIXING TECHNIQUES

MIXING METHOD	LEAVENING AGENT	TYPE OF FAT	RESULT
Creaming	Baking soda, baking powder, air	Softened at room temperature (butter, margarine, lard)	Cakelike texture, moist, tender, rich, springs back when touched
Muffin	Baking soda, baking powder, air	Liquid (melted butter, oil, coconut oil)	Cakelike texture, moist, tender, soft, springs back when touched
Biscuit	Baking soda, baking powder	Cold, solid (butter, lard, margarine)	Flaky, crumbly, breaks apart with little resistance

CHEMICALLY LEAVENED BAKED GOODS

BAKED GOOD	LEAVENING AGENT	MIXING METHOD	TYPE OF FAT	RESULT
Butter Cakes	Baking soda, baking powder, air	Creaming	Softened butter	Moist, tender, soft, fine crumb, springs back when touched
Muffins	Baking soda, baking powder, air	Muffin	Oil, melted butter, coconut oil	Moist, tender, soft, springs back when touched, dome shaped top, even distribution of mix-ins
Loaf breads	Baking soda, baking powder, air	Muffin	Oil, melted butter	Moist, tender, soft, springs back when touched, even shaped and even distribution of mix-ins
Biscuits/ Shortcakes	Baking soda, baking powder	Biscuit	Solid butter, margarine, lard	Light, flaky, tender, crumbles easily
Scones	Baking soda, baking powder	Biscuit	Solid butter, margarine, coconut oil	Light, flaky, tender, crumbles easily
Cookies	Baking soda, baking powder, baking ammonia, air	Creaming	Softened butter, margarine, coconut oil	Tender, chewy or crumbly, cake-like
Brownies	Eggs, air	Creaming or muffin	Softened butter, melted fat, oil	Chewy, fudgy, dense or cake-like

gluten function in baking

Gluten formation is critical to the volume, texture and appearance of a product. When the proteins in the flour are hydrated and the dough/batter is mixed, gluten bonds form, providing structure and elasticity. This happens because the proteins in the dough form linkages and gluten strands are created. As mixing increases, so does the strength of the dough. The amount of gluten formation is dependent on the application. Less gluten formation is desired in a tender cake, whereas high amounts of gluten formation are needed for chewy artisan bread. You can purchase various types of flour with more or less protein, depending on the desired level of gluten-forming potential. Below provides the protein content of flours based on the type and use. You can see how the amount of gluten present in a recipe can affect the texture of the baked goods.

The amount of protein in all-purpose flour can vary among brands, so make sure to check the nutritional labels. This can have more of an impact when kneading and baking bread dough because more protein creates more gluten development, potentially creating a more rubbery texture. This is less of a concern with tender crumb products with higher sugar and fat like muffins, biscuits or cookies. To calculate the percent protein level, divide the grams of protein by grams in a serving size, then multiply by 100. The recipes in this book were developed using all-purpose Gold Medal brand flour that is about 10 percent protein. If using a higher protein content all-purpose flour like King Arthur brand, which is about 11.7 percent protein, there is an easy fix. *Cook's Illustrated* recommends replacing 1 tablespoon (7.8 g) of flour per cup (125 g) with 1 tablespoon (9.4 g) of cornstarch. If within the 10- to 11-percent protein range, there should be less of a noticeable difference in bread recipes.

PROTEIN CONTENT IN FLOURS

FLOUR TYPE	PERCENT PROTEIN	APPLICATION
Cake	6–8	Tender cakes
Pastry	7.5–9.5	Pie crusts, biscuits
All-purpose	10–13	General baking
Bread	12–15	Breads, yeast breads, some cookies
Whole-wheat	13–14	Breads, quick breads, muffins, cookies
High-gluten	14–15	Bagels, add to weaker flours to increase protein
Vital wheat gluten	40–85	Add to weaker flours to increase protein

(Source: *On Baking: A Textbook of Culinary Fundamentals*)

chocolate chip banana bread

CHEMICAL LEAVENING | VEGETARIAN

A delicious banana bread recipe is always a good staple to have in your recipe collection, so that no overripe fruit goes unused! Ripened bananas produce a stronger banana flavor and sweetness in the bread. A traditional quick-bread technique is used for gently folding the wet ingredients into the dry ingredients. The result is a coarse, tender crumb, with slices of banana bread that are soft, moist and flavorful.

SERVES: 1 loaf, about 8 to 10 slices | **PREP TIME:** 20 minutes | **COOK TIME:** 1 hour 15 minutes

½ cup (112 g) unsalted butter

5 very ripe medium-size peeled bananas (16 oz [454 g] total peeled)

2 large eggs

¾ cup (165 g) packed light brown sugar

1 tsp pure vanilla extract

1¾ cups (210 g) all-purpose flour

1 tsp baking soda

½ tsp kosher salt

½ cup (87 g) mini semisweet chocolate chips

½ cup (54 g) walnuts, finely chopped

Adjust the oven rack to the middle position and preheat the oven to 350°F (177°C).

Microwave the butter in 30 second intervals until melted, stirring in between, about 1 minute. Allow to cool at room temperature but not solidify.

Place the bananas in a medium-size microwave-safe bowl. Cover with plastic wrap and microwave until the bananas are tender, 5 minutes. Transfer the bananas to a strainer sitting over a bowl. Press the bananas to release the liquid, stirring occasionally and allowing the banana liquid to drain for 15 minutes.

Collect the banana liquid: it should yield about ½ to ¾ cup (120 to 180 ml), and transfer to a small pan. Over medium-high heat, reduce the liquid to ¼ cup (60 ml), about 5 to 7 minutes.

In a medium-size bowl, mash the cooked bananas and liquid until a purée is created, about ¾ cup (180 ml). The purée should be slightly warm, but not hot, before adding the other ingredients. Whisk in the butter, eggs, brown sugar and vanilla.

In a large bowl, whisk together the flour, baking soda and salt. Stir in the chocolate chips and walnuts. Add the banana mixture into the flour mixture. Use a spatula to fold the ingredients until just combined, being careful to fold the batter just enough to hydrate the flour, yet keep gluten formation to a minimum. A few streaks of flour should remain, but do not overmix.

Grease an 8½ x 4½-inch (22 x 11.4-cm) loaf pan with cooking spray. Place the pan on a small sheet tray. If using a larger 9 x 5-inch (23 x 13-cm) pan, check the cooking time at least 5 minutes earlier as the larger pan will cause the bread to cook quicker.

Transfer the batter into the pan and bake until golden brown, 55 to 70 minutes. After 30 minutes, loosely cover the banana bread with foil to reduce browning and help create a dome shape. Bake until a toothpick inserted in the center of the loaf comes out clean with some crumbs attached. Allow the bread to cool in the pan for 10 minutes. Turn onto a wire rack, flip over and allow to cool 1 hour before serving.

COOK'S NOTE:

If you aren't ready to make banana bread when the ripening time is right, refrigerate the bananas to slow the ripening process and ethylene gas production. The bananas will be around the same sweetness and firmness after about 5 days. The ripe bananas can also be peeled, frozen and defrosted before using. Defrosted bananas do not need to be microwaved because the freezing process ruptures the bananas' cell walls and the liquid will be easily released and ready to concentrate.

RECIPE SCIENCE:

Over time, the natural ethylene gas in bananas is emitted and encourages ripening, causing the conversion of banana starch to fructose (fruit sugar). The right time to add bananas into a quick bread is when the skin is abundantly coated with brown speckles to even black, versus a yellow banana with just a few spots. A clever kitchen trick to increase the banana flavor is to cook them in the microwave, and then separate the solids from the liquid. This allows the ability to concentrate and control the amount of moisture added into the bread for a more predictable baked good.

lemon-raspberry cream scones

CHEMICAL LEAVENING | VEGETARIAN

Sweet ruby red raspberries are gently folded in between layers of moist scone dough, then drizzled with a tangy lemon glaze for the ideal flavor balance. A little brush of butter and a sprinkle of sugar create a nice golden crisp crust on each delightful pastry.

SERVES: 8 | **PREP TIME:** 60 minutes | **COOK TIME:** 15 minutes

2 cups (240 g) all-purpose flour, plus more for dusting

1 tbsp (13 g) double-acting baking powder

½ cup plus 2½ tsp (106 g) granulated sugar, divided

½ tsp kosher salt

2 tsp (1 g) lemon zest

7 tbsp (98 g) unsalted butter, chilled, cut into ¼-inch (6-mm) cubes, divided

1 cup plus 1 tbsp (255 ml) heavy whipping cream, chilled, divided

1½ cups (215 g) raspberries

¾ cup (78 g) powdered sugar, sifted, divided

1 tbsp (15 ml) lemon juice

COOK'S NOTE:

Frozen raspberries can be used and do not need to be defrosted. Scones can be made the day before and refrigerated once cut into triangles, using the same baking procedure.

Adjust the oven rack to the middle position. Preheat the oven to 425°F (218°C).

In a medium-size bowl, mix together the flour, baking powder, ½ cup (99 g) of granulated sugar, salt and lemon zest. Add 5 tablespoons (70 g) of cubed butter a few pieces at a time to the flour mixture, and toss to coat. Use your fingers to break the butter into pea-size pieces. Transfer the bowl to the freezer and chill the flour mixture for 5 minutes.

Gradually stir 1 cup (240 ml) of whipping cream into the flour mixture with a spatula, until the mixture just comes together in large crumbles with little to no loose flour.

Lightly flour the work surface and turn the dough onto the surface. Knead the dough until the dried bits of flour become incorporated into the dough, 6 to 8 kneads; do not overmix. Lightly dust the rolling pin, dough and rolling surface with flour. Shape and roll the dough into a 10 x 10-inch (25 x 25-cm) square, about ½ inch (1.3 cm) thick.

Fold the dough into thirds like a book, approximately a 10 x 4-inch (25 x 10-cm) rectangle. Fold the shorter ends of the dough over in thirds again, into about a 4 x 4-inch (10 x 10-cm) square. Transfer dough to a plate and freeze for 5 minutes.

Lightly flour the rolling pin, dough and surface, and roll the dough into a 10 x 10-inch (25 x 25-cm) square.

In a medium-size bowl, gently mix together the raspberries and 2 teaspoons (8 g) sugar, until the sugar is dissolved. Scatter the raspberries evenly on top of the dough, leaving at least a ½-inch (1.3-cm) border on the edges. Roll the dough into a tight log, seam side down.

Lightly flour board and surface of the dough as needed. Gently roll the dough into a 12 x 4-inch (30 x 10-cm) rectangle. Cut the dough into 4 even rectangles, approximately 4 x 3 inches (10 x 7.6 cm) each. Cut each rectangle into 2 smaller triangles to create 8 scones. Transfer the scones to a plate and freeze for 5 minutes or chill in the refrigerator 10 minutes before baking.

Line a sheet pan with parchment paper. Evenly space out the scones, at least 2 inches (5 cm) apart.

Melt 2 tablespoons (28 g) of butter. Brush the tops of the scones with the butter. Use ½ teaspoon of sugar to evenly sprinkle on the tops of the scones. Bake until the scones are golden brown, 15 to 17 minutes. Cool the scones on a sheet tray.

In a medium-size bowl, whisk together the powdered sugar and lemon juice. Add 1 tablespoon (15 ml) of cream and whisk until smooth. Drizzle the lemon glaze on top of the scones. Allow to set and dry for a few minutes before serving.

RECIPE SCIENCE:

For maximum leavening and flakiness use cold butter and break into pea-size pieces to ensure pockets for gas to puff up the dough. A folding and rolling technique similarly applied to laminated doughs is used. Working swiftly to gently knead the dough and then applying a "book folding" technique, rolling and folding the dough over itself, exponentially creates multiple thin butter layers distributed between the dough. The result is a more delicate crumbly pastry.

blueberry almond muffins

CHEMICAL LEAVENING | **VEGETARIAN** | **QUICK (30 MINUTES OR LESS)** | **FREEZER-FRIENDLY**

Blueberry muffins are my top pick, and a little almond crunch adds some delightful texture to each bite. These gorgeous muffins have a sweet almond flavor and the blueberries pop like little bursts of jam with each bite.

SERVES: 12 | **PREP TIME:** 15 minutes | **COOK TIME:** 17 minutes

2 oz (56 g) unsalted butter

2½ cups (355 g) all-purpose flour

2½ tsp (10 g) double-acting baking powder

1 tsp kosher salt

1⅛ cups plus 1 tsp (227 g) granulated sugar, divided

2 large eggs

¼ cup (60 ml) vegetable oil

1 cup (240 ml) buttermilk

1 tsp almond extract

½ tsp pure vanilla extract

1½ cups (210 g) blueberries, fresh or frozen, divided

6 tbsp (45 g) sliced almonds, divided

Adjust the oven rack to the upper-middle position and preheat the oven to 425°F (218°C).

Melt the butter in the microwave for 45 seconds, and allow to cool at room temperature.

In a large bowl, whisk together the flour, baking powder and salt.

In a medium-size bowl, whisk together 1⅛ cups (223 g) of sugar and eggs until smooth and pale yellow, 1 minute. Slowly whisk the melted butter and vegetable oil into the egg mixture, until incorporated. Whisk the buttermilk, almond extract and vanilla extract into the egg mixture.

Add the egg mixture, 1¼ cups (175 g) of blueberries and ¼ cup (30 g) of almonds to the flour mixture. Gently fold into the flour mixture, until just moistened, lumpy and with some dry flour spots remaining. Do not overmix the batter.

Spray muffin cups with cooking spray or line with paper cups. Fill each cup to the top and mounded slightly, about ⅓ cup (75 g) batter per muffin cup.

Evenly divide and sprinkle 1 teaspoon of granulated sugar on the surface of each muffin. Add the remaining ¼ cup (24 g) of blueberries on top, about two to three berries per muffin. Press berries lightly into the batter. Evenly distribute 2 tablespoons (15 g) of sliced almonds on top of the muffin batter, crushing some on top.

Bake the muffins for 10 minutes. Rotate the muffin pan and bake until the muffins are golden brown, 6 to 7 more minutes. Allow the muffins to cool in the pan for 5 minutes. Use a spatula to carefully release the muffins from the tin and transfer to a cooling rack.

COOK'S NOTE:

Add a little extra crunch to the muffin tops with a sprinkling of granulated sugar. The high temperature of the 425°F (218°C) oven allows the layer of sugar to gradually melt and harden. Baking the muffins in the upper section of the oven, where heat has risen, yields a nice golden crust and gives a little extra boost of heat for a nicely rounded top.

RECIPE SCIENCE:

The baking powder and eggs play a lead role in muffin-top creation. The minute the sodium bicarbonate and acids in the leavening agent and buttermilk come into contact, gas is formed in the batter and gets trapped. The muffin batter needs to bake soon after to prevent losing too much leavening power. Double-acting baking powder is used for insurance, so that the initial gas creation will be followed up by a secondary rise when the muffin batter is heated in the extremely hot oven to guarantee those pretty peaks. As the proteins set in the eggs during baking, they help to trap the gases formed to help further leaven the muffin. To achieve a moist muffin yet coarse crumb, a combination of butter and oil is used for flavor and moistness. Since oil is void of water, it can effectively coat the flour proteins and act as a barrier to prevent some water absorption and gluten formation when mixing the batter. Sugar acts as a tenderizer in the batter, while both the emulsifying agent lecithin in the egg yolk and sugar slow down protein bonding. The moment the liquid comes into contact with the proteins in the wheat flour, gluten formation will begin. Physical agitation like stirring or folding encourages and strengthens the protein network. Minimizing contact time and gentle folding will help yield a tender, and not rubbery, muffin.

flaky country buttermilk biscuits

CHEMICAL LEAVENING | VEGETARIAN | FREEZER-FRIENDLY

Tender, flaky, crunchy-topped biscuits are a culinary masterpiece. A good country-style biscuit may seem simple and unassuming, yet there are so many recipe factors that greatly determine the texture and flavor. To achieve the highly sought-out distinctive layers, the ingredients, temperature and technique make all the difference. Biscuits are a type of chemically leavened quick bread. The chemical leavening provides instant lift for light and layered pieces, creating grooves and rougher areas that will grab any gravy or butter.

SERVES: 9 (2.5-inch [6.4-cm]) biscuits | **PREP TIME:** 60 minutes | **COOK TIME:** 10 minutes

3½ cups (497 g) all-purpose flour, plus more for dusting

1 tbsp (11 g) double-acting baking powder

½ tsp baking soda

2 tsp (12 g) kosher salt, plus more for topping

2 tsp (10 g) granulated sugar

1 cup plus 2 tbsp (254 g) unsalted butter, chilled, divided

1 cup plus 2 tbsp (270 ml) buttermilk, chilled

Adjust the oven rack to the lower-middle position. Preheat the oven to 450°F (232°C).

In a medium-size bowl, whisk together the flour, baking powder, baking soda, salt and sugar.

Cut 1 cup (237 g) of butter into ⅛-inch (3-mm) thick pieces. Add a few butter slices at a time into the flour mixture and toss to coat. Press each slice of butter between the floured thumb and pointer finger, pressing and breaking the butter off into flat, nickel-size pieces. Repeat the process with the remaining pieces of butter, then toss to combine. Freeze the mixture in the bowl until chilled, 15 minutes.

Gradually add the buttermilk into the chilled flour mixture, stirring with a fork until incorporated. Knead the biscuit mixture in the bowl a few times until a shaggy dough forms; it will look slightly dry. If needed, add an extra 1 to 2 tablespoons (15 to 30 ml) of buttermilk so that most of the flour is hydrated and can be kneaded into the dough.

Lightly dust a working surface with the flour. Turn the mixture onto the floured surface and shape and press with hands until combined into a 1-inch (2.5-cm) thick square, about 8 x 8 inches (20 x 20 cm). The dough will not be sticky. Cut the dough into 4 even-shaped squares. Stack the squares as evenly as possible on top of each other.

Lightly flour a rolling pin and roll the dough out into a 1-inch (2.5-cm) thick square, about 8 x 8 inches (20 x 20 cm).

Leave about a ¼-inch (6-mm) border along the edges when cutting the biscuits to give even layers. Using a 2½-inch (6.4-cm) floured biscuit cutter, press the cutter straight down into the dough, without turning. Transfer to a parchment paper–lined sheet pan. Repeat with the remaining dough. Refrigerate the biscuits for 30 minutes before baking.

(continued)

COOK'S NOTE:

It's critical to allow the cut biscuits to rest and chill before baking. This allows the gluten network to relax after all of the kneading and rolling, and keeps that butter cold for layer building. Relaxing the dough also helps the biscuits rise evenly during baking so the heights are more symmetrical and not fallen over.

Add the buttermilk to the chilled flour mixture.

Cut the dough into four equal squares and stack.

Roll the dough into 1-inch (2.5-cm) thickness.

Transfer the biscuits to a new parchment paper–lined sheet pan. Make sure that the biscuits are at least 1 inch (2.5 cm) apart on the sheet pan. Melt 2 tablespoons (28 g) butter. Brush the butter on top of each biscuit and sprinkle the tops with salt. Bake the biscuits until golden brown, 10 to 11 minutes. Cool for 5 to 10 minutes before serving.

RECIPE SCIENCE:

Baking soda promotes browning and rise, and also helps neutralize the acid in the buttermilk to reduce some natural tanginess. Baking powder is added for additional gas formation in the presence of heat from the oven, a double lift! Butter is a crucial staple in biscuits because it provides flavor and lots of mini layers. The butter must be chilled so that it is easy to press into large flat discs to create thin sheets of butter between the dough. Freezing and chilling the biscuit dough in between stages keeps the butter from melting into the protein network as it is mixed, rolled and shaped, ensuring separate layers before it even goes into the oven. The small pieces broken up into the dough create small pockets as those bits of butter melt into the dough during baking. The holes left by the butter allow steam and gas created by the liquid and leaveners in the dough to expand and make layers in between. Using all-purpose flour adds just enough protein (10 to 12 percent) to provide structure from the gluten network for those layers to separate for a light interior, yet crisp exterior. To add more layers to the dough, it's rolled out and cut into four equal-size squares, stacked on top of each other, flattened to 1 inch (2.5 cm) thick, then cut into rounds. The dough may seem slightly dry initially, but the uneven, lightly floured and rigid surface adds wonderful texture to the tops of the biscuits.

nutella cheesecake brownies

CHEMICAL LEAVENING | VEGETARIAN

As a child, I would always look forward to the winter holidays because of a special sweet delivery from our dear family friend Margaret McIntyre. What always arrived was a plate piled high with chocolate swirl cake! This Nutella cheesecake brownie recipe was inspired by this divine dessert, but has a denser chocolate texture and hazelnut flavor. This dessert is the best of both worlds: creamy Nutella cheesecake and intense chocolate fudge cake.

MAKES: 9 large pieces, 16 smaller pieces | **PREP TIME:** 20 minutes | **COOK TIME:** 40 minutes

BROWNIE

3 oz (87 g) unsweetened chocolate, broken into pieces

6 tbsp (84 g) unsalted butter, cut into 8 pieces

1 cup (198 g) granulated sugar

2 large eggs, room temperature

½ tsp vanilla extract

½ tsp hazelnut extract, optional

½ cup (71 g) all-purpose flour

¼ tsp baking soda

¼ tsp kosher salt

CHEESECAKE

8 oz (227 g) cream cheese, softened to room temperature

¼ cup (50 g) granulated sugar

1 large egg, room temperature

1 tsp vanilla extract

½ cup (148 g) Nutella

2 tbsp (30 g) semi-sweet chocolate chips

Adjust the oven rack to the lower third position and preheat the oven to 350°F (177°C).

Fold two long pieces of foil into 8-inch (20-cm) wide pieces with enough length to overhang the sides of the pan. Lay the sheets in an 8 x 8-inch (20 x 20-cm) pan perpendicular to one another, with extra foil hanging over the edges of the pan. Push the foil into the corners of the pan and up the sides, creating a smooth foil flush to the pan. Grease the foil with baking spray and set aside.

For the brownies, melt the chocolate and butter in a medium-size heatproof bowl over a pot filled halfway with barely simmering water. Stir occasionally until the mixture is smooth, about 5 minutes. Alternatively, in a medium-size microwave-safe bowl, heat the chocolate and butter for 1 minute. Stir and heat until the chocolate is melted, 30 seconds. Stir to combine.

Take the chocolate off the heat, or remove from the microwave, and whisk in the granulated sugar. Add the eggs 1 at a time, whisking after each addition until combined, 30 seconds per egg. Whisk in the vanilla and hazelnut extracts (if using) for about 15 seconds.

In a medium-size bowl, whisk the flour, baking soda and salt. Add the flour to the chocolate mixture in 3 additions. Gently fold with a spatula until the batter is just moistened with the flour streaks just disappearing. Do not overmix. Transfer the batter to the prepared pan, smoothing the surface.

For the cheesecake, whisk the cream cheese in a large mixing bowl on high speed until smooth, scraping sides as needed, 1 minute. Add the sugar and whisk on medium-high speed until combined, 30 seconds. Whisk in the egg and vanilla, and mix on medium-high speed, until combined, scraping the sides of the bowl as needed, 30 seconds.

Add the cheesecake topping over the brownie layer. Use a spatula to smooth the cheesecake layer evenly over the brownie layer.

Add the Nutella to a microwave-safe bowl and heat for 30 seconds to make it spreadable. Drop spoonfuls of the Nutella on top of the cheesecake layer, to create a checkered pattern. Use a knife to make shallow swirls, creating marbled patterns throughout the topping. Evenly sprinkle chocolate chips on top of the brownies.

Bake until a toothpick inserted in the center comes out with just a few moist crumbs attached, 35 to 40 minutes, and rotate the pan halfway through baking. After 20 minutes of baking, loosely cover and tent the brownie with foil. The foil should not touch the surface.

(continued)

nutella cheesecake brownies (cont.)

Cool the cheesecake brownies in the pan on a wire rack until they reach room temperature, 2 hours. Use the foil to help remove the brownies from the pan. Use a knife dipped in hot water and then wiped down in between each slice to give nice clean cuts. Cut into squares.

Store the brownies in an airtight container in the refrigerator for up to 3 days if not eating the same day.

chewy cranberry oatmeal cookies

CHEMICAL LEAVENING | VEGETARIAN

The contrast in textures from the plump, sweet and tart cranberries, hearty oats and crunchy pecans makes each bite more addictive than the last. The best thing about these oatmeal cookies is that they stay soft days after they are baked.

MAKES: 15 large cookies | **PREP TIME:** 20 minutes | **COOK TIME:** 20 minutes

1½ cups (360 ml) water

1 cup (122 g) dried cranberries

1 cup (122 g) pecans

1¼ cups (108 g) old-fashioned rolled oats

1¼ cups (178 g) all-purpose flour

¾ tsp baking powder

½ tsp baking soda

½ tsp kosher salt

1 tsp ground cinnamon

12 tbsp (168 g) unsalted butter, softened to 68°F (20°C)

1½ cups (330 g) packed dark brown sugar

1 large egg

1½ tsp (7.5 ml) vanilla extract

COOK'S NOTE:

Rehydrating the berries in water for 10 minutes before adding to the dough allows them to plump up slightly, so they provide a soft, pleasing fruit texture to the cookies.

Adjust the oven rack to the middle position and preheat the oven to 350°F (177°C). Line 2 baking sheets with parchment paper.

Microwave the water for 2 minutes so that it is warm. Add the cranberries and allow to sit and plump up for 10 minutes. Drain the cranberries, squeeze out excess water and dry well with a paper towel.

Heat a small pan over medium heat. Add the pecans and toast until fragrant and crunchy, 3 minutes. Toss the pecans every 30 seconds so they don't burn. Transfer to a cutting board and roughly chop. In a small bowl, combine the pecans, cranberries and oats.

In a medium-size bowl, whisk together the flour, baking powder, baking soda, salt and cinnamon.

Using a stand mixer fitted with a paddle, beat the butter and sugar at medium speed until no lumps of sugar remain, about 1 minute. Scrape the sides of the bowl as needed.

Add the egg and vanilla, and beat on medium-low speed until combined, about 30 seconds, scraping the sides of the bowl as needed.

Reduce the mixer speed to low and add the flour mixture, mixing until just combined, 15 seconds. Gradually add the oat mixture and mix until just combined, 10 seconds. Use a spatula to give the cookie dough a final stir to ensure no flour remains and the ingredients are evenly dispersed.

Measure ¼ cup (70 g) of the dough and roll it into a ball. Place it on a baking sheet. Repeat with the remaining dough, spacing the cookies 2½ inches (6.4 cm) apart. Press each ball into 1 inch (2.5 cm) thick cookies.

Bake the cookies until medium brown in color with set edges and soft centers that look slightly underdone with a wet shiny appearance, 14 to 16 minutes. Rotate the sheet pan after 10 minutes of baking.

Cool the cookies on the baking sheet for 5 minutes. The cookies will continue to cook when removed from the oven. Transfer to a wire rack to cool at room temperature. Store the cookies in a resealable plastic bag for up to 3 days.

This recipe makes 15 large 4-inch (10-cm) cookies. The cookies can be made smaller into 2 tablespoon (35 g) portions, baked for 11 to 12 minutes, making 30 small 3-inch (8-cm) cookies.

RECIPE SCIENCE:

To keep the cookies moist and chewy, dark brown sugar is used as a humectant and a water binder. Brown sugar contains about 6.5 percent molasses (dark brown syrup) and more invert sugar (glucose and fructose) compared to granulated sugar. This causes more moisture to be attracted to the sugar and less hardening during baking. Baking soda creates a crispy outside and baking powder puffs up and lightens the cookie for soft dense centers.

classic pineapple upside down cake

CHEMICAL LEAVENING | VEGETARIAN

Do you want to know the secret to a happy marriage? Make the person you love their favorite cake for their birthday! Pineapple upside down cake is a nostalgic dessert that my husband, Jason, looks forward to each year. His Grandma Rose and mom, Joan, baked up this stunning cake for special occasions and visits. I was lucky enough to learn Grandma's secrets when visiting a few years back. The shining star of the cake is the caramelized tropical fruit topping there is no need for extra frosting and decorations when it's all baked right into the cake. This cake base is versatile enough to use for any sliced fruit, like apples and peaches, if you are looking to switch up the flavors. This recipe is our family tradition and we cannot wait until our children can make it for us!

SERVES: 8 to 10 | **PREP TIME:** 30 minutes | **COOK TIME:** 40 minutes

TOPPING

½ cup (113 g) unsalted butter, room temperature

4½ tsp (22 ml) honey

1 cup (198 g) packed dark brown sugar

¼ tsp vanilla extract

7 canned pineapple slices, 3 inches (8 cm) wide

14 maraschino cherries

¼ cup (28 g) walnut halves, chopped

CAKE

1⅓ cups (157 g) cake flour

2 tsp (8 g) double-acting baking powder

½ cup (113 g) unsalted butter, softened yet cool, 60 to 65°F (16 to 18°C)

½ cup plus 2 tbsp (123 g) granulated sugar

½ tsp vanilla extract

2 large eggs, room temperature

4 tsp (20 ml) whole milk, room temperature

Adjust the oven rack to the middle position and preheat the oven to 350°F (177°C).

For the topping, use a handheld mixer or stand mixer fitted with a paddle attachment, and combine the butter, honey, brown sugar and vanilla over medium speed in a medium-size bowl, 30 seconds.

Lightly grease the bottom and sides of an 8½ x 3-inch (22 x 8-cm) or 9 x 2-inch (23 x 5-cm) round pan. Evenly spread the brown sugar mixture over the bottom of the pan.

Place one of the pineapple slices in the middle and 6 around the edges on top of the brown sugar mixture. Add two cherries in the center of each pineapple ring. Add the walnuts to the edges of the pan where the brown sugar mixture is exposed and add small broken pieces in the center between the rings. Set aside.

For the cake, sift the flour and baking powder in a medium-size bowl. Whisk to combine.

In a separate medium-size bowl, add the softened butter and granulated sugar. Using the paddle attachment, mix on low speed until just combined, 20 seconds. Increase the speed to medium and mix for 3 minutes until the mixture is light and creamy. Scrape down the sides as needed.

Add the vanilla and mix on medium speed for 10 seconds. Add the eggs one at a time, on medium speed until creamy, 30 seconds. Scrape the bowl and repeat with the second egg. Add the milk and combine on medium speed, 15 seconds.

On low speed add the flour mixture in 3 batches, mixing until just combined, 10 seconds each interval. Scrape the sides as needed. Pour the batter into the pan over the pineapples; it will be thick. Use a spatula to spread evenly in the pan.

Bake until the cake is golden brown, springs back when touched and a toothpick inserted in the center comes out clean with a few crumbs attached, or center of the cake registers about 185 to 190°F (85 to 88°C), about 30 to 40 minutes. The bake time will depend on the size of your pan.

(continued)

Allow the cake to cool in the pan on a cooling rack for 45 to 60 minutes. The cake will still be slightly warm, but will set as it will continue to cook in the pan. Do not cool completely in pan or the topping will stick to the bottom.

Run a knife around the edges of the cake, invert onto a serving platter and serve warm. Leftover cake can be stored at room temperature in an airtight container for 1 day.

COOK'S NOTE:

To maximize cake rise, use cool butter between 60 and 65°F (16 and 18°C) for creaming together with the sugar. Unique miniature needle-like beta prime fat crystals are formed in the butter fat at this temperature range, perfect for aerating the butter and trapping it inside the batter. Too cold and air cannot get whipped in, too warm and the butter will not trap the air. An instant-read thermometer works best to check the temperature, or it should feel cool to the touch and slightly dent when pressed. It will take 30 to 60 minutes to soften when left on the counter from the refrigerator.

RECIPE SCIENCE:

It all starts with layering the bottom of the pan with a buttery brown sugar smear. Typically, recipes call for melted butter and sugar, but I've found that whipping the sugar with softened butter makes it easier to spread and has a more even coating on the cake and fruit when baked. As the cake bakes, the high temperature of the oven causes the sugars to caramelize around 320°F (160°C), creating a jaw-droppingly sweet and sticky sauce on the pineapples and walnuts. After testing different types of cakes and methods, the classic creaming technique worked the best. This method provides a strong, nicely risen cake that is able to hold the weight of the pineapple topping once slightly cooled and flipped over. Creaming cool butter and sugar helps the cake rise because the sugar helps to create mini pockets of air in the butter. These pockets get filled with carbon dioxide gas as the sodium bicarbonate in the baking powder reacts with the milk, expands in size to make the cake rise and gets trapped by the fat and gluten protein network in the batter as it cooks. Cake flour is used because its lower protein content allows for reduced gluten formation, to achieve a tender crumb and not a rubbery texture.

strawberries and cream cake

If there is one thing I can't resist it's a big slice of cake! I grew up eating chiffon cakes from our favorite Chinese bakeries for celebrations, so I've created something similar for you to share with your loved ones. This dreamy dessert is all about layers of light and moist yellow cake, fluffy whipped cream and an easy homemade strawberry jam. When the tender sponge cake is combined with the lightly sweetened cream and vibrant strawberry jam, it is ready to be the star of the party!

SERVES: 12 | **PREP TIME:** 1 hour 30 minutes | **COOK TIME:** 30 minutes

STRAWBERRY FILLING

4 tsp (14 g) low-or-no-sugar-needed fruit pectin

¼ cup (50 g) granulated sugar

2 cups (286 g) strawberries, hulled and sliced in half

CAKE

1¾ cups (200 g) cake flour, plus more for dusting

½ cup (120 ml) whole milk, room temperature

4 large eggs, room temperature

2 tsp (10 ml) vanilla extract

1½ cups (297 g) granulated sugar

2 tsp (8 g) baking powder

¾ tsp kosher salt

1 cup (226 g) unsalted butter, softened to 68°F (20°C), cut into 16 pieces

WHIPPED CREAM

1½ cups (360 ml) heavy whipping cream

2 tbsp (24 g) granulated sugar

½ tsp vanilla extract

TOPPING

1 cup (143 g) strawberries, cut in half

For the strawberry filling, whisk together the pectin and sugar in a small saucepan. Add 2 cups (286 g) of sliced berries to the pan and mash together with a potato masher until pulpy and the sugar is dissolved. Bring the strawberry mixture to a boil over medium-high heat. Cook until thickened, stirring occasionally, 2 minutes. Reduce the heat to medium if needed.

Add the cooked strawberries to a fine-mesh strainer set over a medium-size bowl. Stir and press the berries to extract the juice. Discard the solids and seeds. Cool the sauce in the refrigerator until set, 1 to 1½ hours. Use a whisk to break up the filling, until smooth and spreadable.

Adjust the oven rack to the middle position and preheat the oven to 350°F (177°C).

For the cake, grease the bottom of two 9-inch (23-cm) round cake pans. Line each pan with about a 9-inch (23-cm) round piece of parchment paper. Grease the paper and sides of the pan. Dust the bottom and sides with cake flour, removing any excess flour that does not coat the pan.

In a medium-size bowl, whisk the milk, eggs and vanilla.

In a large mixing bowl or bowl of a stand mixer, whisk together the flour, sugar, baking powder and salt.

Using a stand mixer fitted with a paddle or handheld mixer on low speed, add the butter one piece at a time, and mix until pea-size pieces remain, about 60 to 90 seconds.

Set aside ½ cup (120 ml) of the egg mixture. Add the rest of the egg mixture to the flour mixture. Mix on medium-high speed and beat until light and fluffy, 1 minute. Reduce the speed to medium-low and add the remaining ½ cup (120 ml) of the egg mixture. Beat until incorporated, 30 seconds. Use a spatula to give the batter a final stir. The batter may look slightly curdled as all of the butter may not be completely dissolved.

Divide the batter evenly into the two pans. Smooth the tops of the cake with a spatula.

Bake the cakes side by side on the same rack until tops are lightly brown and a toothpick inserted in the center comes out with a few crumbs attached, 20 to 22 minutes.

Cool the cakes on a wire rack for 10 minutes. Use a knife or small metal spatula to carefully release the sides and bottom edges of the cake from the pan. Remove the cakes from the pans and discard the paper. Cool completely on the wire rack before frosting. You can make the cake 1 or 2 days ahead, wrap cakes in plastic wrap and then foil and store at room temperature.

(continued)

To create a silky smooth and voluminous whipped cream, the sugar should be added to chilled cream at the very beginning of whipping. This allows the sugar granules to fully dissolve once whipping is complete, to reduce any chance for a gritty texture. The cold fat in the cream helps to hold and stabilize the air whipped into the cream. In a large chilled bowl, beat the chilled cream, sugar and vanilla on medium-low speed until frothy, 1 minute. Turn the speed to high and whisk until medium to stiff peaks form and look smooth, thick and spreadable and almost double in volume but not clumpy, about 2 to 2½ minutes. Refrigerate until ready to use.

To assemble, place one of the cake layers on a plate or cake stand.

Place the jam in a piping bag or small plastic resealable bag. Cut a ¼-inch (6-mm) opening in the bag. Pipe a circle along the perimeter of the cake, leaving a ⅛-inch (3-mm) border. Fill in the center of the circle with enough jam to fill the center. Smooth the jam with a spatula if needed.

Place 1½ cups (360 ml) of whipped cream into a piping bag fitted with a large round tip (806 tip). Pipe a circle over the jam, leaving a ⅛-inch (3-mm) space from the edge of the jam border. Fill in the circle with more whipped cream. Use a spatula to smooth the surface into an even circle. Place the second cake layer on top.

Pipe or spread with a spatula some whipped cream circles in the center of the cake. Top with 1 cup (143 g) of sliced berries. Serve immediately or refrigerate. Cake can be stored for up to 1 day in the refrigerator.

COOK'S NOTE:

Pectin is a carbohydrate naturally found in fruit. When purchasing pectin for the jam recipe, select "low-or-no-sugar-needed fruit pectin." This product has been formulated to contain dextrose (sugar), the fruit pectin and citric acid all in one to improve set time and reduce the need to add extra ingredients for the jam to solidify successfully once cooled. The pectin thickens the mashed strawberries so that they can hold together in between the cake layers and be spreadable. When heated with sugar and acid, pectin molecules bind together to help trap water and to form a gel-like texture in the fruit.

RECIPE SCIENCE:

To create a slightly spongy, sturdy cake that does not crumble when decorating, a reverse-creaming method (or high-ratio method) is used. It requires more liquid than flour to produce a smooth tender crumb, and reduces the amount of air incorporated into the batter and gluten formation. In order to achieve these tender layer cakes, the butter must be around 68°F (20°C) before adding it to the flour, sugar, baking powder and salt mixture. This gives a softened butter with reduced fat crystals, so that less air is trapped in the batter. The butter is gradually incorporated into the flour mixture and coats the wheat proteins in the flour, minimizing gluten formation once the milk and eggs are added. This technique is great for layer cakes because it gives a finer moist crumb so the cake can support the weight of the filling, and reduces the rise of the cake so the top is flat and easier to cut and layer.

yeast leavening

A FOOLPROOF WAY TO RISE UP

It may seem like magic, but the yeast fermentation process works hard at the microscopic level to expand and rise into a pliable, airy dough in just a few hours. Let's explore the science of creating doughs for sweet breads, rolls and buns.

the simple science

The art of bread making is a timeless craft combining flour, yeast, water and salt to create highly desirable and irresistible products like baguettes, freshly baked dinner rolls, breakfast pastries and artisan breads. What used to take hours, days and lots of muscle fatigue can now incorporate kitchen equipment and yeast technologies that home cooks can use for a more practical approach to their favorite breads. No matter if you are making simple breadsticks or flaky croissants, it all comes down to one key ingredient for leavening success: yeast.

yeast leavening basics

Fermentation: The strain of yeast used in baking is called *Saccharomyces cerevisae*. Just like us, yeast are living organisms that love to eat carbohydrates. After a large meal feeding from starches and sugars in the bread dough, two things are produced by yeast: carbon dioxide gas in the form of bubbles and alcohol. Yes, you guessed it, it's the same process as making beer! Developing a strong gluten protein network from the flour and moisture in the dough and through kneading helps to trap the gas formed during fermentation, the time to allow the dough to rise. All of those captured tiny bubbles are responsible for the leavening, lift and texture in the bread. What happens to the alcohol? It evaporates with the high temperatures of baking. Fermentation builds natural characteristic flavors into different types of bread, so sometimes a longer fermentation period is desired to develop the right taste.

Temperature: Here's the deal: Because yeast are alive, you can kill them. Using a thermometer to correctly measure the temperature of the liquid ingredients is crucial for fermentation and dough rise. If you've ever wondered why your bread ended up flat, it's most likely because liquids in the dough were too high and the poor fungi did not survive to start fermenting. Just like hot liquids can kill them, using liquids that are too cold can slow their activity. Yeast are inactive at 34°F (2°C), so do not use cold refrigerated liquids. Yeast ferment optimally at 75 to 95°F (24 to 35°C), around room temperature or slightly higher if you have a proof box during the rise stage. Yeast die at 138°F (59°C), therefore adding very warm or boiling liquids to the dough is not recommended.

yeast selection: how to choose

Proofing yeast: Waking up the yeast to ensure it's alive. Some sugar as food for the yeast is added with warm water, then stirred and allowed to sit for about 10 minutes. If you see bubbles form and double in size, the yeast is okay to be used, otherwise discard. This is not required for active dry or instant dry yeast. Proofing process and amount of water and sugar used are dependent on the brand used.

Compressed yeast: Fresh yeast that combines yeast, starch and about 70 percent moisture. The appearance is white and crumbly and must be stored in the refrigerator. Before using, it is softened in two times its weight of warm water (100°F [38°C]), then can be added to the dough. Not as practical to use in home baking because it requires refrigeration and is sold in large 1-pound (454-g) blocks. Requires twice as much if using instead of active dry yeast.

Active dry yeast: A convenient dried dormant yeast product that is shelf stable. Requires rehydrating in warm 100 to 110°F (38 to 43°C) water. Requires two rise steps, initial rise after kneading for dough to double in size, then rising after shaping; overall longer time compared to instant dry yeast. Typically over 2 hours for both rise steps. May be substituted for fresh compressed yeast, as it is two times as strong.

Instant dry yeast: A popular yeast product to use for quicker rise of bread products. Also labeled as bread machine yeast and rapid-rise. Does not require proofing before use; it is added directly to the dry ingredients and only requires one rise step. The liquid used in the recipe activates the yeast, incorporated between 120 and 130°F (49 and 54°C) for most products. After kneading, the dough rests for 10 minutes to relax the gluten in the dough; it's then shaped and allowed to rise until double in size. Rise time is much faster, usually an hour or less. Can use as a substitute for active dry yeast, however, may rise slightly less. Two times as strong as compressed yeast. May not be optimal in dried breads like bagels or croissant dough because it may not all dissolve in the lower-moisture formulas.

YEAST	PROOFING	TEMPERATURE	FERMENTATION/TIME
Compressed (Proofing)	Yes	100°F (38°C)	Rise: 1 to 1½ hour / Shape: 1 hour
Active Dry	No	100–110°F (38–43°C) (Rehydrate)	Rise: 1 to 1½ hour / Shape: 1 hour
Instant Dry (Bread Machine)	No	120–130°F (49–54°C) (Added liquid)	Rest: 10 minutes / Shape: 30 to 60 minutes

FORMULAS FOR SUBSTITUTING YEAST PRODUCTS

SUBSTITUTE FOR	MULTIPLY QUANTITY BY	SUBSTITUTE WITH
Compressed Fresh Yeast	0.5	Active Dry Yeast
Compressed Fresh Yeast	0.33	Instant Dry (Bread Machine) Yeast
Active Dry Yeast	2	Compressed Fresh Yeast
Active Dry Yeast	0.75	Instant Dry (Bread Machine) Yeast
Instant Dry (Bread Machine) Yeast	3	Compressed Fresh Yeast
Instant Dry (Bread Machine) Yeast	1.33	Active Dry Yeast

Example: 7 grams active dry yeast $\times$ 0.75 = 5.25 g instant dry yeast
(Source: *On Baking: A Textbook of Culinary Fundamentals*)

lean or rich: two types of leavened dough

Depending on the desired texture and flavor of the bread, more or less fat and sweetener can be added to the dough. Those seeking crusty surfaces of country-style loaves or who are sourdough obsessed will like lean doughs. Typically they are a simple combination of flour, liquid and salt as the base plus specific mixing and proofing methods. When fat from butter, shortening or eggs is combined with sugar in the dough at varying levels, beloved breads like cinnamon rolls, croissants and brioches can be created with a softer and more tender crumb.

how to create your own proof box for yeast bread

To create a proof box for fermenting the dough, follow these easy instructions. Microwave or heat on the stove top 3 cups (720 ml) of water until nearly boiling, at least 200°F (93°C). Cover and place the dough on the middle rack of the oven. Place an 8- or 9-inch (20- or 23-cm) round or square pan on the bottom rack of the oven. Carefully pour the hot water into the pan. Close oven door and allow the oven to heat and become humid. Try not to open the door unless needed. This will create the perfect warm and moist environment for the dough to rise, between 75 and 95°F (24 and 35°C). Before preheating the oven for baking, remove the hot water pan and wipe the oven door with a towel to remove any excess moisture buildup.

salted caramel apple cinnamon rolls

Cinnamon rolls are the ultimate breakfast indulgence, and this caramel apple version takes them to the next level! Some hesitate to make these sweet rolls from scratch because of the length of time it takes to prepare and allow the dough to rise by yeast fermentation. This recipe cuts the time down by half to about 90 minutes from start to finish; it's magical! That's because by using dried instant yeast, which has added enzymes and additives to make it rise faster, the rolls only need one rise after rolling and shaping, then they're ready to bake. The combination of tart apples, sweet cinnamon sugar filling and salted caramel drizzled over the hot, tender rolls will convince anyone to wake up in time for breakfast!

SERVES: 12 | **PREP TIME:** 60 minutes | **COOK TIME:** 30 minutes

2¾ cups (330 g) all-purpose flour, plus more for dusting

2¼ tsp (7 g) instant or rapid-rise yeast

1 tsp kosher salt

¼ cup (50 g) granulated sugar

2 tbsp (28 g) unsalted butter

½ cup (120 ml) water

¼ cup (60 ml) whole milk

1 large egg

½ cup (60 g) pecans, roughly chopped

FILLING

7 tbsp (98 g) unsalted butter, softened, divided

2 cups (260 g) diced Granny Smith apples, ¼-inch (6-mm) cubes

⅓ cup (75 g) packed dark brown sugar

⅓ cup (66 g) granulated sugar

2 tbsp (16 g) all-purpose flour

1 tbsp (4 g) ground cinnamon

CARAMEL SAUCE

1 cup (198 g) granulated sugar

¼ cup (60 ml) water

¾ cup (180 ml) heavy cream

4 tbsp (56 g) unsalted butter

¾ tsp kosher salt

For the rolls, whisk together the flour, yeast and salt in a large bowl or bowl of a stand mixer.

In a medium-size microwave-safe bowl, combine the sugar, butter, water and milk. Microwave in 20-second intervals until the mixture reaches 120 to 130°F (49 to 54°C), and whisk to combine.

Gradually stir the liquid mixture and egg into the flour mixture using a spatula, until a soft, sticky dough forms. Using the dough hook attachment of a stand mixer, set the mixer on the lowest setting above stir and mix until dough becomes smooth and elastic, 4 minutes. If not using a mixer, knead by hand on a lightly floured surface for 5 minutes. Cover the dough with plastic wrap or a towel and allow to rest for 10 minutes.

Heat a medium-size pan over medium-high heat. Add 1 tablespoon (14 g) of butter and allow to melt. Add the apples and sauté until tender, 5 minutes. Transfer the cooked apples to a plate and chill in the freezer until cold, but not frozen, 10 minutes, or refrigerate 20 minutes.

Adjust the oven rack to the lower-middle position and preheat the oven to 375°F (191°C).

Make the filling in a small bowl, stirring together the brown sugar, granulated sugar, flour and cinnamon. Add 6 tablespoons (84 g) of softened butter and mix until smooth. Set aside.

Roll out the dough on a lightly floured surface into a 16 x 9-inch (41 x 23-cm) rectangle.

Evenly spread the filling over the dough, leaving a ½-inch (1.3-cm) border on all sides. Evenly sprinkle the diced apples over the filling. Tightly roll the dough into an 16-inch (41-cm) long log. Trim the thinner edges off the roll. Cut into 12 even size pieces.

(continued)

COOK'S NOTE:

When making caramel sauce, a thermometer can be used to check the temperature. Target between 320 and 350°F (160 and 177°C) and not above, or do a simple visual check for changes in color. Keep a close watch to prevent the syrup from burning; it will quickly change from caramel to smoky in seconds. Once you see the color change to the desired level, remove the sauce from the heat to reduce the cooking temperature of the sugar.

Carefully add the heavy cream to the caramel sauce.

Evenly spread the cinnamon sugar filling and apples over the dough.

Cover and allow the rolls to rise for 30 minutes.

Place the rolls in a lightly greased 9 x 13-inch (23 x 33-cm) baking pan, spaced out about ½ inch (1.3 cm) apart, 3 rolls per row. Leave about ½ inch (1.3 cm) of space along the edges of the pan. Loosely cover the rolls with plastic wrap or a kitchen towel and allow to rise in a warm draft-free area until doubled in size, 30 minutes.

Bake the rolls until lightly golden brown in color, 15 to 17 minutes. Slightly cool the rolls for 5 to 10 minutes.

For the caramel sauce, heat the sugar and water in a small saucepan over medium-low heat. Allow the sugar to dissolve without stirring. If needed, use a wet pastry brush to wash down any undissolved sugar on the side of the pan.

Increase the heat to high and bring it to a boil, allowing the sugar to caramelize without stirring to a deep amber color, 5 to 7 minutes, between 320 and 350°F (160 and 177°C). Adjust the heat to medium-high if rapidly boiling.

Remove the sugar from the heat; slowly and carefully whisk in the heavy cream. The caramel will bubble as the cream is added, so allow to subside and gradually incorporate. Whisk in the butter and salt. Allow the sauce to cool to room temperature; it will continue to thicken as it cools. The sauce can be stored for 1 week refrigerated in an airtight container.

Drizzle the rolls with the caramel sauce and top the rolls with chopped pecans.

RECIPE SCIENCE:

Fresh apples were tested to reduce some of the cooking required, but it caused too much liquid from the cells of the apple flesh to be expressed once mixed with sugar, causing the rolls to be soggy. Therefore, a quick 5 minute precook to the diced apples helped to soften and remove some excess moisture before fermentation and baking. Creating a caramel sauce may seem like a challenge, but it's actually a very simple science of controlling heat when cooking sugar and water to purposely brown the mixture. Cooking the sugar syrup causes water to evaporate, and the sugar concentration increases and the temperature rises. Sugar will turn to a honey golden color between 320 and 335°F (160 and 170°C), and a reddish amber color up to 350°F (177°C). Be very careful as you add the cream; gradually whisk it in as it will bubble up from the extremely hot sugar syrup. Once you practice the caramelization technique, it will be something you can use for various cooking and baking applications to elevate any recipe.

chinese steamed custard buns

YEAST LEAVENING | VEGETARIAN

Growing up in the San Francisco Bay Area, my family ventured to Oakland Chinatown nearly every weekend for a delicious dim sum brunch, and it's still a tasty tradition whenever we get a chance to get together. These light and airy buns were my favorite childhood treat to order as the huge metal steam carts would pass by. I still look forward to breaking open a hot bun filled with warm and gooey egg custard filling. The process is a labor of love, however, worth each moment to create right at home. The bun base works great with other fillings such as Chinese barbecued pork (char siu), pork meatballs or even as buns that can be filled with Peking duck. Once you make your first batch of steamed custard buns, you will be hooked!

MAKES: 24 buns | **PREP TIME:** 3 hours | **COOK TIME:** 30 minutes

STEAMED BUNS

½ cup plus 1 tbsp (111 g) granulated sugar, divided

¼ cup (60 ml) warm water, 100 to 110°F (38 to 43°C)

2¼ tsp (7 g) active dry yeast

4 cups (480 g) all-purpose flour, plus more for kneading

2 tbsp (31 g) shortening

1 cup (240 ml) warm whole milk, 100 to 110°F (38 to 43°C)

1 tbsp (15 ml) vegetable oil

1 tbsp (17 g) baking powder

4½ tsp (22 ml) cold water

CUSTARD

1½ cups (360 ml) whole milk

½ cup (120 ml) heavy cream

½ cup (100 g) granulated sugar, divided

5 large egg yolks

¼ cup (38 g) cornstarch

¼ cup (57 g) cold unsalted butter, cut into 4 pieces

1½ tsp (7.5 ml) vanilla extract

For the dough, dissolve 1 tablespoon sugar (12 g) with warm water (100 to 110°F [38 to 43°C]) in a small bowl. Sprinkle the yeast over the top and let stand 3 minutes. Stir to combine and let stand until the mixture starts to foam, 10 minutes. If no foaming has occurred, the yeast is inactive. Start the steps over if needed, as keeping the yeast alive is crucial for proper rise of the dough.

In a large bowl, sift the flour. Make a well in the center and set aside.

In a medium-size bowl, whisk together the shortening, ½ cup (99 g) of sugar, yeast mixture and warm milk. The fat will not completely dissolve in the liquid.

Add the liquid mixture to the flour, and gradually use your hands to incorporate the flour into the liquid to make the dough. Knead the dough for 10 minutes, sprinkling with additional flour as needed.

Drizzle the dough with oil to grease the outside of the dough. Transfer to a bowl and cover with plastic wrap and let rest in a warm area until doubled in size, 1½ hours. Punch the dough down and flatten out to about ¾ inch (2 cm) thick on a flat surface once it has completed rising.

In a small bowl, combine the baking powder and cold water. Spread the baking powder mixture evenly over the dough. Gather the corners of the dough into the center and roll the dough into a ball; knead until smooth and satiny, 10 minutes. Transfer the dough to a bowl and cover with plastic wrap. Allow the dough to rest for 30 minutes.

For the custard, add the milk and cream in a medium-size saucepan. Bring to a simmer over medium heat. Whisk in ¼ cup (50 g) of sugar, until dissolved and then turn off the heat.

In a medium-size bowl, whisk together the egg yolks and ¼ cup (50 g) of sugar until smooth.

Add the cornstarch to the egg mixture, and whisk until incorporated.

Remove the simmering milk mixture from the heat. Measure ¼ cup (60 ml) of the milk mixture, then gradually add it to the egg mixture, whisking constantly to temper. Gradually add the tempered egg mixture to the remaining milk mixture, whisking constantly.

Place the saucepan on the stove and heat over medium-high heat. Whisk constantly until the mixture slightly thickens, 3 minutes.

Turn off the heat and remove the saucepan from the stove. Whisk in the cold butter and vanilla until incorporated. Cover with plastic wrap and refrigerate until chilled and set, at least 2 hours. The custard can be made a day in advance.

(continued)

Divide the dough into four equal parts. Roll one part by hand to form a rope approximately 9 inches (23 cm) long and 1¼ inches (3 cm) in diameter. Mark the dough into 6 equal parts, 1½ inches (4 cm) long. Continue with the other three dough sections.

Holding the dough with one hand, grip at the first mark with your thumb and index finger of the other hand, and tear away briskly to break off a small dough piece. Continue the process with the other pieces of dough until you have about 24 pieces that are about 1½ to 2 ounces (43 to 57 g).

Flatten each piece of dough with your palm. Using a rolling pin, roll each into a round disk, making a quarter turn with each roll, leaving the center slightly thicker. The thinner edges will be easier to pleat. The dough should make 4-inch (10-cm) rounds.

Place the rolled dough in the palm of your hand. The custard will be set after chilling, so form into a ball before placing into the dough. Place about 2 to 3 teaspoons of filling in the center of each dough round, flat side up.

Gather the edges by first pleating counter clockwise, and then twisting to securely seal. Place the bun round, smooth side up on a square piece of parchment paper about 2½ x 2½ inches (6 x 6 cm). Let the buns rest, covered with a towel, on a sheet tray for 30 minutes.

Prepare the steamer by adding enough water to cover the bottom of the steamer, about 1 inch (2.5 cm) in depth. The water should not be touching the bottom of the steamer insert. Cover the pot and bring to a boil. If a flat lid is used to cover the steamer, wrap the lid in a kitchen towel to prevent condensed steam from dripping on the buns.

Add the first batch of buns in the steamer, at least 1 inch (2.5 cm) apart. Cover and steam on medium-high heat for 5 to 6 minutes. Do not uncover the steamer during the cooking process. Turn off the steam before opening the lid, remove buns with tongs and then add the next batch of buns. Repeat the steaming process until all of the buns are cooked.

Buns can be refrigerated in a resealable plastic bag for up to 3 days. Reheat the buns in the microwave until softened, 15 to 20 seconds.

COOK'S NOTE:
The custard needs to be brought almost to a boil at 200°F (93°C) for two main reasons. There is an enzyme in egg yolks called amylase that, if it is not destroyed by high heat, will cause the amylose in the starch to break down and result in a runny custard. The high heat also helps the tempered eggs to set and starches to gelatinize; both contribute to thickening the custard into a stiff, yet creamy filling.

RECIPE SCIENCE:
It all starts with proofing the yeast in water with sugar for food to ensure that it will give maximum rise when steamed. To create a soft, yet elastic bun, the dough gets a vigorous 10-minute knead to encourage gluten bond formation with the proteins in the wheat flour. A little bit of shortening and fat from the milk prevents the dough from becoming tough through inhibiting some of the gluten formation, and keeps the bun nice and tender after steaming. The smooth and rich custard filling is made on the stovetop using the tempering method. Tempering is accomplished by adding a small amount of hot liquid like cream and milk to an egg mixture of sugar and starch, then gradually whisking together to slow the rate that the eggs would cook and warm them up. The warmed egg mixture can now be added and whisked into the remaining hot liquid without being shocked by the heat and stay loose. Adding sugar slows down protein unfolding and increases coagulation temperature to 180°F (82°C) compared to 150°F (66°C) of egg coagulation, which helps to stabilize the heated egg proteins. The amylose in the starch granules also releases and coats the egg proteins, preventing those strong bonds from forming and solidifying as the eggs are cooked. This delicate process ensures that the egg in the custard stays creamy and thick, and once cooled, holds its shape in the buns.

italian breadsticks

Cooking for an Italian family requires the occasional homemade breadsticks to appear on the dinner table. My husband, Jason, is a big fan of dipping bread into sauce, so on special nights I'll whip up these freshly baked garlic herb breadsticks to go with our feast. It's a quick and easy recipe that's fun to get other eager eaters involved to help measure, knead and shape. The fragrant aromas of the garlic will make you immediately salivate, while the tender bread with lightly crisp bottoms will make you reach for more!

SERVES: 12 | **PREP TIME:** 60 minutes | **COOK TIME:** 10 minutes

2 to 2¼ cups (240 to 270 g) all-purpose flour, divided, plus more for dusting

1 tbsp (12 g) granulated sugar

2¼ tsp (7 g) instant or rapid-rise yeast

1 tsp kosher salt, plus more for sprinkling, divided

¼ tsp dried oregano

¼ tsp dried basil

¼ tsp dried thyme

¾ cup (180 ml) water

2 tsp (10 ml) olive oil

1 large egg white

1 large egg yolk

1 tbsp (15 ml) whole milk

2 tbsp (28 g) unsalted butter

1 tsp minced garlic

In a large mixing bowl, whisk together 1 cup (142 g) of flour, sugar, yeast, ¾ teaspoon of salt, oregano, basil and thyme.

In a medium-size microwave-safe bowl, combine the water and olive oil. Heat the liquid in the microwave in 20 second increments, until the water is warm and reaches 120 to 130°F (49 to 54°C).

Add the warmed water mixture and egg white to the flour mixture. If using a stand mixer, use the paddle attachment to mix the dough mixture on medium speed for 2 minutes. Scrape the bowl as needed. Add ½ cup (71 g) of flour and beat on high speed for 2 minutes. Stir in ½ to ¾ cup (71 to 107 g) of additional flour into the dough until a ball is formed.

Transfer the dough to a lightly floured surface. Knead until the dough is smooth and elastic in texture. The dough is done kneading when it springs back when lightly pressed with 2 fingers, 6 to 8 minutes. Cover the dough with a towel and allow to rest for 10 minutes.

Portion the dough into 12 equal pieces. Roll dough into 8-inch (20-cm) ropes. Grease a large baking sheet and transfer the breadsticks to the pan.

In a small bowl, whisk the egg yolk and milk together. Brush the tops and sides of the breadsticks with the egg wash. Lightly sprinkle kosher salt over the breadsticks.

Lightly cover the breadsticks with plastic wrap or a kitchen towel and allow to rise in a warm draft-free area until the dough doubles in size, 30 minutes.

Adjust the oven rack to the middle position and preheat the oven to 450°F (232°C).

In a small saucepan, melt the butter over medium heat. Reduce the heat to low and add the garlic and ¼ teaspoon of salt. Cook for 2 to 3 minutes, until the garlic is fragrant but not browned. Turn off the heat and allow the garlic to infuse into the butter while the breadsticks bake.

Bake the breadsticks until golden brown, 8 to 10 minutes. Brush with the garlic butter and serve warm.

COOK'S NOTE:

Mince the garlic just before cooking in the butter to reduce the intense sulfurous garlic aroma that can fill your kitchen. Garlic cloves contain an odorless sulfur-containing amino acid. The moment the garlic is minced, the amino acid and an enzyme called allinase interact to create a flavor compound called allicin, which is responsible for garlic's noticeable taste and aroma. The more the garlic is chopped, the stronger allicin builds, which is desired for maximum flavor infusion into the butter.

RECIPE SCIENCE:

Instant yeast is used to shorten the time needed for yeast fermentation, and is added dry directly with the flour, sugar and herbs. The warmed water helps to activate the yeast instead of needing time for proofing. Dried herbs such as oregano, basil and thyme are added to the dough to add an earthy flavor and attractive appearance. Instead of adding raw pungent and spicy garlic directly into the dough, minced garlic is infused into the butter used for brushing the breadsticks hot out of the oven. Gently cooking the garlic helps to reduce and mellow the harsh sulfur-containing notes from the compound allicin, which gives garlic its characteristic taste and smell and brings out its natural sweetness that is layered on the breadsticks.

whole wheat hamburger buns

YEAST LEAVENING | VEGETARIAN | FREEZER-FRIENDLY

Baking with whole grains allows you to add additional nutrition to each serving of bread. This recipe for whole wheat buns gives a tender product with more texture and chew compared to all-purpose flour alone. Whole wheat flour is the entire red wheat berry, which has been milled and contains fiber-packed bran, germ rich in oils and vitamins, and protein- and starch-containing endosperm. This gives a more natural darker-colored bread, with a nuttier flavor.

SERVES: 8 | PREP TIME: 60 minutes | COOK TIME: 13 minutes

2½ cups (300 g) whole wheat flour

4½ tsp (7 g) instant dry yeast

¼ cup (50 g) granulated sugar

1½ tsp (10 g) kosher salt

¾ cup (180 ml) warm whole milk, 120 to 130°F (49 to 54°C)

3 tbsp (42 g) unsalted butter, softened at room temperature

3 large eggs, divided

1¼ cups (118 g) all-purpose flour

1 tbsp (15 ml) whole milk, for egg wash

Suggested toppings: Sesame seeds (1 tsp), poppy seeds (½ tsp), rolled oats (2 tbsp [14 g]) or sunflower seeds (1 tbsp [8 g])

In a large mixing bowl, whisk together the whole wheat flour, yeast, sugar and salt.

Add the warm milk, butter and 2 eggs to the flour mixture. Use the paddle attachment on a stand mixer on low speed and combine, 30 seconds. Increase the mixer to medium speed, and mix for 2 minutes.

On low speed, gradually add in the all-purpose flour to yield a dough that is not sticky. Use a dough hook attachment on the mixer and knead on low speed for 5 minutes, until elastic and smooth. You can also transfer the dough to a lightly floured board and knead, 5 minutes. Loosely cover the dough with a kitchen towel and allow to rest for 10 minutes.

Divide dough into 8 equal size pieces, about 4 ounces (116 g) in weight, then roll and form each into a ball. Use a flat tool like a bench scraper to flatten the dough into 4-inch (10-cm) round pieces. These buns also make for great mini sliders, yielding about 16 (2-ounce [58-g] size) rolls.

Grease two baking sheets or one large sheet, and evenly space out the buns. Loosely cover the buns with plastic wrap or a towel and allow to rise in a draft-free warm area. Allow to double in size, 30 minutes to 1 hour.

In a small bowl, whisk together 1 egg and 1 tablespoon (15 ml) of milk. Brush the tops and sides of the buns with the egg wash and sprinkle with desired toppings.

Adjust the oven rack to the middle position and preheat the oven to 375°F (191°C).

Bake the hamburger buns until golden brown in color and glossy on the surface, 12 to 13 minutes, until they reach 190°F (88°C) internal temperature. Immediately transfer the buns to a cooling rack. If making small slider buns, bake for 10 minutes.

Serve the buns the same day. The buns can be stored in an airtight container for 2 days, then toasted before serving.

COOK'S NOTE:
Typically, to substitute 100 percent whole-wheat flour for all-purpose flour in a recipe, an additional 2 teaspoons (10 ml) of liquid is needed per 1 cup (125 g) of whole-wheat flour to help hydrate the bran.

RECIPE SCIENCE:
Baking entirely with whole wheat flour can be more dense and dry due to the presence of the bran and germ, which absorb more moisture. The rise may also be reduced due to the sharp whole grains cutting some of the gluten strands when kneaded, which usually trap the gas in the dough to give it a higher lift. These hamburger buns are made primarily with whole-wheat flour for the base, with some all-purpose flour to yield a lighter product. The 10-minute resting process and the fermentation time not only allow the yeast to create carbon dioxide gas, but also allow the whole grains to better hydrate and soften the rough texture. The additional moisture from the milk and eggs helps to prevent the bread from becoming too dry after baking. To ensure a nice rise, the dough is only kneaded for 5 minutes, which reduces cutting of the gluten strands and the starches in the all-purpose flour, keeping a strong gluten network in the bread.

hawaiian sweet rolls

YEAST LEAVENING | VEGETARIAN

Hawaiian sweet rolls are a staple for my family. They are my son's favorite bread so I created a homemade version just for James. These rolls are tender and milky, with a hint of sweetness from pineapple juice and honey. The result is a super-tender interior and crust, light texture, rich buttery flavor and deep golden color from the eggs.

MAKES: 18 rolls | **PREP TIME:** 70 minutes | **COOK TIME:** 20 minutes

5 to 5½ cups (600 to 660 g) all-purpose flour, divided, plus more for dusting

4½ tsp (7 g) instant or rapid-rise yeast

2½ tsp (15 g) kosher salt

½ cup plus 1 tbsp (135 ml) whole milk, divided

1 cup (240 ml) pineapple juice

8 tbsp (112 g) unsalted butter, divided

⅓ cup (80 ml) honey

2 tbsp (16 g) packed dark brown sugar

2 large eggs, divided

1 tsp apple cider vinegar

2 tsp (10 ml) pure vanilla extract

Use a stand mixer fitted with a greased dough hook. Add 5 cups (710 g) of flour, yeast and salt to the bowl, and whisk to combine.

In a medium-size microwave-safe bowl, add ½ cup (120 ml) of milk, pineapple juice, 6 tablespoons of (84 g) of butter and honey, and whisk to combine. Microwave the mixture in 20-second increments until it reaches 120 to 130°F (49 to 54°C), about 90 seconds.

Set the mixer to low speed and gradually add the warmed milk mixture, brown sugar, 1 egg, apple cider vinegar and vanilla to the flour mixture. Scrape the sides of the bowl with a spatula as needed to incorporate the flour.

Knead the dough on low until the dough begins to pull away from the bowl, 2 minutes. Increase the speed to medium low and knead until the dough is elastic and smooth in texture, 7 minutes. The dough should start to clear the sides of the bowl, but will be sticky on the bottom. Add ¼ cup (36 g) of additional flour, mixing on low speed, 1 minute. Add another ¼ cup (36 g) if needed, until the desired texture is achieved and a slightly sticky ball is formed. Use as little added flour as possible. Transfer the dough to a lightly floured surface. Cover and allow to rest for 10 minutes.

Grease a 9 x 13-inch (23 x 33-cm) pan with cooking spray and set aside. Cut the dough into 18 even-size pieces. Roll pieces of the dough into balls with smooth tops, lightly flouring the work surface as needed. Place the dough balls into the greased pan, 3 balls per row, 6 rows total. Leave about ½ inch (1.3 cm) around the corners of the pan.

Loosely cover the pan with plastic wrap or a kitchen towel and place in a warm draft-free place. Allow the dough balls to rise and double in size, 30 to 40 minutes. The buns should be touching each other and nearly filling the pan completely.

Adjust the oven rack to the lower-middle position and preheat the oven to 350°F (177°F).

In a small bowl, whisk together 1 egg and 1 tablespoon (15 ml) of milk. Brush the egg wash on the tops and sides of the buns. Bake the rolls until golden brown and shiny on the surface, 18 to 20 minutes. Make sure to rotate the pan halfway through baking.

Cool the rolls on a wire rack for 10 minutes. Remove the rolls from the tray and brush with 2 tablespoons (28 g) of melted butter. Serve the rolls immediately while warm.

COOK'S NOTE:

For even portioning of the rolls, use a kitchen scale. My method is to weigh the dough after resting. Divide that weight by 18 to get an approximate weight per roll. Use a bench scraper to cut and weigh each dough ball on the scale, adding more or less as needed per roll, then shape into rounds. My rolls were between 2½ and 2¾ ounces (71 and 78 g) each.

RECIPE SCIENCE:

The recipe yields an enriched sweet dough, which contains higher amounts of butter, sugar and eggs compared to lean doughs. The juice and sugars in the formula yield a stickier dough, so light dusting with flour is needed for kneading and shaping the rolls, but too much flour can make the rolls less tender due to too much protein. To reduce the preparation time by half, instant yeast is used so that fermentation is only required once after shaping, and still yields tall and fluffy rolls.

test kitchen tools & tips

What you need to set up a test kitchen right at home! The essential tools and equipment recommendations for fast, flavorful and easy cooking. Tips and guides for measuring and preparing safe and delicious recipes.

essential kitchen tools & equipment

There are so many items to choose from when equipping your kitchen. This list includes the essential tools and equipment I use in my home test kitchen. I have indicated some items and brands that I recommended for your reference. Start with the basics and build from there. If you do not have these already, at minimum, buy an instant-read thermometer, oven thermometer and digital kitchen scale to have the most success with this cookbook. These three items will give you insightful data as you cook, making the process more predictable and consistent.

MEASURING TOOLS	FEATURES	MEASURING
Instant-Read Thermometer	Read in 10 seconds or less.	Range of -40 to 450°F /-40 to 232°C. Water resistant. (I prefer ThermoWorks Super-Fast Thermapen MK4 or Pocket Thermometer.)
Oven Thermometer	Clear numbers and markings. Base or hanging hook.	Range up to 600°F (316°C). (I prefer TruTemp Pro Kitchen Oven Thermometer.)
Digital Oil and Candy Thermometer	Various settings for hot oil and candy. Large LCD monitor, splatter/heat shield, pivoting stainless-steel probe, side hook, signals when ideal temperature is reached.	Range up to 392°F (200°C). (I prefer Maverick CT-03 Digital Oil and Candy Thermometer.)
Digital Scale	Pound and gram conversion. Large platform for weighing. Zeroing button.	At least 7-pound (3.17-kg) capacity. (I prefer OXO Good Grips Stainless Steel Food Scale 11-pound [5 kg].)
Dry Measuring Cups	Stable, stainless steel. Handles level with cup rim.	¼, ⅓, ½, 1 cup (37.5, 50, 75, 140 g); ⅔ and ¾ cup (95 and 105 g) optional. (I prefer OXO Good Grips Stainless Steel Measuring Cup with Magnetic Snaps.)
Liquid Measuring Cups	Clear container with a handle. Cup and milliliter markings. Heatproof.	Measures ¼ and ⅓ cup (60 and 80 ml) amounts. (I prefer Pyrex Glass Measuring Cups: 1-, 2- and 4-cup [240-, 480- and 960-ml] capacity.)
Measuring Spoons	Oval in shape for easier scooping from small containers. Handles level with spoon rim.	I prefer OXO Good Grips Stainless Steel Measuring Spoons with Magnetic Snaps.

CUTTING TOOLS	FEATURES	SIZES
Chef's Knife	Curved blade and lightweight. High-carbon stainless steel. Tang extends into the handle, not separately attached.	8-inch [20-cm] blade. (I prefer Wüsthof Classic 8-inch [20-cm] Chef's Knife)
Paring Knife	Curved blade and pointed tip. Used for cutting smaller items.	3- to 3½-inch (7.62- to 8.9-cm) blade
Boning Knife	Slender and flexible blade. Used for boning meat, poultry, fish.	6-inch (15.24-cm) blade
Serrated Knife	With serrations. Used to cut bread.	10- to 12-inch (25.4- to 30.48-cm) blade
Slicing Knife	Tapered, oval scallops carved into blade. Used to slice large cuts of meat.	12-inch (30.48-cm) blade
Kitchen Shears	Durable stainless steel, come apart for easy cleaning and sharpening.	N/A
Cutting Board	Polypropylene antibacterial or wood with grain running parallel to surface.	Large 18 to 20 inches (45.7 to 50.8 cm) long. (I prefer Farberware Poly Cutting Board 18 x 12 inches [45.72 x 30.48 cm] and John Boos Maple Cutting/Carving Board 18 x 24 x 1½ inches [45.72 x 60.96 x 3.81 cm].)

POTS/PANS	FEATURES	SIZES
Clad Skillets / Sauté Pan	Layered material, aluminum filling and stainless steel outer layer, flared sides.	Sizes: 8-, 10- and 12-inch (20.32-, 25.4- and 30.48-cm). Used for sautéing, pan-frying, searing. (I prefer All-Clad Stainless Steel Tri-Ply Bonded: 8-, 10-, 11- and 12-inch [20.32-, 25.4-, 27.94- and 30.48-cm] French Skillet with Lid.)
Cast-Iron Skillet	Heavy, retains heat well, inexpensive.	Sizes: 8-, 10- and 12-inch (20.32-, 25.4- and 30.48-cm). Used for pan-frying, stewing, baking. (I prefer Lodge Pre-Seasoned Cast-Iron Skillets.)
Nonstick Pan	Do not heat to smoking point as the coating can vaporize and be harmful.	Sizes: 5-, 8-, 10- and 12-inch (12.7-, 20.32-, 25.4- and (30.48-cm). Used for delicate foods prone to sticking like eggs, fish and crepes.
Wok	Can handle high heat. Used for stir-frying, deep-frying, steaming and smoking.	Carbon steel, 12 to 14 inches (30.48 to 35.56 cm) wide, a 4- to 5-inch (10- to 12.7-cm) flattened bottom and sloped sides .
Dutch Oven	Heat-proof handles and knobs. Used for braises and stews.	Stainless steel or enameled cast iron. 6-quart [5.6 L] minimum size, 9-inch [23-cm] diameter. (I prefer Le Creuset 7¼-quart [6.8 L] Round French Oven.)

POTS/PANS	FEATURES	SIZES
Sauce Pans	Made of clad materials. Used to make sauces, soups, steaming.	Sizes: 2-, 2⅓-, 3- and 4-quart (1.89-, 2.20-, 2.83- and 4.78-L) capacity
Roasting Pan	Large with deep sides, Made of stainless steel with aluminum core, side handles, fitted V-rack. Used for roasting large items like chicken, turkey, beef.	Around 15 x 11 inches (38 x 28 cm) in size
Baking Sheets	Rimmed, light-colored surface, thick and sturdy. Double-thick aluminum with rolled edges. Have two of each. Darker sheets tend to bake items faster. Used for sweet and savory applications.	Half sheet (18 x 13 inches [45.72 x 33 cm]) and quarter sheet (13 x 9 inches [33 x 22.86 cm]), about ¾-inch (2-cm) sides

BAKING ESSENTIALS	FEATURES	SIZES
Muffin Tin	Nonstick helps with even browning and easy release. Use muffin liners if not using nonstick. Have 2 to make up to 24 muffins or cupcakes to quickly bake the next batch.	Capacity of ½ cup (64 g)
Loaf Pan	Glass for easier monitoring or dark nonstick, both evenly brown and easy release. Use baking spray for glass. The wider size cooks faster and may have less doming.	Have 8½ x 4½-inch (21.59 cm x 11.43-cm) and 9 x 5-inch (22.86 x 12.7-cm) sizes
Baking Pans	Metal with nonstick surface for even browning and easy release. Glass baking dish for casseroles and cobblers. Used for cakes, brownies, cinnamon rolls, quick breads and bar cookies.	Sizes: 8-inch (20.32-cm) and 9-inch (22.86-cm) square; 13 x 9-inch (33.02 x 22.86-cm). Glass, 13 x 9-inch (33.02 x 22.86-cm)
Round Cake Pans	Anodized aluminum pans or nonstick, straight sides. 3 inches (7.62 cm) high preferred for standalone cakes. Have a set of 2.	Sizes: 8- and 9-inch (20.32- and 22.86-cm) pans at least 2 inches (5.08 cm) to 3 inches (7.62 cm) high
Pie Plate	Glass for easier monitoring and even browning.	½-inch (1.27-cm) rim, and shallow angled size. Size: 8- to 9-inch (20.32- to 22.86-cm) round
Cooling Rack	Grid-style or line with heavy-gauge bars. Have between 2 and 4 racks.	Fit inside an 18 x 13-inch (45.72 x 33-cm) baking pan
Rolling Pin	Tapered sides okay for long pins. Marble rolling pins also an option.	Straight barrel, about 19 inches (48.26 cm) in length and 1 to 1½ pounds (0.45 to 0.68 kg).
Bench Scraper	Stainless steel. Used for cutting and shaping dough, cleaning board and transferring small food items.	6-inch (15.24-cm) size, with inch markings
Pastry Prep Board	Often will have length markings (inches), or circular dimensions for easy measuring when working with dough or crusts.	A large 16-inch (40.64-cm) square, ¾-inch (0.75-cm) thick wooden board

APPLIANCES & EQUIPMENT	FEATURES	WATTAGE/CAPACITY
Blender	Variable speed blender for control, stainless steel blades at the bottom of the cup. Used for sauces, soups, purées.	At least 700-watt motor, 62-ounce capacity. (I prefer Vitamix CIA Professional Series Blender, 64 ounce.)
Food Processor	Used for quick chopping, breaking down proteins into smaller uniform pieces, pie doughs.	5-cup (40-ounce) capacity minimum. (I prefer Cuisinart 8-cup [1.8 kg] Food Processor.)
Mixer	Handheld with variable speeds and attachments for mixing batters, frosting or eggs. Stand mixer with whisk, dough and paddle attachment. Used for batters and breads, plus more attachments.	At least 450-watt motor, variable speed and 5- to 6-quart (4.7 to 5.6 L) capacity. (I prefer KitchenAid Professional HD Stand Mixer, 5-quart [4.7 L] , 475-watt motor.)
Slow Cooker	Programmable, oval shape. High, low, warm settings. Time setting and automatic shutoff. Used to make soups, braises, stews, steaming, sweets, desserts and beverages.	6-quart (5.6 L) capacity. (I prefer Crock-Pot 6-quart [5.6 L] Programmable Cook & Carry Stainless Steel Slow Cooker.)
Grill	Gas or charcoal with a large grilling area. Gas with two to three burners for controlled heat settings. Purchase a long grill brush with stainless steel scrubbing pad to scrape and clean grill plate before and after use.	N/A

HELPFUL TOOLS	FEATURES	SPECIFICATIONS
Oven Mitts	Silicone, waterproof, nonslip. Best for preventing burns and easy to clean. Have at least one pair.	Withstand heat and steam at least 480°F (229°C)
Fine-Mesh Strainer	Used for desserts, sifting, straining, washing small particle ingredients, making fine purées.	Large and small sizes: Around 3⅛-inch (7.93-cm), 5½-inch (13.97-cm) and 7⅞-inch (20-cm) sizes
Tongs	Concave pincers, scalloped edges. Have multiple on hand.	12 inches (30.48 cm) in length
Potato Masher	Handheld, flat mashing area with holes to create purées with some remaining smaller particles	N/A
Spoons	Long wooden and heat-stable spoons for stirring hot foods, sauces, dry ingredients. Slotted spoons to help separate cooked foods from liquids, or skimming stocks.	N/A
Spatulas	Large and small rubber heatproof spatulas for scraping and folding ingredients. Metal fish spatula for flipping fish. Nonstick spatulas for egg cookery.	N/A

HELPFUL TOOLS	FEATURES	SPECIFICATIONS
Whisks	All-purpose that has at least 10 wires for mixing ingredients and sauces. A small whisk for mixing smaller volumes. Large balloon whisks with multiple wires to incorporate air into eggs or cream.	N/A
Bowls	Mini prep size for small items. Small, medium and large heat-stable metal, glass or ceramic bowls for mixing.	N/A
Graters	Large paddle-style grater with large holes for cheeses and vegetables. Long rasp grater (Microplane) for fine-size grating like hard cheese, ginger, garlic or citrus zest.	N/A
Vegetable Peeler	Sharp carbon steel blade, 1-inch (2.54-cm) space between blade and peeler. The swivel peeler has a vertical blade and the Y-peeler has a horizontal blade; it is personal preference. Choose one that has a sturdy and comfortable handle.	N/A
Spiralizer Vegetable Peeler	A larger apparatus with different blades to cut sturdy and thicker vegetables and fruits (no large center pit) into various shapes and sizes. Creates volume and extends length of the produce. Popular for making vegetable noodles.	N/A
Parchment Paper	Can be cut to fit into cake pans or pots for poaching or braising. Rolls can be used as well.	Pre-cut 16 x 12-inch (40.64 x 30.48-cm) pieces of parchment paper. Fits on half sheet trays for baking cookies.
Disposable Gloves	Powder-free latex or vinyl gloves for handling raw meat or cutting strong-smelling herbs and vegetables, or foods that stain. Can usually be found in the medical aisle at grocery stores.	N/A
Storage Containers	Airtight glass or plastic containers for storing cooked foods. Various-size airtight plastic containers for storing dry ingredients like flour and sugar with large enough openings to easily scoop and directly measure ingredients.	I prefer OXO Good Grips Airtight POP Containers.

the importance of measuring

Measuring ingredients may differ between people or even day to day, affecting the final taste and texture of a recipe. This can especially be true with even the slightest variation in more precise processes like baking. The reason for variability is that each food has a different density, its mass per unit volume, and varies with temperature and pressure. The variance is typically smaller for solids and liquids, but powders like flour can be tricky. This is where bulk density, the mass of the particles of the material divided by the total volume they occupy, comes into play. The volume that an ingredient can occupy may be sensitive depending on how it is added into the cup. Some ingredients have more void spaces between particles, so it can aerate easily or compact with more pressure. The technique you use to measure with standardized measuring tools like cups and spoons can create more or less total volume and impact the actual amount of the ingredient added to the recipe. There are ways to make measuring a more predictable and standardized process that reduces the rate of error.

TIPS FOR ACCURATE MEASURING

Use the right tools for measuring. Use dry measuring cups (typically ¼-, ⅓-, ½- and 1-cup [32-, 43-, 64- and 128-g] sizes, ⅔- and ¾-cup [85- and 96-g] are nice to have) for dry ingredients only like flour, herbs, chopped ingredients and sugar. Even though very tempting, do not use these cups for liquids. Use clear liquid measuring cups with indicator markings on the side (usually cups, ounces and metric milliliter amounts) that have a handle and spout. Use measuring spoons for small quantities (⅛ teaspoon, ¼ teaspoon, ½ teaspoon, 1 teaspoon, 1 tablespoon [0.66 g]), for dry and wet ingredients.

Use the same measuring technique every time. I tested several methods to measure 1 cup (128 g) of flour, knowing the target weight. I found that the "dip and sweep" technique gave me the least amount of variability between measures for dry ingredients based on volume; however, it must be performed a certain way. Depending on the type of food measured and amount, the right technique and tool should be used.

How to measure volume with the dip and sweep method. Gently dip the dry measuring cup into the container (flour, sugar and cocoa for example) and use a straight-edged knife or spatula to sweep away the excess, creating a level, flat surface on top. Whenever I buy a new bag of flour or sugar, I like to transfer it into an airtight container with a lid and a large enough opening to accommodate the largest dry measuring cup size. This keeps the product fresher longer and makes it easier to measure.

How to measure liquids. Place the liquid measuring cup on a flat and even surface. Get down to eye level with the marking of the desired amount of liquid. Pour ingredients until the bottom of the meniscus (the curved surface of the liquid, not the edges) is level with the measurement marking. This may seem less accurate than using a dry measuring cup, but because there is not a chance for spilling or guessing, it's a better way to measure.

How to use measuring spoons. Dip the spoon into the container for dry ingredients, or pour ingredient into a small bowl if the opening is not large enough. Make sure to level and sweep off any excess dry ingredients on the spoon just like measuring cups, because a "heaping" spoonful can give inconsistent results. Carefully measure liquid ingredients into the spoon.

Use a scale to measure weight instead of volume. This method reduces the chance for error, because using calibrated equipment and known weights can give more consistent results each time. For weights for commonly used baking ingredients see page 209. Using weight (ounces or grams) is a common practice in the food industry. The weights of ingredients should not drastically change unless things like flour and sugar have been improperly stored and pick up a large amount of moisture. It's best to buy fresh ingredients if the quality of your ingredients is questionable. If you decide to measure by weight, have the conversion table handy in the kitchen so you can quickly convert the quantities and know exactly how much of each ingredient to add (see Conversions & Equivalents on page 207).

the knife: your best friend

In culinary school, we were taught to always have a good, sharp knife. It is the extension of your hand, allowing you to physically transform foods for a specific application. Chefs use a lexicon for knife cuts to have a common language for the desired shape and size of the ingredient. The cut and how consistent you can make it impacts the taste and texture of the final dish. In this book, I have noted the size of the cuts so you don't have to memorize them, but these key terms will come in handy with other recipes and increase your culinary knowledge.

CHART: COMMON KNIFE CUTS AND TERMS

CUT	SHAPE	SIZE/DESCRIPTION
Julienne	Matchstick	⅛ inch x ⅛ inch x 2 inches (3 mm x 3 mm x 5 cm)
Bâtonnet	Stick	¼ inch x ¼ inch x 2 inches (6 mm x 6 mm x 5 cm)
Brunoise	Small cube	⅛ inch x ⅛ inch x ⅛ inch (3 mm x 3 mm x 3 mm)
Small dice	Cube	¼ inch x ¼ inch x ¼ inch (6 mm x 6 mm x 6 mm)
Medium dice	Cube	½ inch x ½ inch x ½ inch (1.3 cm x 1.3 cm x 1.3 cm)
Large dice	Cube	¾ inch x ¾ inch x ¾ inch (2 cm x 2 cm x 2 cm)
Paysanne	Square	½ inch x ½ inch x ⅛ inch (1.3 cm x 1.3 cm x 3 mm)
Tourner	Football	¾ inch to 1½ inch wide x 2 inches (2 cm to 3.8 cm x 5 cm)
Chiffonade	Strips	To cut into very thin strips. Often used for fresh herbs like basil
Slice	Flat pieces	⅛ inch (3 mm) or less for thin slices
Mince	Irregular	⅛ inch (3 mm) or smaller pieces
Chop, fine	Irregular	⅛ inch to ¼ inch (3 mm to 6 mm) pieces
Chop, medium	Irregular	¼ inch to ½ inch (6 mm to 1.3 cm) pieces
Chop, coarse	Irregular	½ inch to ¾ inch (1.3 cm to 2 cm) pieces
Cut, crosswise	N/A	Perpendicular cut to the length of the food
Cut, lengthwise	N/A	Length cut of the food from end to end
Cut, on the bias	Oval or diagonal	Cut across the food with knife held at 45-degree angle to the food

salt: the ultimate flavor enhancer

The essential ingredient in the kitchen and used in nearly every recipe. The simple ionic compound sodium chloride creates a crystalline salt structure able to penetrate foods, change food structure, add depth of flavor and moisture, and even prolong shelf life. The taste of salt is affected by the size, texture and mineral content. The particle size and shape varies between types of salt, and even by brand. Make sure to adjust accordingly based on the type you buy and use in a recipe. Morton brand kosher salt was used for the recipes in this cookbook.

Quick Conversion: 1 tsp table salt = 1¼ tsp Morton kosher salt* = 2 tsp Diamond Crystal kosher salt

*The top kosher salt brands Morton and Diamond Crystal vary significantly in quantity when using the same volume-measuring tool. Increase the amount by about 60 percent if using Diamond Crystal brand. For example, for 1 teaspoon of Morton brand, substitute 1½ teaspoons to 1⅝ teaspoons of Diamond Crystal brand.

COMMON SALTS USED IN COOKING

SALT	APPEARANCE	USE
Table salt	Fine, evenly shaped, dense crystals	Baking, cooking and last-minute seasoning
Kosher salt	Course, asymmetric larger grains	Cooking, baking and overall seasoning
Sea salt	Larger, unevenly shaped flakes	Finishing seasoning

using temperature for flavorful and safe cooking

HOW TO MEASURE FOOD TEMPERATURE

Calibrate the thermometer, especially if it's new or it's been a long period of time.

Clean and dry the probe before use.

Insert the probe into the center or thickest part of the item, about 1 inch (2.5 cm) into the food on a digital thermometer, but do not let the probe exit the food. Avoid bones and cavities as they may give false readings. Test different areas of larger items, as areas can cook at different rates.

When measuring thinner food like steak or chops, either transfer the food to a plate or lift the food from the cooking surface and take the reading from the side of the food. If the probe touches the heated surface it will give high results.

Give the thermometer time to stabilize. It is taking average readings along the sensing part of the probe. Some thermometers can read as fast as two to three seconds, and others need more time.

SIMPLE WAYS TO CALIBRATE A THERMOMETER

Ice point method: Add cold water and ice to a drinking cup, and allow it to stabilize for a few minutes. Insert the probe into the center of the glass, only touching the ice water. Allow the temperature to stabilize. If it does not reach 32°F (0°C), press the "calibrate" button on the digital thermometer and set to 32°F (0°C), or turn dial-face thermometers to 32°F (0°C).

Boiling point method: Boil water to 212°F (100°C). Add to a glass measuring cup and insert the probe into the hot water. If it does not reach 212°F (100°C), press the "calibrate" button on the digital thermometer and set to 212°F (100°C), or turn dial-face thermometers to 212°F (100°C).

EASY WAYS TO KEEP FOOD SAFE DURING COOKING AND REHEATING

Storage: Store raw foods separate from cooked foods, vegetables or ready-to-eat items to avoid cross contamination. Raw foods are best stored in the bottom of the refrigerator.

Meal prep: Never use the same cutting board for cooked foods and raw foods, and do not place cooked foods on the same plate as raw foods if possible. Do not rinse meat or poultry with water as it could spread contamination in the sink. Do not reuse marinades; discard after use.

Thawing: Never thaw on the counter! Defrost frozen foods in the refrigerator or submerged under cool running water at 70°F (21°C). Do not allow the internal temperature of the food to exceed 40°F (4°C), or it will be at risk of harmful microbial growth. A microwave can also be used for thawing if cooking immediately.

Holding: Keep hot foods at 135°F (57°C). Cold foods should be held at 40°F (4°C) or below.

Serving: In hot weather above 90°F (32°C), do not let food sit out for more than one hour. Discard food left out for more than two hours. Refrigerate leftover foods within two hours. Cooling: The U.S. Food and Drug Administration (FDA) Food Code provides guidelines to cool hot foods from 135°F (57°C) to 70°F (21°C) within two hours, and 135°F (57°C) to 40°F (4°C) within six hours. Do not cool hot foods in the refrigerator, otherwise it can heat the area inside and cause a warmer environment for bacteria to grow.

Reheating: Quickly reheat foods to 165°F (74°C).

Cleaning: Wash dishes in warm water 110°F (43°C) with a detergent to remove debris and dry before storing. If possible, use a dishwasher to help further sanitize the dishes. Clean surfaces with disposable paper towels and an effective cleaner.

KNOW THE TEMPERATURE DANGER ZONE

The most important job in the food industry or cooking at home is to keep the food safe for people to eat. If you leave food out too long at room temperature, harmful bacteria such as *Staphylococcus aureus*, *Salmonella enteritidis*, *Escherichia coli O157:H7* and *Campylobacter* can grow to dangerous levels that can cause foodborne illness. According to the U.S. Food Safety and Inspection Service (FSIS), bacteria grow most rapidly in the range of temperatures between 40°F and 140°F (4.4°C and 60°C), the temperature danger zone, doubling in number in as little as 20 minutes. Harmful bacteria take four hours to grow enough to cause illness. Keep cold foods below 40°F (4.4°C), and hot foods above 140°F (60°C).

heat: the workhouse in the kitchen

Heat is a type of energy. The more present, the higher the temperature in the cooking process. Temperature has a huge role in how fast or slow molecules in water, air, food and materials move, therefore creating more or less heat. It's like a bumper car effect of faster molecules colliding with slower ones, in a chain effect to ultimately create heat. The heat generated in the process of cooking food affects the texture, taste, aroma and appearance of the ingredients. There are different ways that heat is generated and transferred to food in cooking. The most commonly used are conduction, convection and radiant heat, with the potential for a combination of these to occur throughout a cooking process. So next time your cookies burn, just blame the overabundance of energy!

TYPES OF HEAT TRANSFER

Conduction: When heat moves from the surface to the center of the food. Direct contact of heat from one source to another, which causes heat transfer. It can also occur between a heat source and a cooking vessel, then to a food. This also happens within the food itself when the heat is transferred from molecule to molecule. This is a relatively slower heat transfer process. Metals like aluminum and copper are good heat conductors, while water is a better conductor than air.

Convection: When heat is transferred from the heat of a liquid (hot oil or water) or gas (air in the oven) to the food. You can imagine the natural convection occurring in a large pot of soup. As the liquid warms from the burner heating the bottom of the pot, the molecules of liquid closer to the heat source warm up and rise, while cooler ones fall, creating a current of heat. If you want the soup to cook more quickly, add some mechanical convection by stirring the pot with a spoon.

Radiation: When a heat source emits high-energy waves, which are initially absorbed by the surface of the food. The food then finishes cooking on the inside by conduction. This method does not need physical contact with the heat source and food. For infrared radiant-heat cooking, high temperatures radiate from a heating element typically above and interact with the outside of the food. For example, the heating element in an oven used to broil a cheesy dish of lasagna to achieve a golden brown surface or toasting a piece of bread. One very quick and popular type of radiant heat cooking is microwaving. The water molecules in the food move quickly at the same time to generate heat. The radiation from a microwave oven has a much higher penetration depth than other methods (a few centimeters!), creating an extremely fast transfer of heat. No browning occurs in a microwave, but the food will be hot within minutes.

the importance of carryover cooking

As the heat generated from cooking moves from the surface of the food to the inside, heat transfer by convection will continue to cook the food, even when it's removed from the source of heat. This phenomenon is known as carryover cooking and can vary in degree depending on the type of food. This residual heat remaining in the food can be your worst enemy, or your best cooking buddy as long as you know how and when to control it. The chart below has suggested doneness temperatures for chicken, pork, fish, beef and lamb.

DONENESS TEMPERATURE FOR POULTRY, FISH AND MEAT

PROTEIN/ DONENESS	STOP COOKING WHEN TEMPERATURE REACHES	FINAL SERVING TEMPERATURE AFTER RESTING
Chicken: White Meat	160–165°F (71.1–73.9°C)	160-165°F (71.1–73.9°C)
Chicken: Dark Meat	175°F (79.4°C)	175°F (79.4°C)
Pork: Medium	140–145°F (60–62.8°C)	145-150°F (62.8–65.6°C)
Pork: Well-Done	150–155°F (65.6–68.3°C)	155-160°F (68.3–71.1°C)
Fish: Rare	110°F (43.3°C), tuna only	110°F (43.3°C)
Fish: Medium-Rare	125°F (51.7°C), tuna or salmon	125°F (51.7°C)
Fish: Medium	140°F (60°C), white-fleshed fish	140°F (60°C)
Beef & Lamb: Rare	115–120°F (46–48.9°C)	120-125 (48.9–51.7°C)
Beef & Lamb: Medium-Rare	120–125°F (48.9–51.7°C)	125-130°F (51.7–54.4°C)
Beef & Lamb: Medium	130–135°F (54.4–57.2°C)	135-140°F (57.2–60°C)
Beef & Lamb: Medium-Well	140–145°F (60°C–62.8°C)	145-150°F (62.8–65.6°C)
Beef & Lamb: Well-Done	150–155°F (65.6°C–68.3°C)	150-160°F (65.6–71.1°C)

how to choose the right oil for cooking

Selecting an oil depends on the cooking method and desired taste and texture outcome. The flavor of the oil is also a consideration; there are times you want a neutral taste versus a stronger presence in the food. It is important to know an oil's smoke point, the temperature at which oil begins to break down into free fatty acids and visibly produce smoke. Reaching this temperature can become unsafe and create undesirable flavors from the breakdown and release of a chemical called acrolein that gives burnt food its characteristic aroma and taste. Beyond this temperature you can reach the flash point, where volatiles are capable of being ignited. The amount of saturated fat determines how solid or liquid the fat will be at room temperature, the stability of the oil and mouth coating in the fried food. Deep-frying typically occurs between 325 and 375°F (163 and 191°C); above 400°F (204°C) the exterior can brown or even burn too quickly before the inside is cooked. For long frying or cooking times, choose an oil that has a smoke point higher than the recommended frying temperature, around 400°F (204°C). The higher the smoke point and refinement of the oil, the more applications available for cooking.

COMMON COOKING OILS AND SMOKE POINT TEMPERATURES

FAT/OIL	SMOKE POINT*	APPLICATION
Butter	300–350°F (149–177°C)	Sauté, quick pan-fry, baking, roasting
Extra-Virgin Olive Oil	325–410°F (163–210°C)	Sauté, finishing oil, dressings, marinades, baking
Coconut Oil	350–385°F (177–196°C)	Sauté, pan-fry, baking, roasting
Sesame Oil	350–410°F (177–210°C)	Sauté, small amount for stir-frying
Vegetable Shortening	360–410°F (180–210°C)	Baking, sauté
Lard	370°F (188°C)	Sauté, pan-fry, baking, roasting, deep-frying
Grapeseed Oil	390°F (195°F)	Sauté, pan-fry, baking, roasting, dressings
Canola Oil	400–450°F (204–230°C)	Searing, sauté, pan-fry, stir-frying, baking, roasting, grilling, deep-frying
Vegetable Oil**	400–450°F (204–230°C)	Searing, sauté, pan-fry, stir-frying, baking, roasting, grilling, deep-frying
Margarine	410–430°F (210–221°C)	Sauté
Corn Oil	410–450°F (210–232°C)	Searing, sauté, pan-fry, baking, roasting, grilling, deep-frying
Light/Refined Olive Oil	425–465°F (218–241°C)	Sauté, pan-fry, grilling, baking, roasting
Sunflower Oil	440°F (227°C)	Searing, sauté, pan-fry, baking, roasting, grilling, deep-frying
Peanut Oil	440–450°F (227–232°C)	Searing, sauté, pan-fry, stir-frying, baking, roasting, grilling, deep-frying
Clarified Butter	450°F (232°C)	Sauté, pan-fry, baking, roasting
Soybean Oil	450–495°F (232–257°C)	Searing, sauté, pan-fry, baking, roasting, grilling, deep-frying
Safflower	510°F (265°C)	Searing, sauté, pan-fry, stir-frying, baking, roasting, grilling, deep-frying
Avocado Oil, Refined	520–570°F (271–299°C)	Sauté, pan-fry, baking, roasting, grilling, dressings

*This data was compiled from a variety of sources and is meant to be used as a guideline. The reaction temperatures will range depending on the exact type and ratio of fatty acids present and on the brand/manufacturer of the product. The smoke point of fats and oils varies from sample to sample depending on how it has been refined and processed.

**Vegetable oil is typically a combination of different oils, like corn or sunflower, giving a range of smoke points depending on the brand.

key tips for success in the kitchen

· Use indicated time as a guideline, not an exact measurement of doneness. Use all five senses to listen, see, smell, touch and taste what is occurring during the process and determine when the food is ready.

· When seasoning foods with salt, sprinkle about 12 inches (30.5 cm) above the item for even distribution.

· Calibrate your equipment. Do not assume your oven is preheated to the proper temperature. Use an oven thermometer to better gauge how your oven is operating. If it runs too hot or cold, this will affect your recipes. Calibrate your oven and handheld thermometer occasionally as well to make sure things are functioning properly.

· Gain control in your kitchen by using tools designed to provide insightful data. An instant-read digital thermometer, oven thermometer and digital kitchen scale are essential to reduce variability and are affordable items.

· Pay attention to the temperature of ingredients before using them, and follow the recipe instructions. Room temperature is about 70°F (21°C); chilled is 35 to 40°F (2 to 4°C); frozen is 0 to 10°F (-17 to -12°C). There is a scientific reason to incorporate ingredients when called out for a specific result.

· When you need eggs at room temperature, this can quickly be done by adding the whole eggs in a warm bowl of water for about 5 minutes. This is important when making baked products.

· Softened butter is between 60 and 68°F (16 and 20°C), and takes about 1 hour at room temperature. Use a thermometer to gauge, and do not be tempted to microwave to speed up the process. The temperature of butter will affect cake and cookie texture.

· If available, use unsalted stocks and broths so that you have more control over the salt level in the finished dish.

· Be curious!

conversions & equivalents

A helpful reference guide to converting U.S. and metric cooking measurements used in everyday cooking, baking and recipes developed in this book. All conversions are approximate and rounded to the nearest whole number. The U.S. system uses ounces and pounds (weight), cups (volume) and inches or feet (length). The metric system used around the world uses grams (weight), liter (volume) and meter (length).

common volume and weight equivalents*

Dash = ⅛ teaspoon

3 teaspoons = 1 tablespoon (0.5 ounce)

2 tablespoons = 1 fluid ounce

4 tablespoons = ¼ cup (2 fluid ounces)

16 tablespoons = 1 cup (8 fluid ounces)

2 cups = 1 pint (16 fluid ounces)

4 cups = 1 quart (32 fluid ounces)

2 pints = 1 quart (32 fluid ounces)

4 quarts = 1 gallon (128 fluid ounces)

1 gram = 0.035 ounces

1 ounce = 28.35 grams (rounded down to 28 or up to 30 for convenience)

454 grams = 1 pound

2.2 pounds = 1 kilogram (1,000 grams)

1 teaspoon = 5 milliliters

1 cup = 0.24 liters

1 quart = 0.95 liters

1 gallon = 3.80 liters

*In U.S. measurements, liquids are measured in fluid ounces (volume) and dry ingredients in ounces (weight).

MEASUREMENT	KNOWN	MULTIPLY BY	CONVERT TO
Mass (weight)	ounces	28.5	grams
	pounds	0.45	kilograms
	grams	0.035	ounces
	kilograms	2.2	pounds
Volume (capacity)	teaspoons	5.0	milliliters
	tablespoons	15.0	milliliters
	fluid ounces	29.57	milliliters
	cups	0.24	liters
	pints	0.47	liters
	quarts	0.95	liters
	gallons	3.785	liters
	milliliters	0.034	fluid ounces
Temperature	Fahrenheit	5/9 (subtract 32 first)	Celsius
	Celsius	9/5 (then add 32)	Fahrenheit

VOLUME CONVERSIONS

U.S. MEASURES	METRIC MEASURES
1 teaspoon*	5 milliliters
2 teaspoons	10 milliliters
1 tablespoon	15 milliliters
2 tablespoons	30 milliliters
¼ cup	60 milliliters
⅓ cup	80 milliliters
½ cup	120 milliliters
¾ cup	180 milliliters
1 cup	240 milliliters
1¼ cups	300 milliliters
1½ cups	360 milliliters
2 cups	480 milliliters
2½ cups	600 milliliters
3 cups	720 milliliters
4 cups (1 quart)	0.946 liter
1.06 quarts	1 liter
4 quarts (1 gallon)	3.8 liters

* 1 teaspoon (4.929 milliliters) has been rounded to 5 milliliters.

U.S. MEASURES (OUNCES)	METRIC MEASURES (GRAMS)
½	14
¾	21
1*	28
2	57
3	85
4 (¼ pound)	113
5	142
6	170
7	198
8 (½ pound)	227
9	255
10	283
12	340
16 (1 pound)	454

*1 ounce (28.349 grams) has been rounded down to 28 grams, often 30 grams for baking.

CONVERSIONS FOR COMMONLY USED BAKING INGREDIENTS

INGREDIENT	TABLESPOONS	CUPS	OUNCES	GRAMS
Egg, large	N/A	N/A	2	57
Baking powder, baking soda	1	¹⁄₁₆	0.4	12
Cream of tartar	1	¹⁄₁₆	0.4	12
Cornstarch	1	¹⁄₁₆	0.3	9
Gelatin, powdered	1	¹⁄₁₆	0.1	1
Table salt	1	¹⁄₁₆	0.6	18
Kosher salt	1	¹⁄₁₆	0.5	15
Dry spices, ground	1	¹⁄₁₆	0.2	6
Active dry yeast	1	¹⁄₁₆	0.4	12
Fresh compressed yeast	1	¹⁄₁₆	0.5	15
Vanilla extract	1	¹⁄₁₆	0.5	15
All-purpose flour	16	1	5	142
Cake Flour	16	1	4	113
Whole-wheat flour	16	1	5½	156

(continued)

INGREDIENT	TABLESPOONS	CUPS	OUNCES	GRAMS
Granulated sugar	16	1	7	198
Brown sugar (packed)	16	1	7	198
Confectioners' sugar	16	1	3	85
Butter (1 stick, [8 tablespoons])	8	½	4	113
Shortening (solid)	16	1	7.1	192
Coconut oil	16	1	7.7	218
Honey, corn syrup, molasses	16	1	12	384

A HANDY VISUAL GUIDE FOR CONVERTING LIQUID VOLUMES

G = Gallon (128 ounces)

Q = Quart (32 ounces)

P = Pint (16 ounces)

C = Cup (8 ounces)

1 gallon = 4 quarts = 8 pints = 16 cups

COMMON TEMPERATURE CONVERSIONS & KEY INDICATORS FOR COOKING & BAKING

FAHRENHEIT (°F)	CELSIUS (°C)	INDICATOR
32	0	Freezing point of water
34	1.1	Yeast inactive for baking
40	4.4	Start of temperature danger zone*
75	23.9	Optimal yeast fermentation for baking (75–95°F; [23.9–35°C])
100	37.8	Rehydrate active dry yeast (100–110°F; [37.8–43.3°C])
120	48.8	Liquid (120–130°F; [48.8–54.4°C]) to add to instant dry yeast
138	58.9	Yeast die, will not be active for baking
140	60	End of temperature danger zone*, egg whites begin to set
144	62.2	Whole eggs begin to set
150	65.6	Egg yolks begin to set, cheesecake doneness temperature

FAHRENHEIT (°F)	CELSIUS (°C)	INDICATOR
160	71.1	Poaching temperatures (160–180°F; [71.1–82.2°C]), collagen begins to dissolve to gelatin (160–170°F; [71.1–76.7°C])
165	73.9	Safe internal temperatures for whole and ground poultry
170	76.7	Doneness for baked custard (170–175°F;[76.7–79.4°C])
170	76.7	Pastry cream or lemon curds (170–180°F; [76.7–82.2°C])
185	85	Simmering temperatures (185–206°F; [85–96.7°C]), optimum slow cooker liquid cooking temperature
190	87.8	Doneness for sweet yeast bread (190–200°F; [87.8–93.3°C])
200	93.3	Doneness for lean yeast bread (200–210°F; [93.3–98.9°C])
203	95	Maximum swelling of cornstarch for thickening
210	98.9	Doneness of cakes (dependent on type)
212	100	Boiling point of water
300	149	Maillard Reaction (browning occurs)
320	160	Sugars begin to caramelize (320–350°F; [160–177°C])
325	162.8	Oil frying temperature (325–375°F; [162.8–191°C])
350	177	Common baking temperature
375	191	Common baking temperature
400	204	Common baking or roasting temperature
425	218	Common baking or roasting temperature
450	232	Common roasting temperature
475	246	Common roasting temperature
500	260	Common broiling temperature (500–550°F; [260–278.8°C])
550	278.8	Maximum oven temperature

* Keep cold foods below 40°F (4.4°C) and hot foods above 140°F (60°C). See page 201 for more information on the temperature danger zone.

acknowledgments

I never imagined that a passion for food could lead me into so many fascinating, challenging and blissful experiences. I've learned so much and feel immensely grateful that I've been given the opportunity to explore and play, pushing my boundaries and making me hungry for more. This cookbook is a dream come true, a little piece of my heart and soul that I will always cherish.

My life journey has been filled with incredible people who have supported me in so many different aspects along the way. Whether big or small, silly or serious, my squad is the best a girl could ask for, cheering me on no matter what.

To the Page Street Publishing team, thank you for your wonder and interest in the world of culinary science. From the first email communication and me thinking "Is this too good to be true?" to each milestone bringing this cookbook to fruition, you've given me the chance to share my knowledge and art with others. Thank you, Will, for craving a science spin on food. To Elizabeth my incredible editor, allowing me to craft my cookbook vision. Rosie, for designing and bringing the beautiful visual elements together. All of you have made this process seamless and fun!

The amazing Anne Watson, photographer extraordinaire! Thank you for bringing my recipes to life with your beautiful styling and capturing the most delicious moments. I've never had so much fun cooking, collaborating and shooting food. Our bond over '90s hip-hop and R&B, candor and humor made each moment unforgettable. I couldn't wait to hear what your next idea would be, especially when we were both telepathically connected. I'm incredibly impressed by your grit, pursuit for the perfect shot, positivity, mentorship and openness while achieving our food story. #CookbookDreamTeam

Ginny Erickson, your surfaces were the perfect palette for each recipe. Thank you for sharing your craft; it was so much fun creating food scenes with your art. Naomi Robinson, thank you for your food-styling tips and allowing me to raid your prop treasure chest! Your unique collection of dishes and textiles brought interest and playfulness to each photo.

My dear readers, your interest and willingness to learn pushes me each day to create and share. Your questions challenge me and feedback motivates me. Thank you so much for your support and desire to explore in the kitchen, and allowing me to guide you.

To my food science and culinary school teachers and mentors. Your dedication to helping others grow in their passions and careers is incredibly inspiring. I relished every moment that I had the chance to learn from you.

To my friends, you have each brought something extraordinary to my life. Whether it was a bond over food, babies, hikes, time in the kitchen or in the lab, a shared culinary or science class or living the blog life together, I am so grateful every day to have you in my community!

To my soul sisters, Kristina and Jasmin. You ground me, my confidantes and forever Bonaire Bakery girls. No matter the distance, I know I can give you a call to make my day so much better. Thank you for always being real and encouraging me to live my dreams. To Patrice, I will never forget sitting next to you in the front row on the first day of Food Science 101. My roomie and fellow science geek. I never would have survived college without our Michael Jackson dance study breaks and trips to the farmers market. To Karen, our bond for the Bay and weekly steak, chicken cacciatore and enchilada nights as we learned to be grown-ups is priceless. Thank you, ladies, for being my best friends and the strongest women I know!

To the Yee family, our constant pursuit of yumminess is undeniable. When we are together, it's always the important question of "Where should we eat?" and sharing new places to try. Our family has fueled my obsession for food. There are so many great memories we've created together and I can't wait to see what the next food stop will be! Thank you, Dad and Lynne, for your unconditional love and support. Blandon, Mel, Syd, Svet, Jacob, Aidan, Zachary and Hudson, my food soulmates, cheerleaders, Disneyland team and babysitters. Bee and Syd, you are always keeping a watchful eye and encouraging my growth. I know Mom would be proud. My cousins Melissa, Michaela, Michael and Taryn, the original Bashers club. Always using our imagination to create the next game or adventure, never lose that desire to play and dream. My uncles Brian and Daniel and aunts Lynette and Carol, thank for being extraordinary role models.

To my incredible God family, thank you for your love and care. To the Gavin and Puglisi families, your Irish/Italian heritage and culinary teachings have found a special and permanent place in our kitchen. Thank you for your continuous encouragement! My grandparents, Bing, Kam, Cheung and Fay, your bravery and hope to give your family a better life and future is inspiring. I will never forget my roots and your influence on our lives.

To my love bug, James. You have changed me in so many ways. Nothing is better than being your mommy and seeing you grow. My heart fills every time you ask to help in the kitchen, or eat something I've made. You remind me to take breaks and enjoy life's precious moments. Your comic relief always has the best timing, making Mommy and Daddy laugh when we need it the most. You helped me so much when I was recipe testing (especially the dessert section), always looking forward to baking with mommy after school, and spending hours patiently with me writing each chapter. Always remember to be strong, brave, smart, kind and happy. I know you will do something good in this world. I love you so much!

To Olivia. You were in my belly as I wrote this cookbook, I could always tell you liked a recipe when you would kick. Thank you for being my taste tester and coming along for this adventure. Now that you are here, your sweet personality and undeniable strength makes us proud. Your smile lights up a room and our hearts!

To my mom, Janet. If only you could be here to see how our family has grown. Your compassion, love, smile and kindness still shine through each of us. There is not a day that goes by that I don't think of you, wishing for even a few moments to just embrace you or tell you everything on my mind. I will be strong for you and take nothing for granted. Thank you for shining down on me, and being my guiding light.

To my talented husband, Jason. Since the moment I met you, it has been a nonstop adventure. You are the most unselfish and loving person I have ever met. Your integrity never wavers and your relentless pursuit to help your family thrive is remarkable. You challenge and push me to reach my full potential, and to be fearless in the next endeavor. You have taught me how to take risks and not be afraid to try something new. We know that the path we have chosen together is not easy, but we like the thrill. Even through the hard work, dedication, sacrifice and tears, I wouldn't have it any other way as long as I have you by my side. Thank you for being an incredible father and husband; we all love you so much. Home is where you are, babe, so let's keep the adventure going wherever it may take us!

about the author

Jessica Gavin is the charmingly geeky but approachable cook, photographer and scientist behind the popular website, JessicaGavin.com. She uses her superpowers, which include degrees and certifications in agriculture, culinary science and food science, to help her readers get smart about getting dinner on the table.

A teacher at heart, Jessica loves nothing more than unraveling the science behind better, healthier cooking and sharing that know-how with her readers, on her site and in her videos. Her work has been featured on Food Network, The Kitchn, BuzzFeed and more. She lives in Orange County, California, with her husband, Jason, and their two young children, James and Olivia. When she's not in the kitchen, she's likely on the hunt for the world's best, butteriest croissant. Healthy may be the norm in her house, but who doesn't love an exception to the rule!

index

A

Aioli, Lemon Basil, 142–144

Almond Green Beans, Orange Glazed, 73

Almond Muffins, Blueberry, 160

Andouille Sausage and Shrimp Gumbo, 98

Apple Cinnamon Rolls, Salted Caramel, 181–182

apples, in Pork Pappardelle Pasta, 113

Apricot Glaze, 58

arrowroot, 137–138, 149

Asparagus Wrapped in Bacon, Caramelized, 57

Avocado Yogurt Lime Sauce, Blackened Salmon Tacos with, 19

avocados, in Grilled Corn Salad with Cilantro Lime Dressing, 62

B

Bacon, Caramelized Asparagus Wrapped in, 57

bacon, in Chicken Carbonara Pasta, 81–82

baking, 16–17

Mexican Quinoa-Stuffed Sweet Potatoes, 45

baking ammonia/baking powder/baking soda, 154–155

Balsamic Roasted Pork Tenderloin, 34

Banana Bread, Chocolate Chip, 157

Barbecue Sauce, Pulled Pork with, 128

basil, in Pan-Seared Halibut with Tomato Basil Couscous, 41

Basil Aioli, Lemon, 142–144

bean sprouts, in Chicken Egg Rolls, 27–29

beans, black, in Turkey Chili with Quinoa, 123

beans, garbanzo

Indian Cauliflower Curry, 104

Moroccan Lamb Stew, 103

beans, green

Buddha's Braised Tofu and Vegetables, 110

Minestrone Soup, 74

Orange-Glazed Almond Green Beans, 73

Tempura Shrimp and Vegetables, 47–48

beans, kidney, in Minestrone Soup, 74

beans, pinto, in Turkey Chili with Quinoa, 123

beef

Grandma's Ginger Beef Stew, 107

Grandma's Italian Meatballs, 133

Pan-Seared Ribeye with Miso Butter, 30

Red Wine–Braised Short Ribs, 114

Soy Marinated Flank Steak, 65

Beer-Braised Chicken and Vegetables, 109

beets, in Roasted Root Vegetables, 44

bell peppers

Andouille Sausage and Shrimp Gumbo, 98

Kung Pao Chicken, 127

Red Curry Lemongrass Chicken Meatballs, 99

Turkey Chili with Quinoa, 123

Biscuits, Flaky Country Buttermilk, 163–164

Blackened Salmon Tacos with Avocado Yogurt Lime Sauce, 19

Blender Hollandaise Sauce, 139

Blueberry Almond Muffins, 160

boiling, 68–69

Chicken Carbonara Pasta, 81–82

Chinese Sticky Rice, 78

Creamy Macaroni and Cheese, 84

Fluffy Roasted Garlic Mashed Potatoes, 87

Orange-Glazed Almond Green Beans, 73

bok choy, in Buddha's Braised Tofu and Vegetables, 110

braising, 94–95

Beer-Braised Chicken and Vegetables, 109

Buddha's Braised Tofu and Vegetables, 110

Pork Pappardelle Pasta, 113

Red Curry Lemongrass Chicken Meatballs, 99

Red Wine–Braised Short Ribs, 114

breads, quick

Blueberry Almond Muffins, 160

Chocolate Chip Banana Bread, 157

Flaky Country Buttermilk Biscuits, 163–164

Nutella Cheesecake Brownies, 165–166

breads, yeast

Chinese Steamed Custard Buns, 183–184

Hawaiian Sweet Rolls, 191

Italian Breadsticks, 187

Salted Caramel Apple Cinnamon Rolls, 181–182

Whole Wheat Hamburger Buns, 188

broiling, 16–17

Brownies, Nutella Cheesecake, 165–166

browning/searing, 16

Brussels sprouts, in Roasted Root Vegetables, 44

Buddha's Braised Tofu and Vegetables, 110

buns/rolls

Chinese Steamed Custard Buns, 183–184

Hawaiian Sweet Rolls, 191

Salted Caramel Apple Cinnamon Rolls, 181–182

Whole Wheat Hamburger Buns, 188

Burgers, Grilled Salmon, 61

butternut squash

Grandma's Ginger Beef Stew, 107

Turkey Chili with Quinoa, 123

C

cabbage
    Buddha's Braised Tofu and Vegetables, 110
    Chicken Egg Rolls, 27–29
    Fish Katsu with Asian Slaw, 50
Caesar Salad Dressing, Creamy, 141
Cake, Classic Pineapple Upside Down, 170–172
Cake, Strawberries and Cream, 173–175
capers
    Grilled Salmon Burgers, 61
    Pan-Seared Scallops with Garlic Sauce, 24–26
Caramel Apple Cinnamon Rolls, Salted, 181–182
caramelization, of foods, 19, 44
Caramelized Asparagus Wrapped in Bacon, 57
Carbonara Pasta, Chicken, 81–82
carrots
    Beer-Braised Chicken and Vegetables, 109
    Crispy Vegetable Fritters, 38
    Fish Katsu with Asian Slaw, 50
    Grandma's Ginger Beef Stew, 107
    Herb-Roasted Chicken with Vegetables, 54
    Minestrone Soup, 74
    Moroccan Lamb Stew, 103
    Pork Pappardelle Pasta, 113
    Roasted Root Vegetables, 44
cauliflower, in Red Wine Braised Short Ribs, 114
Cauliflower Curry, Indian, 104
Cedar-Planked Mahi Mahi with Pineapple Salsa, 49
cheese
    Chicken Carbonara Pasta, 81–82
    Creamy Macaroni and Cheese, 84
    Mushroom Risotto, 77
    Nutella Cheesecake Brownies, 165–166
chemical leavening, 154–155

Blueberry Almond Muffins, 160
Chewy Cranberry Oatmeal Cookies, 169
Chocolate Chip Banana Bread, 157
Classic Pineapple Upside Down Cake, 170–172
Flaky Country Buttermilk Biscuits, 163–164
Lemon-Raspberry Cream Scones, 159
Nutella Cheesecake Brownies, 165–166
Strawberries and Cream Cake, 173–175
Chewy Cranberry Oatmeal Cookies, 169
chicken
    Beer-Braised Chicken and Vegetables, 109
    Chicken Carbonara Pasta, 81–82
    Chinese Chicken Lettuce Wraps, 23
    Herb-Roasted Chicken with Vegetables, 54
    Honey Hoisin Garlic Chicken, 121
    Kung Pao Chicken, 127
    Moroccan-Spiced Chicken Skewers with Apricot Glaze, 58
    Pan-Roasted Greek Chicken and Vegetables, 33
    Red Curry Lemongrass Chicken Meatballs, 99
    Sticky Asian Chicken Wings, 42
    Yucatán-Style Chicken with Pickled Onions, 124
Chicken Egg Rolls, 27–29
Chicken Udon Soup, 72
chili peppers
    Blackened Salmon Tacos with Avocado Yogurt Lime Sauce, 19
    Kung Pao Chicken, 127
    See also jalapeño peppers
Chili with Quinoa, Turkey, 123
Chinese Chicken Lettuce Wraps, 23
Chinese Steamed Custard Buns, 183–184
Chinese Sticky Rice, 78
Chipotle Sauce, 45
chocolate, in Nutella Cheesecake Brownies, 165–166

Chocolate Chip Banana Bread, 157
cilantro, in Red Curry Lemongrass Chicken Meatballs, 62
Cinnamon Rolls, Salted Caramel Apple, 181–182
Citrus Herb Vinaigrette, 145
Classic Pineapple Upside Down Cake, 170–172
coconut milk
    Red Curry Lemongrass Chicken Meatballs, 99
    Thai Green Curry with Shrimp, 97
conduction and convection cooking, 16–17, 202
conversions/equivalents, 207–211
Cookies, Chewy Cranberry Oatmeal, 169
corn
    Beer-Braised Chicken and Vegetables, 109
    Grilled Corn Salad with Cilantro Lime Dressing, 62
    Turkey Chili with Quinoa, 123
cornstarch, 137–138, 149
    in Asian sauces, 107
    in dumpling filling, 91
    in tempura batter, 47
couscous, in Moroccan Lamb Stew, 103
Couscous, Pan-Seared Halibut with Tomato Basil, 41
Cranberry Oatmeal Cookies, Chewy, 169
Creamy Caesar Salad Dressing, 141
Creamy Macaroni and Cheese, 84
Creamy Miso Sauce, 50
Crispy Roasted Potatoes, 53
Crispy Vegetable Fritters, 38
cucumbers, in Fish Katsu with Asian Slaw, 50
culinary arts/science, defined, 13
currants, in Moroccan Lamb Stew, 103
Curry, Indian Cauliflower, 104
Curry Lemongrass Chicken Meatballs, Red, 99
Curry with Shrimp, Thai Green, 97
Custard Buns, Chinese Steamed, 183–184

D

dairy-free recipes

    Balsamic Roasted Pork Tenderloin, 34

    Beer-Braised Chicken and Vegetables, 109

    Buddha's Braised Tofu and Vegetables, 110

    Cedar-Planked Mahi Mahi with Pineapple Salsa, 49

    Chicken Egg Rolls, 27–29

    Chicken Udon Soup, 72

    Chinese Sticky Rice, 78

    Crispy Roasted Potatoes, 53

    Five-Minute Teriyaki Sauce, 150

    Grandma's Ginger Beef Stew, 107

    Grilled Corn Salad with Cilantro Lime Dressing, 62

    Grilled Salmon Burgers, 61

    Honey Hoisin Garlic Chicken, 121

    Italian Seafood Stew, 100

    Kung Pao Chicken, 127

    Lemon Basil Aioli, 142–144

    Mediterranean Steamed Mussels, 83

    Moroccan Lamb Stew, 103

    Moroccan-Spiced Chicken Skewers with Apricot Glaze, 58

    Orange-Glazed Almond Green Beans, 73

    Oven-Roasted Rack of Lamb with Mint Gremolata, 37

    Pan-Seared Halibut with Tomato Basil Couscous, 41

    Pulled Pork with Barbecue Sauce, 128

    Red Curry Lemongrass Chicken Meatballs, 99

    Red Wine–Braised Short Ribs, 114

    Roasted Root Vegetables, 44

    Shumai Chinese Steamed Dumplings, 91

    Soy Marinated Flank Steak, 65

    Sticky Asian Chicken Wings, 42

    Stir-Fry Sauce, 149

    Strawberry Balsamic Vinaigrette, 147

    Tempura Shrimp and Vegetables, 47–48

    Thai Green Curry with Shrimp, 97

    Turkey Chili with Quinoa, 123

    Wok-Fired Orange Garlic Shrimp, 20

    Yucatán-Style Chicken with Pickled Onions, 124

deep-frying, 17

    Chicken Egg Rolls, 27–29

    Sticky Asian Chicken Wings, 42

    Tempura Shrimp and Vegetables, 47–48

desserts

    Chewy Cranberry Oatmeal Cookies, 169

    Classic Pineapple Upside Down Cake, 170–172

    Nutella Cheesecake Brownies, 165–166

    Strawberries and Cream Cake, 173–175

dressings, salad

    Cilantro Lime Dressing, 62

    Citrus Herb Vinaigrette, 145

    Creamy Caesar Salad Dressing, 141

    Lemon Basil Aioli, 142–144

    Strawberry Balsamic Vinaigrette, 147

dry-heat cooking, 16–17

Dumplings, Shumai Chinese Steamed, 91

E

Easy Pan Sauce, 148

Egg Rolls, Chicken, 27–29

eggplant, in Thai Green Curry with Shrimp, 97

eggs, in Chinese Steamed Custard Buns, 183–184

Eggs Benedict, 71

emulsification, 136–137

    Blender Hollandaise Sauce, 139

    Citrus Herb Vinaigrette, 145

    Creamy Caesar Salad Dressing, 141

    Lemon Basil Aioli, 142–144

    Strawberry Balsamic Vinaigrette, 147

English muffins, in Eggs Benedict, 71

equivalents/conversions, 207–211

F

fennel, in Roasted Root Vegetables, 44

fish

    Blackened Salmon Tacos with Avocado Yogurt Lime Sauce, 19

    Cedar-Planked Mahi Mahi with Pineapple Salsa, 49

    Fish Katsu with Asian Slaw, 50

    Grilled Salmon Burgers, 61

    Italian Seafood Stew, 100

    Pan-Seared Halibut with Tomato Basil Couscous, 41

Five-Minute Teriyaki Sauce, 150

Flaky Country Buttermilk Biscuits, 163–164

flour, types, 156, 188

Fluffy Roasted Garlic Mashed Potatoes, 87

food safety, 201

food science, defined, 13

food temperatures, 200–201, 203, 210–211

freezer-friendly recipes

    Andouille Sausage and Shrimp Gumbo, 98

    Blueberry Almond Muffins, 160

    Chicken Egg Rolls, 27–29

    Flaky Country Buttermilk Biscuits, 163–164

    Grandma's Ginger Beef Stew, 107

    Grandma's Italian Meatballs, 133

    Indian Cauliflower Curry, 104

    Minestrone Soup, 74

    Turkey Chili with Quinoa, 123

    Whole Wheat Hamburger Buns, 188

Fritters, Crispy Vegetable, 38

G

garlic

    Fluffy Roasted Garlic Mashed Potatoes, 87

    Honey Hoisin Garlic Chicken, 121

    Lemon Basil Aioli, 142–144

    Pan-Seared Scallops with Garlic Sauce, 24–26

Wok-Fired Orange Garlic Shrimp, 20

Ginger Beef Stew, Grandma's, 107

gluten-free recipes

    Balsamic Roasted Pork Tenderloin, 34

    Blackened Salmon Tacos with Avocado Yogurt Lime Sauce, 19

    Caramelized Asparagus Wrapped in Bacon, 57

    Cedar-Planked Mahi Mahi with Pineapple Salsa, 49

    Chicken Carbonara Pasta, 81–82

    Crispy Roasted Potatoes, 53

    Five-Minute Teriyaki Sauce, 150

    Fluffy Roasted Garlic Mashed Potatoes, 87

    Grilled Corn Salad with Cilantro Lime Dressing, 62

    Herb-Roasted Chicken with Vegetables, 54

    Honey Hoisin Garlic Chicken, 121

    Indian Cauliflower Curry, 104

    Italian Seafood Stew, 100

    Kung Pao Chicken, 127

    Moroccan-Spiced Chicken Skewers with Apricot Glaze, 58

    Mushroom Risotto, 77

    Orange-Glazed Almond Green Beans, 73

    Oven-Roasted Rack of Lamb with Mint Gremolata, 37

    Pan-Roasted Greek Chicken and Vegetables, 33

    Pan-Seared Ribeye with Miso Butter, 30

    Pan-Seared Scallops with Garlic Sauce, 24–26

    Pork Pappardelle Pasta, 113

    Pulled Pork with Barbecue Sauce, 128

    Red Curry Lemongrass Chicken Meatballs, 99

    Roasted Root Vegetables, 44

    Soy Marinated Flank Steak, 65

    Thai Green Curry with Shrimp, 97

    Turkey Chili with Quinoa, 123

    Wok-Fired Orange Garlic Shrimp, 20

Yucatán-Style Chicken with Pickled Onions, 124

Grandma's Ginger Beef Stew, 107

Grandma's Italian Meatballs, 133

Greek Chicken and Vegetables, Pan-Roasted, 33

Gremolata, Mint, 37

grilling, 16–17

    Cedar-Planked Mahi Mahi with Pineapple Salsa, 49

    Grilled Corn Salad with Cilantro Lime Dressing, 62

    Grilled Salmon Burgers, 61

    Moroccan-Spiced Chicken Skewers with Apricot Glaze, 58

    Soy Marinated Flank Steak, 65

Gumbo, Andouille Sausage and Shrimp, 98

H

Halibut with Tomato Basil Couscous, Pan-Seared, 41

Hamburger Buns, Whole Wheat, 188

Hawaiian Sweet Rolls, 191

Hawaiian-Style Pork Ribs, 130

Herb-Roasted Chicken with Vegetables, 54

Hollandaise Sauce, Blender, 139

Honey Hoisin Garlic Chicken, 121

I

Indian Cauliflower Curry, 104

Italian Breadsticks, 187

Italian Seafood Stew, 100

J

jalapeño peppers

    Cedar-Planked Mahi Mahi with Pineapple Salsa, 49

    Grilled Corn Salad with Cilantro Lime Dressing, 62

    Mexican Quinoa-Stuffed Sweet Potatoes, 45

    Red Curry Lemongrass Chicken Meatballs, 99

    Turkey Chili with Quinoa, 123

K

kale

    Crispy Vegetable Fritters, 38

    Eggs Benedict, 71

Katsu with Asian Slaw, Fish, 50

Kung Pao Chicken, 127

L

Lamb Stew, Moroccan, 103

Lamb with Mint Gremolata, Oven Roasted Rack of, 37

leavening, chemical, 154–155

leavening, yeast, 178–179

leeks, in Italian Seafood Stew, 100

Lemon Basil Aioli, 142–144

lemongrass, in Thai Green Curry with Shrimp, 97

Lemongrass Chicken Meatballs, Red Curry, 99

Lemon-Raspberry Cream Scones, 159

Lettuce Wraps, Chinese Chicken, 23

Lobster Sliders, 88

long beans, in Buddha's Braised Tofu and Vegetables, 110

M

Macaroni and Cheese, Creamy, 84

Mahi Mahi with Pineapple Salsa, Cedar-Planked, 49

Maillard reaction, 16

marinating, meat, 58, 65

measuring, food temperatures, 200–201, 210–211

measuring, ingredients, 198, 207–210

meat

    braising, 94–95

    browning/searing, 16

    collagen, 94

    marinating, 58, 65

    roasting, 16

    simmering, 68

    slow cooking, 119

    stewing, 94–95

Meatballs, Grandma's Italian, 133

Meatballs, Red Curry Lemongrass Chicken, 99

Mediterranean Steamed Mussels, 83

Mexican Quinoa-Stuffed Sweet Potatoes, 45

Minestrone Soup, 74

Mint Gremolata, 37

Miso Butter, 30

Miso Sauce, Creamy, 50

moist-heat cooking, 68–69

Moroccan Lamb Stew, 103

Moroccan-Spiced Chicken Skewers with Apricot Glaze, 58

Muffins, Blueberry Almond, 160

mushrooms

    Balsamic Roasted Pork Tenderloin, 34

    Beer-Braised Chicken and Vegetables, 109

    Buddha's Braised Tofu and Vegetables, 110

    Chicken Udon Soup, 72

    Chinese Chicken Lettuce Wraps, 23

    Chinese Sticky Rice, 78

    Kung Pao Chicken, 127

    Mushroom Risotto, 77

    Red Wine–Braised Short Ribs, 114

    Shumai Chinese Steamed Dumplings, 91

mussels, in Italian Seafood Stew, 100

Mussels, Mediterranean Steamed, 83

N

Nutella Cheesecake Brownies, 165–166

nuts. See pecans; walnuts

O

Oatmeal Cookies, Chewy Cranberry, 169

oils, cooking, 204–205

okra, in Thai Green Curry with Shrimp, 98

olives

    Moroccan Lamb Stew, 103

    Pan-Seared Halibut with Tomato Basil Couscous, 41

one-pan/one-pot meals

    Beer-Braised Chicken and Vegetables, 109

    Buddha's Braised Tofu and Vegetables, 110

    Chinese Chicken Lettuce Wraps, 23

    Mediterranean Steamed Mussels, 83

    Minestrone Soup, 74

    Mushroom Risotto, 77

    Pan-Roasted Greek Chicken and Vegetables, 33

    Pan-Seared Scallops with Garlic Sauce, 24–26

    Wok-Fired Orange Garlic Shrimp, 20

Onions, Pickled, 124

Orange Garlic Shrimp, Wok-Fired, 20

Orange-Glazed Almond Green Beans, 73

Oven-Roasted Rack of Lamb with Mint Gremolata, 37

P

pan-frying, 17

    Crispy Vegetable Fritters, 38

    Pan-Seared Halibut with Tomato Basil Couscous, 41

Pan-Roasted Greek Chicken and Vegetables, 33

Pan-Seared Halibut with Tomato Basil Couscous, 41

Pan-Seared Ribeye with Miso Butter, 30

Pan-Seared Scallops with Garlic Sauce, 24–26

pasta

    Chicken Carbonara Pasta, 81–82

    Chicken Udon Soup, 72

    Creamy Macaroni and Cheese, 84

    Minestrone Soup, 74

    Pork Pappardelle Pasta, 113

pecans

    Chewy Cranberry Oatmeal Cookies, 169

    Salted Caramel Apple Cinnamon Rolls, 181–182

pineapple/pineapple juice

    Classic Pineapple Upside Down Cake, 170–172

    Hawaiian Sweet Rolls, 191

    Pineapple Salsa, 49

poaching, 68–69

    Chicken Udon Soup, 72

    Eggs Benedict, 71

pork

    Balsamic Roasted Pork Tenderloin, 34

    Chinese Sticky Rice, 78

    Hawaiian-Style Pork Ribs, 130

    Pork Pappardelle Pasta, 113

    Pulled Pork with Barbecue Sauce, 128

    Shumai Chinese Steamed Dumplings, 91

potatoes

    Beer-Braised Chicken and Vegetables, 109

    Crispy Roasted Potatoes, 53

    Fluffy Roasted Garlic Mashed Potatoes, 87

    Grandma's Ginger Beef Stew, 107

    Herb-Roasted Chicken with Vegetables, 54

    Indian Cauliflower Curry, 104

    Pan-Roasted Greek Chicken and Vegetables, 33

    See also sweet potatoes

Pulled Pork with Barbecue Sauce, 128

Q

quick recipes

    Blackened Salmon Tacos with Avocado Yogurt Lime Sauce, 19

    Blender Hollandaise Sauce, 139

    Blueberry Almond Muffins, 160

    Chinese Chicken Lettuce Wraps, 23

    Citrus Herb Vinaigrette, 145

    Creamy Caesar Salad Dressing, 141

    Easy Pan Sauce, 148

Five-Minute Teriyaki Sauce, 150

Grilled Salmon Burgers, 61

Lemon Basil Aioli, 142–144

Lobster Sliders, 88

Red Curry Lemongrass Chicken
Meatballs, 99

Stir-Fry Sauce, 149

Strawberry Balsamic Vinaigrette, 147

Thai Green Curry with Shrimp, 97

Wok-Fired Orange Garlic Shrimp, 20

Quinoa, Turkey Chili with, 123

Quinoa-Stuffed Sweet Potatoes, Mexican, 45

R

raspberries, in Lemon-Raspberry Cream
Scones, 159

red bell peppers

Andouille Sausage and Shrimp Gumbo,
98

Kung Pao Chicken, 127

Red Curry Lemongrass Chicken
Meatballs, 99

Turkey Chili with Quinoa, 123

Red Curry Lemongrass Chicken Meatballs, 99

Red Wine–Braised Short Ribs, 114

Ribeye with Miso Butter, Pan-Seared, 30

Ribs, Hawaiian-Style Pork, 130

Ribs, Red Wine–Braised Short, 114

Rice, Chinese Sticky, 78

rice, in Mushroom Risotto, 77

Risotto, Mushroom, 77

roasting, 16–17

Balsamic Roasted Pork Tenderloin, 34

Caramelized Asparagus Wrapped in
Bacon, 57

Crispy Roasted Potatoes, 53

Herb-Roasted Chicken with Vegetables,
54

Oven-Roasted Rack of Lamb with Mint
Gremolata, 37

Pan-Roasted Greek Chicken and
Vegetables, 33

Roasted Root Vegetables, 44

rolls/buns

Chinese Steamed Custard Buns, 183–184

Hawaiian Sweet Rolls, 191

Salted Caramel Apple Cinnamon Rolls,
181–182

Whole Wheat Hamburger Buns, 188

Root Vegetables, Roasted, 44

roux, 98, 138

S

sake, in Chicken Udon Soup, 72

salad dressings

Cilantro Lime Dressing, 62

Citrus Herb Vinaigrette, 145

Creamy Caesar Salad Dressing, 141

Lemon Basil Aioli, 142–144

Strawberry Balsamic Vinaigrette, 147

Salad with Cilantro Lime Dressing, Grilled
Corn, 62

Salmon Burgers, Grilled, 61

Salmon Tacos with Avocado Yogurt Lime
Sauce, Blackened, 19

Salsa, Pineapple, 49

Salted Caramel Apple Cinnamon Rolls,
181–182

salts, types, 200

sauces

Avocado Yogurt Lime Sauce, 19

Blender Hollandaise Sauce, 139

Caramel Sauce, 181–182

Chipotle Sauce, 45

Creamy Miso Sauce, 50

Dipping Sauce, for tempura, 47–48

Easy Pan Sauce, 148

egg-based, 144

emulsifying, 136

Five-Minute Teriyaki Sauce, 150

Orange Dipping Sauce, 27

Stir-Fry Sauce, 149

thickening, 136

Tomato Sauce, 133

Yogurt Sauce, 38

sausage

Andouille Sausage and Shrimp Gumbo,
98

Chinese Sticky Rice, 78

sautéing, 16–17

Balsamic Roasted Pork Tenderloin, 34

Blackened Salmon Tacos with Avocado
Yogurt Lime Sauce, 19

Chinese Chicken Lettuce Wraps, 23

Oven-Roasted Rack of Lamb with Mint
Gremolata, 37

Pan-Roasted Greek Chicken and
Vegetables, 33

Pan-Seared Ribeye with Miso Butter, 30

Pan-Seared Scallops with Garlic Sauce,
24–26

Wok-Fired Orange Garlic Shrimp, 20

scallops

Italian Seafood Stew, 100

Pan-Seared Scallops with Garlic Sauce,
24–26

Scones, Lemon-Raspberry Cream, 159

seafood

Andouille Sausage and Shrimp Gumbo,
98

Blackened Salmon Tacos with Avocado
Yogurt Lime Sauce, 19

Cedar-Planked Mahi Mahi with
Pineapple Salsa, 49

Fish Katsu with Asian Slaw, 50

Grilled Salmon Burgers, 61

Italian Seafood Stew, 100

Mediterranean Steamed Mussels, 83

Pan-Seared Halibut with Tomato Basil
Couscous, 41

Pan-Seared Scallops with Garlic Sauce,
24–26

Tempura Shrimp and Vegetables, 47–48

Thai Green Curry with Shrimp, 97

Wok-Fired Orange Garlic Shrimp, 20

searing/browning, 16

Short Ribs, Red Wine–Braised, 114

shrimp

Andouille Sausage and Shrimp Gumbo, 98

Italian Seafood Stew, 100

Shumai Chinese Steamed Dumplings, 91

Tempura Shrimp and Vegetables, 47–48

Thai Green Curry with Shrimp, 97

Wok-Fired Orange Garlic Shrimp, 20

Shumai Chinese Steamed Dumplings, 91

simmering, 68–69

Minestrone Soup, 74

Mushroom Risotto, 77

Slaw, Asian, 50

Sliders, Lobster, 88

slow cooking, 118–120

Grandma's Italian Meatballs, 133

Honey Hoisin Garlic Chicken, 121

Kung Pao Chicken, 127

Pulled Pork with Barbecue Sauce, 128

Turkey Chili with Quinoa, 123

Yucatán-Style Chicken with Pickled Onions, 124

smoke point, of oils, 204–205

Soup, Chicken Udon, 72

Soup, Minestrone, 74

Soy Marinated Flank Steak, 65

spareribs, in Hawaiian-Style Pork Ribs, 130

spices, blooming/toasting, 19, 104

spinach

Eggs Benedict, 71

Indian Cauliflower Curry, 104

squash

Balsamic Roasted Pork Tenderloin, 34

Grandma's Ginger Beef Stew, 107

Minestrone Soup, 74

Pan-Roasted Greek Chicken and Vegetables, 33

Turkey Chili with Quinoa, 123

starch gelatinization, 136–138

Steak, Soy Marinated Flank, 65

Steamed Custard Buns, Chinese, 183–184

steaming, 68–69

Lobster Sliders, 88

Mediterranean Steamed Mussels, 83

Shumai Chinese Steamed Dumplings, 91

stewing, 94–95

Andouille Sausage and Shrimp Gumbo, 98

Grandma's Ginger Beef Stew, 107

Indian Cauliflower Curry, 104

Italian Seafood Stew, 100

Moroccan Lamb Stew, 103

Thai Green Curry with Shrimp, 97

Sticky Asian Chicken Wings, 42

Strawberries and Cream Cake, 173–175

Strawberry Balsamic Vinaigrette, 147

sugar snap peas, in Wok-Fired Orange Garlic Shrimp, 20

sun-dried tomatoes, in Grilled Salmon Burgers, 61

swai, in Fish Katsu with Asian Slaw, 50

sweet potatoes

Beer-Braised Chicken and Vegetables, 109

Crispy Vegetable Fritters, 38

Mexican Quinoa-Stuffed Sweet Potatoes, 45

Red Curry Lemongrass Chicken Meatballs, 99

Tempura Shrimp and Vegetables, 47–48

Sweet Rolls, Hawaiian, 191

T

Tacos with Avocado Yogurt Lime Sauce, Blackened Salmon, 19

temperatures, food, 200–201, 203, 210–211

tempering, egg mixtures, 183–184

Tempura Shrimp and Vegetables, 47–48

Tenderloin, Balsamic Roasted Pork, 34

Thai Green Curry with Shrimp, 97

thermometers, calibrating, 201

thickening, 136–138

Easy Pan Sauce, 148

Five-Minute Teriyaki Sauce, 150

Stir-Fry Sauce, 149

Tofu and Vegetables, Buddha's Braised, 110

tomatoes

Andouille Sausage and Shrimp Gumbo, 98

Balsamic Roasted Pork Tenderloin, 34

Cedar-Planked Mahi Mahi with Pineapple Salsa, 49

Indian Cauliflower Curry, 104

Italian Seafood Stew, 100

Mediterranean Steamed Mussels, 83

Mexican Quinoa-Stuffed Sweet Potatoes, 45

Minestrone Soup, 74

Moroccan Lamb Stew, 103

Pan-Roasted Greek Chicken and Vegetables, 33

Pan-Seared Halibut with Tomato Basil Couscous, 41

Turkey Chili with Quinoa, 123

Yucatán-Style Chicken with Pickled Onions, 124

Turkey Chili with Quinoa, 123

turnips, in Grandma's Ginger Beef Stew, 107

U

Udon Soup, Chicken, 72

Upside Down Cake, Classic Pineapple, 170–172

V

vegetables

blanching/shocking, 69

preparation, for slow cooking, 119

retaining color, 69

roasting, 44

steaming, 68

vegetarian recipes

    Blender Hollandaise Sauce, 139

    Blueberry Almond Muffins, 160

    Buddha's Braised Tofu and Vegetables, 110

    Chewy Cranberry Oatmeal Cookies, 169

    Chinese Steamed Custard Buns, 183–184

    Chocolate Chip Banana Bread, 157

    Citrus Herb Vinaigrette, 145

    Classic Pineapple Upside Down Cake, 170–172

    Creamy Macaroni and Cheese, 84

    Crispy Roasted Potatoes, 53

    Crispy Vegetable Fritters, 38

    Eggs Benedict, 71

    Five-Minute Teriyaki Sauce, 150

    Flaky Country Buttermilk Biscuits, 163–164

    Grilled Corn Salad with Cilantro Lime Dressing, 62

    Hawaiian Sweet Rolls, 191

    Indian Cauliflower Curry, 104

    Italian Breadsticks, 187

    Lemon Basil Aioli, 142–144

    Lemon-Raspberry Cream Scones, 159

    Mexican Quinoa-Stuffed Sweet Potatoes, 45

    Minestrone Soup, 74

    Mushroom Risotto, 77

    Nutella Cheesecake Brownies, 165–166

    Orange-Glazed Almond Green Beans, 73

    Roasted Root Vegetables, 44

    Salted Caramel Apple Cinnamon Rolls, 181–182

    Stir-Fry Sauce, 149

    Strawberries and Cream Cake, 173–175

    Strawberry Balsamic Vinaigrette, 147

    Whole Wheat Hamburger Buns, 188

vinaigrettes, 136

    Citrus Herb Vinaigrette, 145

    Strawberry Balsamic Vinaigrette, 147

W

walnuts

    Chocolate Chip Banana Bread, 157

    Classic Pineapple Upside Down Cake, 170–172

water chestnuts

    Buddha's Braised Tofu and Vegetables, 110

    Chinese Chicken Lettuce Wraps, 23

Whole Wheat Hamburger Buns, 188

Wok-Fired Orange Garlic Shrimp, 20

Wraps, Chinese Chicken Lettuce, 23

Y

yeast leavening, 178–179

    Chinese Steamed Custard Buns, 183–184

    Hawaiian Sweet Rolls, 191

    Italian Breadsticks, 187

    Salted Caramel Apple Cinnamon Rolls, 181–182

    Whole Wheat Hamburger Buns, 188

yogurt

    Blackened Salmon Tacos with Avocado Yogurt Lime Sauce, 19

    Indian Cauliflower Curry, 104

Yucatán-Style Chicken with Pickled Onions, 124

Z

zucchini

    Balsamic Roasted Pork Tenderloin, 34

    Chicken Udon Soup, 72

    Crispy Vegetable Fritters, 38

    Kung Pao Chicken, 127

    Minestrone Soup, 74

    Pan-Roasted Greek Chicken and Vegetables, 33

Red Curry Lemongrass Chicken Meatballs, 99

Thai Green Curry with Shrimp, 97